SAILORS, SLACKERS
AND BLIND PIGS

Mary —
With many
memories
and love
Kay
February 2003

SAILORS, SLACKERS
AND BLIND PIGS

HALIFAX AT WAR

STEPHEN KIMBER

DOUBLEDAY CANADA

National Library of Canada Cataloguing in Publication Data
Kimber, Stephen
Sailors, slackers, and blind pigs: Halifax at war / Stephen Kimber.

Includes bibliographical references and index.
ISBN 0-385-25993-X

1. World War, 1939-1945—Nova Scotia—Halifax. 2. Halifax (N.S.)—
History—20TH century. I. Title.

FC2346.4.K55 2002   971.6'22503   C2002-902062-X
F1039.5.H17K55 2002

Jacket images: courtesy Maritime Command Museum
Jacket design: CS Richardson
Text design: Daniel Cullen
Printed and bound in the USA

Published in Canada by
Doubleday Canada, a division of
Random House of Canada Limited

Visit Random House of Canada Limited's website:
www.randomhouse.ca

BVG   10 9 8 7 6 5 4 3 2 1

For my parents, who lived it

-CONTENTS-

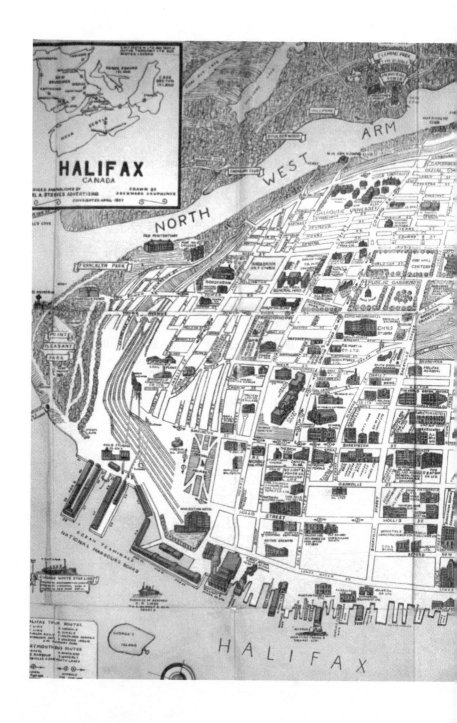

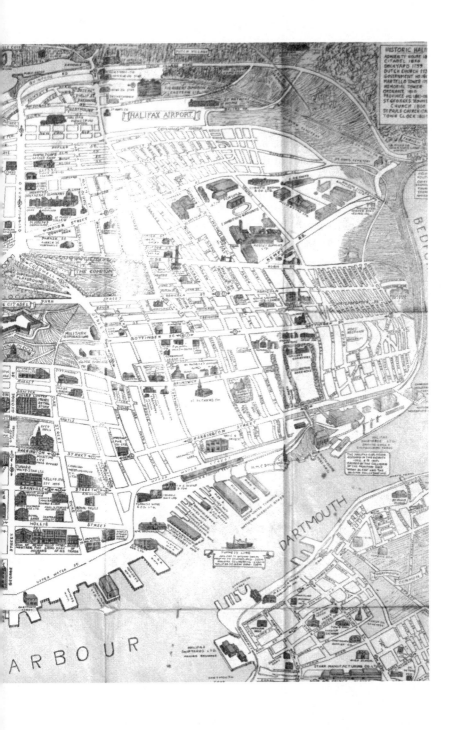

The mayor has stated that he is dismayed
Because of the part the navy has played.
He forgets in the midst of his trouble and tears
That sailors in Slackers had plenty for years.

—FROM "THE BATTLE OF HALIFAX"
BY LEADING SEAMAN R. WALTERS

- A NOTE ON SOURCES -

This is the story about what life was like in Halifax during the Second World War, told as much as possible from the viewpoints of those who lived it. Since it is not intended as an academic history, I've chosen not to include footnotes or exhaustive source notes. The book has been carefully and completely researched nonetheless, and is as true to life as I can make it.

In piecing together the narrative, I had the benefit of extensive interviews with almost all of the book's principal characters, most of whom are still alive and whose memories of those days remain sharp and clear. Wherever possible, I've attempted to verify and supplement their recollections with supporting interviews (see the Acknowledgements on page 333), documents, letters and news accounts, as well as the published work of later historians of the navy, the war, the era and Halifax itself (see Selected Bibliography on page 329).

Two of the book's key characters—Admiral Leonard Murray and Censor H.B. Jefferson—died long before I could interview them. Luckily, both men left behind a treasure trove of material that helped me bring their lives and views into sharper focus. Jefferson was not only a keen, sometimes acerbic observer of life around him, but also an inveterate journal writer and note-maker. His papers, which are stored in thirty uncatalogued boxes in the Public Archives of Nova Scotia, provided unique and invaluable insights into both wartime Halifax and Jefferson himself. Murray was a much more sporadic and not especially revelatory diarist, but the official record as well as the later accounts of his many defenders and detractors helped me put his life too in some perspective.

Perhaps the most useful and balanced account of Murray's long rise to power and sudden dramatic fall from grace came from a thesis the late journalist and author Doug How prepared when he was an MA student at Dalhousie University in the early seventies. Though, regrettably, it was never published as a thesis or a book, How kindly directed me to one of the few remaining copies—at the New Brunswick Public Archives—and, in spite of his own declining health, patiently answered my many questions about Murray and about his own years as a young reporter in Halifax at the beginning of the war.

The epigraph to this book, from "The Battle of Halifax" by Leading Seaman R. Walters, was discovered in Royal Canadian Navy files in Ottawa and quoted by How in his thesis, entitled "Career of Rear Admiral Leonard Murray."

CHAPTER ONE

1939
– Preparations, Expectations and the Phony War –

Eric Dennis stared hard at the dozens of men and women streaming off tonight's Ocean Limited passenger train just arrived from Montreal, searching the platform for familiar faces, faces to which he could put names, names his readers might recognize. He knew he had to concentrate. But how could he? It had finally happened. After weeks of bluster and bluff, feint and fallback, incursion and indecision, war had really begun. He had awakened to the news this morning. British prime minister Neville Chamberlain had gone on the radio to announce officially that England had declared war on Germany. France, Australia and New Zealand followed almost instantly. How soon before Canada did too, Eric Dennis wondered? What would—should—*he* do then?

Eric was twenty-two, tall and thin, with a wispy moustache and thick glasses. He was a general assignment reporter for both the morning Halifax *Herald* and the afternoon *Mail*, the largest circulation daily newspapers in Nova Scotia, both of them owned by his legendary uncle, Senator William Dennis, who in turn was the son of the original, and even more legendary, Senator William Dennis, the *Herald*'s first reporter and the founder of the *Mail*. Newspapering flowed in the Dennis veins. But what of soldiering?

Standing in the middle of the echoing tumult of this cavernous barn of a railway station as arriving passengers met their loved ones, grabbed their bags and hurried off into the cool late summer night, Eric couldn't help but recall a sweltering June day less than three months before. King George and Queen Elizabeth had arrived at this very station aboard a specially decorated royal blue and silver, twelve-coach train for the final stop of what had turned into a triumphant seven-week royal tour of Canada. Although the possibility of war had hung like a storm cloud over planning for the visit—it was very nearly cancelled in the tense aftermath of the Nazi invasion of Czechoslovakia in March—you wouldn't have guessed it by the adoring crowds who gathered inside and outside the station that festive day.

Eric had been one of the reporters assigned to cover the visit. He tagged along as the King, in his Admiral of the Fleet uniform, and the Queen, in her favourite powder blue outfit, toured Halifax's freshly spiffed streets in an open motor car. When, at the end of the day, the royal couple stood on the deck of the *Empress of Britain* proffering their practised royal waves in yet another farewell to yet another adoring crowd, Eric was so caught up in the moment that he waved back.

Who would have believed war was already so close at hand? It was only now that Eric finally began to understand the significance of the visit. Britain's unspoken purpose was to stir up imperialist fervour among Canadians so they would pressure their government to commit to the defence of the mother country should it ultimately come to that. The ploy had worked: everyone knew it was only a matter of time before Prime Minister Mackenzie King officially announced Canada was in the war too.

Dennis initially assumed that war, if there was to be one at all, would be confined to a few little nations on the continent. But in March the Germans had gobbled up Czechoslovakia. In May, Hitler signed his Pact of Steel with Mussolini's Italy. And then, less than two weeks ago, on August 23, 1939, the German leader reached a surprise non-aggression pact with Stalin's Soviet Union that raised fears of a great power showdown. Ever since the German-Soviet deal, in fact, the *Herald*'s daily drumbeat of headlines had created a feeling that a much wider war was inevitable: EMPIRE STANDS WITH BRITAIN, his paper had declared the day after the announcement of the alliance. The next day it was FATE OF WORLD IN BALANCE, followed by a slightly more optimistic DRIFT TO DISASTER IS DELAYED, then a crushing HITLER REFUSES DIRECT TALKS WITH POLAND. By Tuesday, August 29, it had come down to PEACE OR WAR: HITLER HAS HIS CHOICE. The following morning's BRITAIN'S FIRM STAND BRINGS NEW PROPOSALS FROM HITLER seemed encouraging, but was followed by the ominous ARMIES' MIGHT IS INCREASED AS SECRET CRISIS NOTES EXCHANGED, and then—on September 1, the day the *Herald* published its first extra of the conflict—a chilling POLISH BORDER VIOLATED AT 4 POINTS. On Saturday of the Labour Day holiday weekend, the *Herald*'s headline read: HITLER IS GIVEN LAST WARNING.

Tonight, back in the newsroom, Edgar Kelley, the *Herald*'s editor-in-chief, and Bob Rankin, the managing editor, had already settled on tomorrow's main-edition headline: EMPIRE AT WAR, set in the largest type yet. But events were unfolding so quickly that the paper's editors had already had to make room above the *Herald*'s nameplate for another headline, nearly as large: LINER ATHENIA IS TORPEDOED AND SUNK.

War had really begun. Should he—?

Eric Dennis stopped himself, tried to focus on the job at hand. He looked around at the departing passengers. The other regulars were here too, of course, including his opposite number from the *Chronicle*. Like Dennis, he was scouring the faces in the crowd. Like Dennis, he showed no indication he recognized anyone. A good sign?

Germaine Pelletier and her boyfriend were at their usual posts near the baggage counter. Pelletier operated the city's most popular brothel, in a red brick building opposite the lieutenant-governor's official residence a couple of blocks north of the station, on Hollis Street. Each evening, she would walk down to the station to meet the arriving trains in order to discreetly advertise the existence of her establishment and determine if any of the passengers might wish to partake of the services her girls had to offer. War, Eric thought, would probably be good for her business.

The railway station was part of Eric Dennis's regular beat. He stopped by each day to see who was who among the arriving passengers. His job was to find out if any of them were interesting enough to write about for the paper's "Yesterday I Saw . . ." photo feature. During his five years at the paper he'd befriended everyone from the baggage handlers, who would alert him to expensive-looking luggage, to the conductors and porters, who often knew their most prominent passengers by name. But these days he was much more careful to check and recheck every snippet of information they provided. Three years earlier, "Yesterday I Saw . . ." almost cost him his job. He'd been told the mayor of Shelburne, a small town on the province's south shore, was visiting Halifax. Since the paper already had a photo of the mayor on file, Dennis, who hadn't been able to track him down to talk to him personally, wrote it up anyway. "Yesterday, I saw the Mayor of Shelburne," the caption under the photo began.

After the piece appeared, Eric's uncle, William, approached him in the newsroom. "Yesterday, you saw—" the publisher began, pausing a beat for emphasis, "—a man whose funeral I attended ten years ago." Another pause. "How was he?"

It turned out the passenger Eric Dennis had written about was actually the unremarkable son of the town's late mayor. Eric was suspended for two weeks without pay. He might have been fired if he hadn't been the publisher's nephew and, perhaps just as importantly, if he hadn't been named for William Dennis's beloved son, Captain Eric Reginald Dennis, who was killed during the Battle of Vimy Ridge in 1917. When Eric was born a month later, his mother named him in honour of his late cousin. Uncle William had been so touched, he wrote immediately to Eric's parents, commending them for choosing the name and adding, "When this boy finishes school, I want him to come and work for me at the paper."

By the time Eric completed high school in 1934, his family had settled in British Columbia, where his father operated a struggling, thirty-acre farm in the Fraser Valley. There was no money for university; it was still the Depression, and most of Eric's friends who'd gone on to university were unemployed or building roads through the mountains. He decided to take his uncle up on his offer.

Although he had no formal journalism training—or any training of any sort beyond high school composition, in which he'd got good marks—his uncle put him to work as a night reporter for twelve dollars a week. Since there weren't enough reporters to cover all the day-side beats, Mike Ryan, the night editor, instructed Eric to begin his four-to-midnight shift each day with a quick stop at Magistrate's Court to find out if there had been any cases worth reporting that day. Later, he would go to the CNR station to meet incoming trains, make the first of two stops to find out what was happening at the police station, and then check in with the desk clerks at all the major local hotels to see who among the newcomers might be worth a story.

The guests were somewhat less talkative at Snow & Company, the undertakers, which was also part of his beat, but the folks who worked there always seemed happy to see Eric. Sometimes they'd even invite him into the back room to help them prepare a body for showing.

He'd stop in at the undertakers on his way back to the office tonight, he thought. Maybe someone interesting had died. The train station was certainly dead tonight. Not that anyone back in the newsroom would care. Tomorrow's paper would be full to bursting with war news. There wouldn't be much space or interest for "Yesterday I Saw . . ." anyone, alive or dead.

If he finished work early, perhaps he'd stop in for a late evening snack at Norman's, or head back to the boarding house to continue his conversation with his roommate, Colin Campbell. He and Campbell, who worked at a small investment house on Hollis Street, had been talking a lot lately about whether they should enlist in the navy together. Now that it seemed just a matter of time before Canada joined the conflict, they should make their plans. Should Eric go through with it? It would be an adventure. There was nothing to keep him in Halifax. Although he was the publisher's nephew and had been at the paper for five years, he was still being paid twelve dollars a week.

But what about Maxine? What would she think? He'd met Maxine Mabee just a few months before, during a visit home to his parents in British Columbia. His mother had arranged for him to go out on a blind date with Maxine. By the time Eric returned to Halifax, they were an item. They'd been corresponding almost daily ever since. Perhaps he would write to Maxine tonight, ask her what she thought he should do.

He took one last look around the station. Nothing here.

"BEND OVER, MONT." The deep voice boomed off the bare walls of the cavernous room, making it seem to ten-year-old Billy Mont even louder and more ominous than it actually was. "And get those pants down. Now!"

The Gad! He was going to get the Gad! That's what he'd heard the other boys call the wide leather strap used by the authorities at the Halifax Industrial School to discipline the boys. He didn't know why they called it that. Billy had never been strapped before. Now he was about to feel the bite of the leather on his backside too. And for what? For flushing the toilet. How was he supposed to know it would overflow?

At home in Greenbank, there had been no flush toilets, only an outdoor privy. The water didn't come out of a tap, either. When Billy's family needed water, his grandfather would send him down Clarence Street to the Young Avenue bridge, where a spring bubbled up from under the ground. As he filled his bucket, Billy could look up and see the mansions on Young Avenue where the rich folks lived. There was a real castle up there; he'd seen it with his own eyes.

There were no castles in Greenbank. Greenbank was a shanty-town, a jumble of shacks hastily slapped together to house the hundreds of workers brought in to build a harbourside complex of modern piers and sheds in the late twenties. The shacks were sup-posed to have been torn down after the terminals opened, but they survived. Families took them over, put additions on. Other folks built new cottages nearby. Some of the land those cottages squat-ted on was bought up by the local gentry, who regarded the strate-gically situated shantytown, just west of the CNR train station and the new international Ocean Terminals complex, as a wise long-term investment. Billy's grandfather paid five dollars a month for their two-bedroom cottage, which had no running water, sewage or other city services, to Susan Mack, the widow of a prominent Halifax doctor.

During the thirties, Greenbank had become a grudgingly accepted Halifax address. At least, it was accepted by some, but certainly not by its closest neighbours. The problem was that Greenbank sat rudely, inconveniently, incongruously smack in the middle of Halifax's most exclusive streetscape.

By 1939, Halifax's lines of social demarcation were immutable. The northeast quarter of the peninsula belonged to the poor and the working class, with Africville—a poorest-of-the-poor segregated community of about four hundred that was the black equivalent of Greenbank—anchoring the farthest north end, where the harbour met Bedford Basin. The gentry, which had originally favoured the downtown core for homes as well as businesses, had long since abandoned it to commerce and the dregs of the waterfront, devel-oping their own deliberately closed residential neighbourhoods in the southern and western quarters of the peninsula. Even Germaine Pelletier, the madam who operated her prostitution busi-ness at 51 Hollis Street in the seedy downtown waterfront district, knew better than to live there; her house was in a comfortable neighbourhood in the city's west end.

By general agreement the most prestigious street in town was Young Avenue in the city's south end. Back in 1896 the provincial legislature had passed a law making the broad, boulevarded roadway leading to lush Point Pleasant Park one of Halifax's first officially restrictive neighbourhoods. Under the terms of the legislation, intended "to provide that a certain class and style of house be built," every house on the street had to cost at least $2,000 for a wooden structure, $3,000 for a brick one, this at a time when houses in the north end sold for $600 to $700. In addition, no one could put up any other building within 180 feet of the street without the approval of city council; and no one could ever use any such building for a "hotel, house of entertainment, boarding house, shop, or for sale of liquor."

To make Young Avenue even more attractive to Halifax's turn-of-the-century upper class, the city spent thousands of dollars to develop and grade the boulevard, not to mention contributing $50,000 for a new sewer system. At the time it was built, the sewer system served the disposal needs of just five houses. City fathers willingly, eagerly committed such resources to the care and comfort of the affluent at a time when most streets in the working-class north end of the city were in desperate need of repair.

Such favouritism did not go unnoticed. In a letter to the editor of the Halifax *Chronicle* in April 1899, one correspondent, who signed himself "Maynard Street" after a working-class, north-end street, complained that "before it was criminal for a poor man to live therein, I had often enjoyed a stroll [along Young Avenue] . . . The songs of the birds gladdened the heart and the scent of the foliage was pleasing to the smell. [Now] I know that no common north-ender is supposed to set foot within the sacred precincts of this south-end swelldom."

This legislative attempt to keep the neighbourhood free from riff-raff didn't last long. It was dealt its first severe blow in 1912, when the Tory prime minister of the day, Sir Robert Borden, announced plans to expropriate a swath of prime residential real estate that sliced right through the heart of Young Avenue. The confiscated land, which ran from the harbour west through Young Avenue and then hugged the edge of the pristine Northwest Arm for six miles, to the edge of the city, was gouged out to make way for railway tracks leading to a new south-end train station. There were those among the Halifax aristocracy who still cursed Borden, a native Nova Scotian who should have known better, for marring the peninsula with his "volcanic fissure, miles long, filled with deep rumblings and wild whistle whoops, and emitting smoke and steam." Worse, the construction workers not only built their temporary shacks on the edge of the railway line, smack up against Young Avenue, but those shacks had the temerity to stay, eventually becoming Greenbank.

Although he was still only a child, Billy Mont already knew he didn't belong up on Young Avenue. Or even in Tower Road School, where the children of Greenbank uneasily shared space with the sons and daughters of the south-end swells. The latter kids were going places. Robert MacNeil, who would grow up to be the famous international news correspondent and host of PBS's *MacNeil/Lehrer Report*, had been in Billy's class at Tower Road. So was David MacKeen, the son of one of the city's most successful corporate lawyers, who would eventually serve as an alderman and important backroom Conservative operative. Billy's future, it seemed, had been sealed last year, in second grade, with the pencil incident: his step-grandmother had sent him off to school without any pencils.

"They'll give you pencils there," she said.

But they didn't. "No, we don't supply pencils," the teacher told him. "Go home and get them."

Home again. Back to school again. Home again. After a while Billy gave up. He didn't go back to school. Eventually, the police picked him up and took him before J. Elliott Hudson, the judge in charge of the city's youth courts.

The judge stared down at Billy from a great height. "Did you play hooky from school, young man?" he demanded.

"Yes," Billy answered, not knowing what else to say.

Judge Hudson sentenced him to five years in the Halifax Industrial School. Billy was nine.

The Industrial School, an imposing, flat-roofed, four-storey building on Quinpool Road in the city's west end, was a cross between an orphanage and a reformatory. Founded as the Ragged and Industrial School in 1853 by a prominent socialite, its goal was to rescue street urchins and transform them into at least modestly productive members of society. The young ones attended school while the older boys learned barbering, shoemaking, the care and feeding of horses, and a variety of other skills that might one day make them marketable. As Isabella Binney Cogswell, the school's "philanthropic Miss," explained in one early annual report: "Many of these poor lads are fatherless, with drunken mothers, or motherless with drunken fathers, or in many cases abandoned by both parents . . . These unfortunate lads are often compelled to seek shelter in some house of ill fame, or gain a precarious living by begging or stealing or playing the tambourine at some low public house in the upper streets."

Billy Mont, who was small for his age, with olive skin and an impish grin, could have been a poster boy for the Industrial School. His biological father, a Lebanese-born boxer with the Anglicized name of Jerry Allen, had frozen to death in a refrigerated freight car outside Moncton, New Brunswick, in December 1935, when Billy was six. "Promoted by a spirit of adventure," the front-page obituary in the newspaper declared, "Gerald 'Jerry' Allen, 25-year-old Halifax boxer, rode freight trains in safety on a 10,000-mile trip from Nova Scotia to California and back, but death rode with him when he attempted a 300-mile trip from Saint John to Halifax."

In the obituary Billy wasn't even listed as next of kin. By then, Jerry and Billy's mother, Mary, had long since gone their separate ways. Mary's own troubles had less to do with the alcohol Isabella

Binney Cogswell fretted about than with a simple lack of maturity. After running off to Shawinigan, Quebec, chasing after some guy or another, she and Billy eventually moved into the cottage in Greenbank with his grandfather, William Mont, a crane operator and sometime policeman at the Halifax Shipyards, and his second wife, Alice. A hard-as-nails Newfoundlander, Alice wasn't keen on sharing what little they had with her husband's ne'er-do-well daughter and grandson. She didn't seem unhappy, Billy noticed, when the judge sentenced him to the Industrial School.

Neither, truth to tell, was Billy. The food, much of which came from the school's own garden, turned out to be better and more plentiful than it had ever been at home. The kids were much more like him than those effete snobs at Tower Road had been. The boys, perhaps a hundred altogether, lived in dormitories, six or eight to a room. They ate in the cafeteria, roughhoused in the big gym, attended classes in the schoolroom. There were even pencils in the Industrial School's classroom that he was allowed to use. Surprisingly for a boy who'd been considered slow at Tower Road, Billy discovered not only that he liked to learn but also that he was good at it.

In fact, for the first ten months of his five-year sentence he had been content at the Halifax Industrial School. Not once had he been punished for anything—until tonight. The toilet? How could he have known what would happen?

"Hold still, Mont," the voice boomed again. Billy could sense rather than see the man swing his right arm back over his shoulder. Even before the first blow landed, he could feel the tears welling up.

In the larger world beyond the punishment room, beyond the grounds of the Industrial School, war had finally begun. For Billy Mont, however, the war was the least of his worries.

JANET MACNEILL LOOKED again at the *Herald*'s front page. EMPIRE AT WAR. Edith had been right! Worse still, LINER ATHENIA IS TORPEDOED AND SUNK. What if . . .? The one thing Janet Macneill knew for certain this morning was that if she hadn't listened to Edith, her oldest sister, she would not be sitting here in the living room of her parents' comfortable home on Young Avenue, in Halifax's south end, reading the newspaper and listening to the cheering, cheery voice of her four-year-old daughter, Anne, wafting in from the kitchen, where Janet's mother was preparing the girl's breakfast. Janet used to tell her friends she'd been born under a "lucky star." Until this morning she had not known how lucky.

Earlier that summer, Edith, a thirty-four-year-old newspaper columnist who wrote "letters" home to Canadian newspapers about her travels, had visited Danzig to see first-hand what life was like in a city that had become a key diplomatic battleground in the growing war of words between Britain and Germany. On her first morning in Danzig, Edith fell into conversation with an American newspaper correspondent over breakfast, who warned her to "take your articles and get out of here *now*. Did you hear the noise last night?"

She had.

"Tanks," he explained. "And that's just the first of them. In two weeks the Germans are going to make their big move here and this city will be a battleground. So will all of Europe. Get out of here while you still can, and go back to Canada before it's too late."

Frightened, she returned immediately to London, where she informed Janet they must leave for Canada *now*. At first, Janet was dismissive. "Oh, don't be silly," she told Edith breezily. "There's not going to be any war." Besides, she added, she had things to do before she could leave. She planned to travel back to Halifax to visit her parents soon anyway; she'd booked passage for her and her daughter on a ship leaving Liverpool in less than a month. She'd leave then.

"No, Jannie," Edith insisted, exasperated that her little sister didn't seem to grasp the gravity of the situation. "Look, for once listen to what I have to say. Call that fellow you know, Eric Bowater, and see if he can help you find a ship that's leaving sooner."

Sir Eric, who owned a huge pulp and paper company with ships and a mill in Newfoundland, was happy to oblige. The fourteen-day voyage from London to Corner Brook was pleasantly uneventful. The seas were so calm and the weather so bright and clear, the crew even rigged up a swing on the deck for Anne. Three days after docking in Corner Brook, on September 3, Janet, Anne and Edith arrived by train in Halifax to the news that, earlier that day, England had declared war on Germany.

Janet was stunned. But that was nothing to what she felt the next morning, when she saw the front page of the *Herald*. In what was being described as the first act of war, the Germans had torpedoed and sunk the *Athenia*, a British liner, which had just left Liverpool the day before on its regular run across the Atlantic to Montreal. Many among the 1,400 passengers and crew had drowned, and hundreds were still missing. Janet Macneill read the story, and then read it again. Still she couldn't quite comprehend it.

She and Anne had been booked on the *Athenia*.

She refused to allow herself to think any more about it. She thought instead about her lucky star. She gave thanks for it, and for her sister Edith. She was safe now at her parents' home in Halifax, an ocean away from the madness in Europe. The war could not touch her here.

Janet Macneill would turn out to be wrong about that. Indeed, she was already wrong.

HALIFAX HAD BEEN GEARING UP for this war since long before anyone in authority in Canada was willing even to concede publicly that war was inevitable. Given that Halifax would almost certainly be on the front lines of any new conflict, just as it had been throughout its history, that probably shouldn't have been surprising.

In November 1938, just a little over a month after British prime minister Neville Chamberlain's infamous "peace in our time" accord with the Germans at Munich, the Royal Canadian Navy had quietly reactivated a recently retired lieutenant-commander (turned insurance agent) named Dick Oland to develop secret plans for convoying men and supplies from Halifax to Europe "in case of an emergency." Three months later—before Hitler sent troops into Czechoslovakia and before Britain put him on notice not to do the same in Poland—the head of the Royal Canadian Mounted Police's H Division met privately with senior officials of the Nova Scotia Light & Power Co., the province's largest gas and electrical company, to draw up plans for protecting its strategically important power generating facilities "in the event of an emergency." By dawn on September 1, 1939, the day the first German tanks rumbled into Poland, NSLP's main waterfront steam-electric plant was already completely surrounded by high, floodlit steel fencing, and armed company guards were fanning out to take up their assigned positions at every vital or vulnerable spot in NSLP's gas and electrical system network across the city.

By September 5, three days after Britain declared war but five before Canada signed on, Halifax's sixty thousand residents had been put through the paces of their first blackout drill. The city's Provincial and Civic Air Raid Precautions Committee announced it would sound steam whistles to alert residents in the event of a German air attack. Eaton's, the department store, began advertising specially made green blackout curtains to help keep light from leaking out into the night and giving away building locations to enemy aircraft. Civic officials began debating how the city should deal with possible gas attacks. "Where can we get sixty thousand gas masks?" asked one school board member plaintively.

This almost frantic gearing up for war in Halifax made a sharp contrast with the seeming nonchalance with which the impending conflict was being greeted in the rest of the country. On the day after the Soviet-German pact—the day the Halifax *Herald*'s main headline fairly screamed EMPIRE STANDS WITH BRITAIN— the Toronto *Star*, Canada's largest circulation newspaper, didn't consider that far-off news to be nearly as important as its own lead story: TORONTO MAN NEW SALVATION ARMY HEAD.

When the Canadian Press issued a bulletin shortly after noon on Sunday, September 10, announcing that Parliament had approved the declaration of war, the national CBC radio network, which had been carrying an NBC show from Philadelphia called *Music for Moderns*, did break into "Smoke Gets in Your Eyes" with the news. But after the announcer read the brief news story, the CBC returned to regular programming so that Canadians, who'd just been told they were at war, could hear Kenneth Martin's band play "Inka Dinka Doo."

Canada was not ready for war for a number of reasons. For starters, Canada's prime minister, Mackenzie King, had initially downplayed Hitler's potential for mischief in Europe. After meeting him in 1937, King had dismissed Hitler to one journalist as "a simple peasant" and written reassuringly to the governor general, "I am perfectly certain that the Germans are not contemplating war." King's political self-interest may have coloured his views. Canada was already deeply split along linguistic lines. While English-speaking Canadians would likely support the mother country, French-speaking Quebecers, who generally voted for King's Liberals, would probably rebel if conscripted into yet another war on behalf of Britain, as they felt they had been in World War I. If King championed Canada's involvement in such a war, he might pay a steep political price.

As well, the country's experience in World War I—sixty thousand Canadians had been killed—made others, including many in English Canada, chary of becoming caught up again in someone else's far-off war. During one parliamentary debate over proposed increases in the military budget, J.S. Woodsworth, the socialist CCF leader, argued, with the quiet support of some among the governing Liberals, that "Canada should remain strictly neutral [in any war] regardless of who the belligerents might be." This isolationist spirit was reinforced by the reality that the country was still suffering through an economic depression that showed no signs of lifting. Besides, there seemed little need to invest scarce funds in home defence: the Americans had made it plain they would not, as President Franklin Roosevelt put it, "stand idly by" if some other power decided to invade Canada. The result, as the Government Leader in the Senate smugly put it, was that Canada had become "a fireproof house free of inflammable material."

How free? Well, by the time Canada suddenly found itself in need of a military in mid-1939, it almost didn't have one. Defence spending had shrunk to about one-half of 1 percent of national income. (Despite the criticism that Canada spends far too little on defence today, the defence budget in terms of gross domestic product in 2000 was twice as high as in 1939.) The air force had few aircraft that could fly, which was not such a problem as it didn't have any bombs for them to carry. The army, which finally got its first tank in 1938, had enough ammunition on hand for ninety minutes' worth of fire in the enemy's direction before its obsolete field guns would fall silent. The navy's total strength was 6 destroyers, 5 minesweepers, 2 training vessels, and 1,819 officers and men. Not that Canadians thought this lack of firepower necessarily a bad thing. During the twenties and thirties, as RCN Captain Leonard Murray put it, "Canadians would be quite pleased if someone would take the whole navy out in the middle of the ocean and sink it without trace or memory."

Some Canadians probably felt the same about Halifax itself. There had been a time when Halifax was among the most prosperous and important port cities in the world, but by 1939 that time seemed in the distant past.

HALIFAX WAS FOUNDED in 1749 as a strategic British wedge driven into the heart of the French colonial stronghold of Acadia. From the beginning, war was the city's raison d'être—and the source of its sporadic prosperity. It's easy to understand why the British picked this particular spot to establish their new colonial outpost. To begin with, it was the closest port to Britain on the North American continent. Better still, its four-mile-long harbour, which spilled into a basin three miles long by one and a half miles wide that was capable of comfortably accommodating a vast armada, was sheltered from the ravages of the unpredictable North Atlantic. And the icing on the cake, the water in the harbour was deep and ice-free, too.

Halifax itself was situated on an 1,800-square-hectare, 2½-mile-wide horse's head of land, a peninsula bordered on three sides by water and joined to the mainland by a narrow, easily defended neck of land at its northwest corner. The top of the hill that rose up from the harbour, and upon which the city's founder, Colonel Edward Cornwallis, soon set about building a citadel, commanded a strategic view of the entrance to the harbour mouth.

During the Seven Years' War with France, Halifax became Britain's prime North American naval and military depot. It played a similar role in every conflict that followed. After the American Revolution, Halifax's stock as Britain's last naval stronghold in North America rose considerably. Later, after Prince Edward, the Duke of Kent and son of King George III, became Britain's commander-in-chief in North America and set up his headquarters in Halifax, the city became even more important to the Empire. Thanks to the Duke's connections and clout, the British dotted the city with new military fortifications and completely rebuilt the Citadel. The Duke's presence also gave the city a certain cachet among the Empire's colonial outposts. Halifax society came to be so dominated by British officers and their families that Charles Dickens, during a visit to the city in 1842, described it as "like looking at Westminster through the wrong end of a telescope."

By the middle of the nineteenth century Halifax had become smug about its importance in the imperial scheme of things, as well as cocky about its own bright future on the world stage. The military continued to goose the local economy—especially during the United States' Civil War, when British fears that the American North–South conflict could escalate to engulf its own northern colonies prompted another buildup of military forces in Halifax.

But the city's good fortune continued even after war and the threat of war subsided. During the Golden Age of Sail in the mid-1800s, when "to live by the sea was to dwell on the highway of the world," Nova Scotia's shipbuilding and shipping industries prospered and the city was "glutted with money . . . These were the days," as writer Thomas Raddall noted more than a century later, "when sailing ships, flank to flank at the wharves, raised a thicket of spars along the Halifax waterfront, and their long, sharply steeved bowsprits and jib booms literally made a roof above the sheds of Water Street."

The date many choose to mark as the beginning of the end of Halifax's golden age is 1867, the year Nova Scotia and three other British North American colonies came together to form the Dominion of Canada. "The saddle of the Dominion, like any other, was placed in the middle and he who sat there rode the horse, commercially and politically," Raddall wrote. The federal government, based in Ottawa and dominated by the more populous provinces of Ontario and Quebec, brought in a new National Policy that discouraged Nova Scotia's traditionally profitable north-south trade with New England while promoting the development of more country-building east-west commercial links. The problem for Halifax was that those links seemed to run only one way. Ontario had no interest in the fish, coal and lumber Nova Scotia was pitching, but Nova Scotians became a prime market for the far broader range of products being shipped out of the factories of rapidly industrializing Ontario. According to Raddall, "A flying column of sharp and thrusting drummers from the factories and great mercantile houses of Toronto and Montreal" made their way east on the new Intercolonial Railway, another "gift" of Confederation, scooping up business from complacent local merchants. To make matters worse, wind and wood were finally giving way to steam engines and iron ships, and Nova Scotians were left behind in the changeover.

In 1876, the year the Intercolonial Railway reached the east coast, wrote Raddall, "Halifax stood on a crest, glancing back with a sigh upon fifty years of phenomenal progress and facing a long and indefinite decline."

Shortly after the beginning of the twentieth century the British decided it was time to redeploy their forces. By 1905 the Royal Navy had abandoned Halifax entirely to the beneficence of the Government of Canada, which seemed not the least interested in maintaining a navy, or a coastal defence system, or even Halifax itself. "The Dockyard became a place of rust and ghosts,"Raddall concluded. "Admiralty House was closed and the furniture sold. The outer forts were manned for brief gunnery exercises in summer and left in the hands of military janitors the rest of the year. The inner forts were carefully locked against thieves and abandoned to time and weather."

World War I brought the welcome return of the Royal Navy, which used Halifax not only as its North American refuelling base but also as an examining port to look into the holds of neutral ships carrying cargo destined for countries bordering Germany. Halifax also became the marshalling yard for close to 285,000 Canadian soldiers destined for Europe. That brought the city a brief fiscal reprieve, but it also led indirectly to a disaster that would leave a disastrous physical and psychological legacy.

After German submarines began to range the North Atlantic, picking off not only enemy naval targets but supply-filled merchant ships as well, the British responded by devising a convoy system in which merchant vessels would assemble and proceed across the North Atlantic under the watchful eyes and ready weapons of a naval escort. Where better to assemble convoys than Halifax's commodious Bedford Basin?

On the morning of December 6, 1917, the French steamship *Mont Blanc*, loaded down with a "devil's brew" of munitions, sailed up the harbour on its way to Bedford Basin to join a convoy assembling there. As she passed through the Narrows, she was struck by a Belgian relief steamer, the *Imo*, heading in the opposite direction. That otherwise innocuous collision punctured some steel drums of highly flammable benzol on the *Mont Blanc*'s deck. A small fire resulted and then, a few minutes later, at 9:05 a.m., there was a massive explosion. White smoke and shards of ship shot up to a mile into the air above the city, and the ear-splitting noise echoed more than a hundred miles in every direction. The Halifax Explosion, the largest and most destructive man-made blast to that point in history, killed more than 1,400 Haligonians and levelled the entire north end of the city, including much of what had passed for the city's military establishment.

The Explosion was a blow from which neither the military nor the city had fully recovered by 1939. That was largely because Ottawa, which was still trying to cope with the effects of the Great Depression, didn't consider the navy or Halifax a priority. A 1938 federal government report on the state of the Halifax dockyard, for example, described it as being in a "peculiarly bad state . . . A portion of the barracks is unsafe and should not be used for human habitation." As for Halifax's long-term future as a naval or port city, powerful federal Liberal cabinet minister C.D. Howe argued in a 1938 speech that there was "no future for Halifax except as an occasional port of call for tramp freighters."

The lingering impact of the Explosion, the ravages of the Depression, the inexorable post-Confederation shift of trading patterns from north-south to east-west, which favoured Central Canada over the hinterlands, and the careless indifference of Ottawa to both defence and port facilities all conspired to make Halifax less than ready to assume its suddenly vital role in the world in September 1939.

But ready or not, fit for human habitation or not, the dockyard's barracks were soon spilling over with freshly minted naval ratings. They hung their hammocks in the dockyard's gym, in the skating rink, and in other assorted buildings and sheds. When these too filled up, they spread out across the city, renting every available room or closet in every rooming house in the city.

As for those tramp freighters C.D. Howe had spoken of, they took on a surprising new importance. As did Halifax.

NO ONE COULD FIGURE out what was going on, let alone what any of it meant. Why had three of Britain's best fighting ships been tied up alongside Halifax's Ocean Terminals piers for two days, offloading explosives from their ammunition lockers, when they could be escorting a vital convoy back across the Atlantic? And why had their captains, who never took much interest in such routine matters as loading and unloading, personally supervised the movement of the boxes from their ships to a waiting train, which seemed in such a hurry to be off that it was already belching smoke from its funnel while the unloading progressed? And why had civilians in bankers' suits stood beside the captains, dutifully noting the numbers on the boxes (Z298, Z299, Z300 . . .) and then signing a receipt for each one? And why, finally, had a hundred or more gun-toting Mounties stood menacingly on the ships' decks and the wharves while the cargo was being transferred?

It wouldn't have helped to ask the ships' crews. They were as mystified as everyone else. More so, in fact.

Almost two weeks earlier, on October 4, a month after Chamberlain declared war, the crews of the British battle cruisers *Emerald*, *Enterprise* and *Caradoc* had been mustered at Plymouth, England, and issued with white canvas tropical clothing. Captain Augustus Wallington Shelton Agar, the skipper of the *Emerald*, told his 650 crewmen they would be given a brief leave with their families before embarking on their new mission. Normally a secretive sort, Agar surprised his men by telling them he had no objection if they told their loved ones they'd soon be frolicking in the tropics.

Twelve hours after the ship left Plymouth, however, the captain made an entry in the ship's log: "Sailed for Halifax with *Caradoc* and *Enterprise*," it stated simply.

What was going on? The ship's gun lockers were invariably filled with munitions of one sort or another, but the captain didn't usually oversee their loading. This time he'd not only supervised personally, but he also hadn't returned the locker key to its usual spot in the bulkhead cabinet, where all the ship's keys were kept.

Instead, he put it in his pocket and kept it in his possession for the entire ten-day Atlantic crossing.

There was good reason for caution: the "explosives" were in fact £2 million worth of gold bars being shipped secretly to Canada to buy arms and supplies from the United States under its cash-and-carry-only policy. (They weren't the first. In June, shortly before the war began, the British had used the royal visit to Canada as a cover to secretly spirit gold bullion out of England aboard the navy cruisers that accompanied the King and Queen.) This time the British Admiralty not only misidentified the ships' cargo to avoid detection, but it also concocted the elaborate subterfuge of issuing the crews with tropical gear in hopes that loose lips might leak the word to enemy agents, who would then transmit false information back to Berlin. The plan had worked wonderfully well, except for the fact that the ships' crews had had to cross the frigid Atlantic wearing little more than their summer lights. The return journey promised to be even colder.

When Agar confided his concerns for his crew's comfort to a Bank of Canada official—one of those "civilians in bankers' suits" who'd signed for the gold bars—the man told him not to worry and immediately contacted a friend in the local Red Cross. Within forty-eight hours the ships' crews were unloading Red Cross cartons filled with warm horsehide gloves of the kind worn by Canadian lumbermen, thick woollen scarves, seaboot stockings, leather headgear lined with wool and fur to protect the ears, and enough woollen underwear for every member of the crew.

Thirty-six hours after arriving in Halifax, the three ships departed with their convoy of merchant ships. Shortly after the *Emerald* cleared the harbour mouth, Captain Agar and a few members of his crew tuned in to listen to Lord Haw-Haw's shortwave radio broadcast. Lord Haw-Haw (real name William Joyce) was an American-born Englishman who'd fled to Germany just before the war and was now doing daily Nazi propaganda broadcasts. Though they weren't supposed to listen, Agar and his sailors couldn't help themselves. It wasn't that they bought Haw-Haw's line—far from it. He was just good for a laugh. "Jarmany calling . . . Jarmany calling," he began in the poor imitation of an aristocratic English accent that had prompted a British journalist to give him his mocking nickname. After a suitable pause Lord Haw-Haw continued: "The British cruiser *Emerald* is now leaving Halifax harbour with a large convoy of ships carrying American war material to England."

How could he know that? the sailors wondered. Most of the convoy hadn't even cleared the harbour yet. Captain Agar knew. He had been warned there were German spies operating in Halifax. All a spy had to do was see the convoy forming up in Bedford Basin and telephone that information to the German embassy in Washington, which could then relay it instantly to Berlin. Agar was only grateful they hadn't learned in advance of the *Emerald*'s arrival in Halifax or, more importantly, of its real mission.

But the Germans certainly knew enough now to have their submarines in position to attack the *Emerald* and its convoy. And although Agar's ships took action to avoid their pursuers, the German U-boats would manage to sink two vessels before the convoy reached its destination.

"JANNIE?" DESMOND PIERS began hesitantly, not quite certain after all these years that the voice at the other end of his telephone line was really Janet Macneill's.

How many years had it been? Seven? It was difficult to believe that seven eventful, life-shaping, world-changing years had passed since that morning at the railway station back in the summer of 1932. Piers was just nineteen then, fresh-faced and flushed with excitement at the adventure ahead of him. He was about to take the train from Halifax to Montreal, then hitch a ride on a Cunard steamship to England, where he would spend the next five years training to become a full-fledged officer in the Royal Canadian Navy. That was his dream, and he was going to chase it. Jannie, along with his mother, father, brother and sister, had come to the railway station that morning to say their goodbyes and good-lucks. Jannie had been his . . . what? His girlfriend? His friend? He couldn't be sure.

He'd heard from friends that she too was back in Halifax now, living with her parents. He decided to phone her there.

"Yes?" Janet Macneill answered politely, warily. She didn't recognize his voice.

"Jannie, it's Debby. Debby Piers." Everyone called him Debby, the result of a childhood mispronunciation of his original nickname, Desy. He didn't mind, but he did insist on pointing out that it was spelled with a masculine *y* and not a feminine *ie*.

Growing up, he and Janet had been part of the same teen incrowd. They swam and sailed together at the Waegwoltic Club, a popular summer playground for well-to-do families, played tennis and flirted with each other at the south-end courts, were good friends, boyfriend-girlfriend, then just good friends again. He was always, it seemed, more interested in her than she in him. He had been smitten, in fact, since the moment he'd first laid eyes on her up on the stage at the old Majestic Theatre on Barrington Street. She was a six-year-old fairy waving a green sparkler wand in a British touring company's production of *A Midsummer Night's Dream*. The company, which made yearly visits to Halifax, offering local audiences their annual dose of one Shakespeare, one comedy and one mystery, managed to keep costs down and generate community interest by hiring locals to play bit roles in the productions. Janet was one of a group of dancers from a local company who'd been invited to do brief turns in *A Midsummer Night's Dream*. Debby was in the audience, a reluctant seven-year-old dragooned into attending the performance by his parents, who believed he needed a little culture to leaven his boyish physicality. After the show, when his parents asked him what he'd liked about it, Debby could only talk about the little fairy with the green sparkler wand. "I like that one," he said. He still did.

Jannie had grown up to be a dark-haired, dark-eyed young woman whose beauty might have seemed brooding were it not for her constant smile and coquettishness. Debby always found her more than a little hard to read. The summer he'd left for England, she told him he was all right but that they were too close in age to be more than friends. She preferred older boys; they were more exciting. But she'd kissed him goodbye at the railway station anyway. He'd thought about that kiss plenty of times in the years since, wondered from time to time what might have been. But their lives had spun off in different directions.

She'd moved to London, married a Beaverbrook, had a child, separated, made a life for herself in London society, and then reluctantly escaped that life just before war was declared. He had spent five years with the Royal Navy, earning his way up the ranks—cadet, midshipman, sub-lieutenant—while serving aboard British warships and studying at the Royal Naval College. Finally, in 1937, he'd returned to Canada as a first lieutenant aboard the Royal Canadian Navy's newly acquired British destroyer HMCS *Restigouche*, which was based in British Columbia. A few days before Britain declared war on Germany, Ottawa ordered *Restigouche*, along with two other British Columbia–based destroyers, to steam down the west coast to the Panama Canal and then up the eastern seaboard to Halifax. The vessels would be assigned to North Atlantic convoy escort duty, Canada's already agreed-upon role in the coming conflict. The *Restigouche* was due to leave port the day after tomorrow, accompanying a convoy of merchant ships filled to overflowing with war supplies and bound for England, but he was under orders not to disclose the details to anyone, especially over the telephone, where "who knows who" could be listening.

Debby Piers had not been without girlfriends in the years since he and Janet kissed each other goodbye. He was bright and witty, and young men in uniform, especially officers' uniforms, still held their cachet for young women in port cities the world over. But Debby had never quite managed to put Janet totally out of his mind. They still seemed, in ways he couldn't quite articulate, to fit together.

"I'm back in Halifax," Debby Piers explained over the phone. "But not for very long. Would you like to get together?"

In part, of course, they fit together because of their shared heritage. They were both members in good standing of old Halifax society. Debby Piers could trace his roots back to Halifax's founding; Janet's grandfather was the first Conservative premier of Nova Scotia. "Halifax was a queer town," Janet would explain many years later. "It was very military in one element, and then there was the university crowd, and the Halifax establishment—the old 400 of Halifax, people used to call it. It was all very gracious, a very Victorian kind of life." Their families fit comfortably into that life. Debby's father was a prominent businessman, Janet's father a well-known professor who did double duty as registrar at Dalhousie University.

Though Debby's mother, a doctor, had wanted him to go to Dalhousie and become a doctor or a lawyer, Debby wasn't ready to abandon his young manhood to book learning. After graduating from high school in 1930, he enrolled at the Royal Military College in Kingston, Ontario. Two years later, after spending a summer training with the Royal Canadian Navy in Halifax, Piers told his startled family he had decided to abandon his studies at RMC and join the then almost moribund Royal Canadian Navy. He'd decided on the navy, he would admit later, largely because he was so impressed with the commander in charge of his summer training aboard HMCS *Saguenay*, another Royal Navy–trained Nova Scotian, Leonard Murray. "I thought he was the greatest thing on two feet." Murray helped Debby convince his father the navy would be the right career for him.

Janet Macneill had attended Dalhousie for a year, but university life wasn't for her either, which is how she had come to abandon Halifax for the brighter lights of London two years after Debby. Now, she was back home again, a single mother at loose ends.

She happily agreed to meet her old beau for coffee.

HAROLD BRUCE JEFFERSON peered into his binoculars, slowly playing them along the sleek black hull of the luxury vessel that was executing a graceful mid-harbour turn before falling into line behind her predecessor. It was December 22, 1939, and the second troop convoy of the war was finally departing for Europe. At both bow and stern, blazing gold lettering proudly proclaimed this vessel to be the *Andes*, a ship barely out of her builder's yard. Unlike some of the other ships in today's convoy, which had at least painted their superstructures a dull war grey and blacked out their towering funnels, the *Andes* not only broadcast its name for all the world to see but also continued to flaunt its Caribbean cruise colour scheme of black, white and buff. What ever happened to camouflage, Jefferson wondered?

Jefferson—H.B. as he signed his official papers, Jeff to everyone who knew him—was a squat, balding, middle-aged ex-journalist whose rimless glasses did nothing to camouflage the fact that his right eye wandered. It always seemed to be looking off to the side. Some people thought it made him seem like he wasn't paying attention to them. But he was. In fact, very little escaped his notice.

Jefferson put down the binoculars and picked up a pen. On a pad at his desk he added the name *Andes* to the growing list of ships' names. He had already written "HMS *Revenge*," the name of the lead British naval escort, at the top of the page, followed by the flotilla of ocean liners, all of which had only recently been converted into troopships: the *Chobry, Almanzora, Reina del Pacifica, Batory, Ormonde* and now *Andes*. He made a careful note of each ship's name, its place in today's convoy, its time of departure and, if possible, some interesting tidbit about it. Today he noted that the *Chobry* and *Batory* were "orphans of the seas," Polish ships that, thanks to Hitler, no longer had a home port to call their own; and also that the *Almanzora*, the slowest ship in the convoy, had performed similar soldier-carrying services in the last war.

Through the window Jefferson could hear ships' bands playing as their vessels passed his observation post, and even snatches of the songs—"Hail, Hail, the Gang's All Here," "South of the Border," "Beer Barrel Polka"—the soldiers were singing lustily to amuse themselves as they bid their final farewells to the shores of North America. The fact that there were few on the wharves to hear their singing didn't seem to deter them.

Perhaps, Jefferson thought, looking out the window again, he should try to snap a last photograph of the *Andes* before she disappeared into the spitting snow and mist and fog at the harbour mouth.

He smiled to himself. Picture taking, ship watching, list making—these had long been among his diverse pleasures, some might even say passions. What would his new official self make of a man sitting alone in an office high above Halifax harbour, carefully documenting the supposedly top secret departure of Canada's second troop convoy?

He certainly wasn't the only one whose hobbies, even offhand remarks, might be subject to sinister interpretation. As Frank Doyle, the often acerbic managing editor over at the *Mail*, had put it, the local police court these days "looked like a Halifax Who's Who as the notables, who should have known better, appeared in the dock charged with having written or telephoned information of value to the enemy." Three days ago, in fact, five more Halifax men had been charged with violating Defence of Canada regulations through their indiscretion in mentioning military matters in letters they'd written to people in the United States.

As embarrassing as that might have been for those good citizens of Halifax, getting caught would be far worse for Jeff Jefferson. He was barely a month into his new position as the Canadian government's Regional Director of Censorship (Press and Radio) for the Maritimes.

On September 1, 1939, Mackenzie King's federal government passed Order-in-Council PC 2481, which declared that "no person shall print, circulate or distribute a book, newspaper, periodical, pamphlet, picture, or document of any kind containing any material, report or statement, false or otherwise intended or likely to cause disaffection to His Majesty, or to interfere with the success of His Majesty's forces, or of the forces of any Allied or associated power, or to prejudice His Majesty's relations with foreign powers, or intended or likely to prejudice the recruiting, training, discipline or administration of any of His Majesty's forces, or which would or might be prejudicial to the safety of the state or the efficient prosecution of the war." To help translate this sweeping prohibition into a workable, practicable reality in the newsrooms of the nation, the government appointed Walter Scott Thompson, a three-hundred-pound former Fleet Street reporter who'd become the official press agent for the CNR, as the Chief Censor for Canada for the duration of the war that had not yet been declared.

As an ex-newspaperman, Thompson decided his press censors should be experienced journalists acceptable to the most skeptical reporters. His first choice was Wilfrid Eggleston, a veteran parliamentary press gallery journalist and self-described "John Stuart Mill follower" who believed that censorship was, at best, a necessary evil. Eggleston became the chief press censor for the country, and he in turn recruited equally strong-minded journalists in Toronto, Montreal and Vancouver, as well as the especially strong-minded Jefferson in Halifax to oversee the regional press.

Given the Maritimes' geographical closeness to the conflict and the key role that Halifax was expected to play in it, Eggleston initially planned to hire local censors to handle Saint John and Charlottetown. He soon changed his mind, however, concluding (rightly) that Jefferson, who was famed for his prodigious memory, his devastating wit and his insatiable appetite for work, could handle the Maritimes by himself. It was no easy task. There were sixteen daily newspapers, ten radio stations, seventy-seven weeklies, two wire services, and assorted magazines and publications in his territory, not to mention visiting journalists filing stories to elsewhere. Jefferson's job was to read in advance every newspaper story and radio broadcast that was submitted, and then offer advice on whether the story should—or could—be told.

Canada's censorship system, like that of the British, was essentially voluntary. The editors themselves decided which stories they'd ask Jefferson to rule on. And Jefferson couldn't forbid them to publish or broadcast anything; he simply interpreted the current law and regulations, and explained what harm publishing a particular nugget of information might do to the war effort. It was then up to the editors to decide what to publish, knowing that if they made the wrong decision, their papers could be banned and they could end up in jail.

The problem was that no one, including Jefferson and his fellow censors, really understood what the law was or, more importantly, what it meant. Within two months of the declaration of war *The Clarion*, a Toronto-based communist newspaper, had been banned. While that was not surprising—*The Clarion* supported Stalin, who'd thrown his lot in with Hitler—other, more mainstream newspapers found themselves stifled too. The Victoria newspapers, for example, complained when the Vancouver censor ruled they shouldn't report on the departure of the Princess Patricia Regiment, the first detachment from the city to head overseas, even though the soldiers had marched openly through the city's downtown streets and *The New York Times* had published a photo of the parade.

To make matters worse—for the censors and those they were supposed to censor—government officials themselves often ignored their own rules. The day after Ottawa issued an edict banning newspapers from mentioning actual or expected troop movements, Vincent Massey, Canada's High Commissioner in London, told the world in a shortwave broadcast that "in a few weeks a full division will be leaving Canadian shores for service in France." Even though the CBC broadcast Massey's declaration, the censors refused Canadian newspapers permission to publish it, just as they had said no less than a week earlier when Winston Churchill broke a Canadian embargo on news that the first convoy from Halifax carrying Canadian army troops had docked in England. "Yesterday," Churchill had declared in a stirringly patriotic statement broadcast everywhere in the British Empire but not reported in Canada, "the leading division of the Canadian army, strongly escorted over the ocean, disembarked safely and smoothly in one of our harbours."

Luckily, Jefferson had so far escaped criticism from the editors he dealt with. Perhaps that was because he was already well known and respected. Born in 1893, he had begun his reporting career in his hometown of Moncton in 1912 before setting out on a peripatetic, two-and-a-half-decade journalistic journey around the Maritimes, with stops—sometimes more than once—in Fredericton, Saint John, Yarmouth, Charlottetown, Sydney and Halifax. As a reporter he seemed to have a knack for being in the right place at the right time. He joined the staff of the Halifax *Herald*, for example, just in time to cover the Halifax Explosion and the military riots that occurred near the end of the Great War. A mob of sailors and soldiers rampaged through city streets, beating policemen and attacking civic institutions like police headquarters and city hall. That riot was quelled only when a British cruiser landed an armed force in the city to take control of the situation. Tension between locals and the military, Jefferson knew from that experience, was an almost inevitable by-product of the pressures of war on Halifax.

By the beginning of the turbulent 1920s, Jefferson had landed in Sydney, where he became news editor of the *Post-Record* just as labour troubles in the coal mines there turned violent. While covering the colliery strikes, legend had it that he worked fifteen straight days without sleep. In the late 1930s, after an unsuccessful three-year sojourn as the editor and publisher of two weekly newspapers he'd leased in southwestern Nova Scotia, Jefferson returned to Halifax to become an editorial writer and columnist for the *Chronicle* just as the city was gearing up for war. But this move may have had less to do with his search for the next big story and more with a desire to put some distance between himself and his creditors. In 1938 a Yarmouth coal company tracked him down to his new job in Halifax to dun him for payment of an overdue account. If he didn't pay up by July 11, declared the shirty letter from the accountant at L.E. Baker and Co., "I will immediately put the matter in the hands of a lawyer and possibly call up Angus L. on the telephone, as your letters refer to him." That was another thing about Jefferson: he knew everyone who was anyone in the region, including Angus L. Macdonald, the premier of Nova Scotia, and he wasn't afraid to let others know of his relationships with the powerful.

Now, at forty-six, it seemed he had finally become powerful himself. Not that you would know it by his office, a cramped, newspaper-strewn workspace in what was popularly referred to as "the knob," a small, largely ornamental four-storey dome on the roof of the eight-storey Post Office Building on Bedford Row, the tallest office building in the downtown. Though his furnishings were standard government issue—a flat-top office desk with brass handles on the drawers, a wooden swivel armchair, an oak typewriter desk, four gooseneck lamps, an already-the-worse-for-wear Underwood typewriter and a black telephone whose headset seemed never to remain long in its cradle—Jefferson at least had the compensation of a stunning view of the harbour all the way from the Narrows in the north to the harbour mouth in the south, as well as east across the harbour to Dartmouth and west across the downtown and up to the Old Town Clock on the eastern slope of Citadel Hill.

Jefferson didn't have a secretary, but he didn't need one. He not only knew where he kept every note and file and newspaper, but he could also—thanks to his years as a journalist—type faster than any secretary. He typed, and kept copies of, everything: notes of his telephone calls, reports of his rulings, his official as well as unofficial correspondence, his daily journal, his random observations on life in the city, and, of course, his careful lists of everything from what was contained in the many photographs he'd taken to the names and details of the ships in the convoys that passed by his office window.

Later tonight, back in his room at the Nova Scotian Hotel, he would, as usual, write about what he'd observed today. "It is

December 22, 1939, and the second flight of Canada's active service force is on its way. No crowds assemble. No shore bands play. Only a few score people fortunate enough to possess residences or offices overlooking the port really see put in motion the forces which may soon upset nations and profoundly change the course of history."

Strange, he thought to himself, how little it seemed like war. Perhaps that was because the troopships in today's convoy looked more like luxury liners than military transports. Until very recently, all but two of the conscripted cruise ships in this convoy had catered to the tourist trade in the sunny south. Jefferson had visited the *Andes* after it docked earlier this week. The ship, he had noted in his journal, boasted Australian walnut, rosewood and ash ornamentation, not to mention modern indirect illumination, chromium, tapestry, and expensive leather in profusion. Canada's first troops were going to war in style, some even sleeping in staterooms with their own private baths, which would have set the ordinary traveller back up to fifty dollars a day. The only problem was that these vessels weren't equipped with the familiar steam heat, so the soldiers aboard them spent many chilly hours while they figured out how to make the tricky newfangled electrical controls heat their cabins.

This past week, while the convoy was assembling—thousands of troops had poured into the city by the trainload—Jefferson had spent whatever spare time he could carve out from his censorship duties hanging out with the newspaper correspondents who accompanied the troops. They were a jovial lot. Sam Robertson, the Canadian Press correspondent, had acquired a bosun's whistle and learned to blow it well enough to pipe them all aboard the ship they were scheduled to sail on. Later, the reporters gathered in the wardroom to present the officer assigned to look after them with an impressive-looking brassard, or arm band, which, when unfolded, declared in formidable gold letters, *Steward Barovsky*. That translated roughly, Robertson would later tell Jefferson, as bar steward.

How long might they all be gone, Jefferson wondered? Would Canadian soldiers even be needed to defeat Hitler? It seemed less and less likely. He glanced at the newspapers on the desk in front of him. ALLIES SMASH NAZI SUB FLEET, declared the main headline on the December 20 *Mail*, over a wire service story quoting French estimates that the Allies had sent more than fifty German submarines to the bottom of the North Atlantic since the war began. Yesterday's *Mail* lay opened to another equally upbeat story: UNHAPPY HOLIDAY FOR HITLER, it read, TIDE OF BATTLE TURNS HEAVILY AGAINST NAZIS.

His job, Jefferson felt, might be over before he'd even learned what it was. As satisfying as that might be for the country as a whole, he wasn't certain he wanted his new career to end quite so soon.

He looked up again from his desk and out the window at the harbour. The snow was coming down harder and thicker. As the last of the big troop transports cleared the harbour mouth, a powerful but deceptively yacht-like warship flying the French flag slipped its moorings and fell in behind. This was the *Dunkerque*, possibly the handsomest warship afloat. "The whirligig of time," Jefferson would write that evening, "brings few changes stranger than the partnership under which France and Britain unite to convoy the soldiers of the young Dominion over which they fought tooth and nail less than 200 years ago."

He'd already made a note that this convoy had taken a "bare" thirty-five minutes to get underway in formation while the first departing troop convoy, two weeks ago, needed a full one hour and fifty-five minutes to accomplish the same.

The war, he thought, was going very well.

THE WAR, IN TRUTH, was not going nearly as well as Jefferson supposed, at least not so far as staff at naval headquarters in Ottawa was concerned. *Naval headquarters.* Now that was a joke. The Royal Canadian Navy operated out of the second and third floors of a three-storey building on Queen Street in the nation's capital. The building's more important tenant was a grocery store. The offices, as one officer described them, were "an extremely inconvenient rabbit warren," so overcrowded that the only place for the officers and their subordinates to have coffee was in the anteroom where the female staff hung their coats.

Nova Scotia–born Captain Leonard Murray arrived at naval headquarters in January 1939. His new appointment, as Director of Operations and Training, was bittersweet because, though it was a promotion, it was also a reminder: he was still one step behind the man he called his "running mate." George Jones had been promoted too. The two men were engaged in a bitter, career-long competition that had begun in 1913, the year they graduated from the three-year training program at the Royal Naval College in Halifax. By virtue of his higher standing in the class, Murray had managed to stay one step ahead of his rival until 1938, when their boss, Vice Admiral Percy Nelles, the Chief of Naval Staff, appointed them both captain but chose to promote Jones one day ahead of Murray, effectively leapfrogging Jones into pre-eminence for future promotions.

Murray's rivalry with Jones was no secret in naval circles. In 1931, when Canada's tiny four-ship destroyer fleet trained together in the West Indies, Murray, the commander of the east coast's two-vessel flotilla, and Jones, in charge of the two west coast destroyers, got into a heated argument one night on the deck of one of the destroyers. Though no one would later be able to recall what the argument was about, one officer said that both men "yielded to mutual animosity in harsh unbridled language . . . A feud had blossomed."

Murray still wasn't sure why Nelles had chosen to humiliate him by publicly favouring his rival, but there were plenty of theories among his underlings. The most popular was that the real target of Nelles's wrath was not Murray at all but his wife, Jean, a failed opera singer six years his senior, who, many suggested snidely, was the real captain in the family. The daughter of a wealthy Ontario physician, Jean spent her teenaged years in Europe becoming "more British than the King," as one acquaintance put it. Two of her sisters married British officers, one of whom, Jean would note with familial pride, became a private secretary to King George VI. Jean and Leonard sent their own eldest son, fourteen-year-old Alexander, to study at the naval college in Dartmouth, England, in 1939. When Eric Dennis called to interview Jean for a story he planned to write for the *Herald* about her son, the up-and-coming young "Nova Scotian naval officer," Jean replied stiffly: "He is not a Nova Scotian naval officer. He is a *British* naval officer."

Even though Murray, who'd trained with the Royal Navy himself, was also much enamoured of all things British ("He's pro–Royal Navy, even to the detriment of the RCN," Nelles wrote in one critical evaluation) and spoke with what some described as an affected English accent, he was not above mocking their foibles. He liked to tell a joke about a proper British officer who had just listened to an impassioned speech by a naval chaplain in which he discussed the awful things that might befall sinful navy men when they arrived at the pearly gates. Shaken by what he'd heard, though not in the way the speaker had intended, the officer later approached the chaplain. "Do you mean," he demanded, "that officers and ordinary sailors will have to share the same heaven?"

Murray remained personally popular with those under him, in part because he seemed so unlike the butt of that joke. He'd played hockey and rugby with ratings on local navy teams wherever he was stationed. But if that earned him the loyalty of those below decks, his incessant stream of petty complaints to head office, especially after Jones overtook him in rank, eventually made him a pariah among some of the brass hats in Ottawa.

Nevertheless, in 1939, Murray's new job put him at the very centre of the navy's planning for war—and, not coincidentally, at the right hand of Nelles. Whatever their personal feelings towards one another, Nelles and Murray turned out to be a well-matched team. They won the first key battle of the war before war was even declared. Some of their more ambitious colleagues wanted Canada to buy battle cruisers or build its own fleet of submarines, but Murray and Nelles argued that the navy's real job in the coming war would be to ferry men and materials to Europe. They proposed that

Canada develop a convoy escort navy instead, one built around the corvette, a small, relatively inexpensive vessel to build and operate. Though the vessel "bucks like the hammers of hell in weather," Murray noted that corvettes were also "very easy to handle, good sea boats whose machinery could be handled by the merest novice." Better yet, they could be built by Canadian shipyards for less than $700,000 each.

Nelles and Murray eventually carried the day, thanks in part, Murray would claim later, to the sinking of the *Athenia*. They were able to use that first-day disaster to convince Prime Minister King that Canada's navy should focus on escort duties and protecting shipping. The sinking of the passenger liner had another unexpected but welcome consequence: it focused public attention on the importance of the navy and goosed recruiting across the country. Canadians, Murray would explain, were "not navy-minded in 1939, but that incident helped prevent a recurrence of World War I in which by far the greatest stress had been on the army." Given that the navy began the war with just 1,819 officers and men, attracting recruits was a crucial part of Murray's job. So too was building, almost from scratch, the fleet of ships that would enable Canada to fulfill its new commitment to convoy escort and anti-submarine warfare.

By September 10, when Canada's parliament finally voted to go to war, Murray had been promoted to Deputy Chief of Defence Staff. With Nelles temporarily absent from headquarters to be with his ill son, who had gone to the United States for surgery, many of the early decisions about the conduct of the war fell to Murray.

During the summer, he travelled from coast to coast, meeting with retired officers to inform them what he would expect of them if and when war came, as well as visiting shipyards to see which ones could build how many new ships and how quickly. The answer was, not enough and not quickly enough. That made one of the navy's most urgent needs a fleet of small, fast vessels to patrol Canada's thousands of miles of coastline. The quickest and most efficient way to get them would be to buy diesel-fuelled, steel-hulled yachts and convert them for war use, but there weren't any suitable vessels in Canada. There were plenty in private hands in the United States, of course, but openly selling the yachts to the Canadian government would have put their owners in violation of the U.S. Neutrality Act.

So Murray devised a clever ruse. He called a number of east coast businessmen, including Sidney Oland, a brewery owner he'd met in Halifax. Are you still prepared to do your patriotic duty, Murray wanted to know? Although a veteran of the Great War, Oland was now fifty-seven and certainly not expecting to play any direct role in this conflict. But Murray had other ideas. He had an important covert mission for him, he told Oland. The Canadian government was about to confiscate his yacht as a naval coastal patrol vessel. Since he was sure Oland wouldn't want to be without a sailing vessel, he would need to buy a replacement right away. Murray had a suggestion for a vessel Oland might want to buy. When he brought this newly acquired American yacht—steel-hulled and diesel-powered—back to Canada, Murray explained, the government would immediately seize it and return his old boat to him. Ingenious, really—Oland would get to keep his yacht, Canada would have an appropriate coastal patrol vessel, and the American sellers would have lived up to the letter of the Neutrality Act.

Oland, like other well-heeled yachtsmen Murray contacted, was more than willing to do his bit for King and country. Shortly after Ottawa seized his yacht, Oland travelled as directed to Houston, where he bought the 140-foot *Mascotte* and sailed her back to Halifax. Luckily, the two brothers who'd owned the vessel and used it primarily for entertaining had accidentally left a "generous amount of Scotch" aboard. That, as Oland explained to Murray, had made the long journey infinitely more pleasurable.

ERIC DENNIS COULDN'T BE SURE if McNab really meant what he said or if his promise was just the liquor talking. It was, after all,

New Year's Eve, and the booze was flowing freely, if clandestinely, in the cavernous ballroom of the Nova Scotian Hotel. Eric knew that McNab's father, Archibald P. McNab, was the lieutenant-governor of Saskatchewan, so perhaps he really could, as McNab claimed, help Dennis get into the Royal Canadian Air Force.

Should he tell McNab the truth, he wondered?

Eric looked around the ballroom. It was full of freshly scrubbed young men in fancy, full-dress uniform—Brits, Canadians, even a few Frenchmen with red pompoms above their pie-plate hats. All of them, it seemed, at least from Eric Dennis's still unhappily civilian vantage point, were surrounded by attractive, eager-to-please young women. They were talking, laughing and dancing, and who knew what else they'd be up to before the night was through. There were rumours—Dennis had heard them himself—that navy medical officers were now handing out condoms like candy. Unofficially, of course; officially, sailors had no need for such protection.

Also officially, thanks to the new censorship rules, newspapers could no longer identify Halifax in their war-related stories; it was now "An East Coast Port." Of course, everyone, including the Germans, knew "An East Coast Port" usually meant Halifax, but that didn't matter to the men who made the rules. If you bought that there was such a place as "An East Coast Port," you might also accept the official line that there were no bars or taverns in that mysterious place. But everyone knew there was no shortage of either alcohol or places to drink it in Halifax, if you knew where to go and what to ask for.

Consider tonight, for example. Even though the hotel ballroom was overflowing with happy drunks, not one of them had purchased alcohol legally at the hotel. Tonight's party-goers bought only mix from the hotel waiters, surreptitiously—or not so surreptitiously, since no one paid the least attention—adding alcohol from the flasks they kept concealed in their dates' purses or in the inside breast pockets of their uniform jackets. That was because the hotel wasn't allowed to sell alcohol of any sort. Nor were bars or taverns permitted to operate. All these regulations were a hangover from the days of real Prohibition, which had officially ended in Nova Scotia nearly a decade before.

But there were ways around the rules. Some of tonight's revellers had bought their liquor from one of the hotel bellhops, who ran a lucrative sideline tending to the alcohol needs of guests and dance patrons. Others had purchased their poison in advance, either from one of the government-operated liquor stores or—because the liquor stores never seemed to be open when people wanted to buy alcohol (a happenstance some insisted was more than coincidental)—from one of the city's dozens of bootleggers. The bootleggers not only kept better hours than the government stores, but they were also, thanks to increasing demand, conveniently located at just about every downtown street corner.

There were also more than two dozen private clubs in Halifax that catered to well-to-do civilians, who would purchase alcohol legally at the liquor commission and keep it in their own personal lockers at their clubs. The bartenders, who held the keys to the lockers, would mix their patrons' drinks using alcohol from the patrons' lockers. And Royal Navy captains were more than welcome to enjoy a wee dram or two, or three or four more, at the Halifax Club, the city's oldest and most exclusive downtown businessmen's gathering spot. Recently, club members, in a moment of patriotic passion, had voted to make them honorary members of the club.

But not ordinary sailors. In fact, there was nowhere in the city for them to drink legally. Under provincial liquor laws no one was allowed to be outside with an open bottle of liquor. The only acceptable place to drink was at home—but most sailors had no home in Halifax. They weren't even allowed to bring liquor they'd bought legitimately at the government liquor store back to their barracks. So, many sailors ended up drinking their fill at waterfront brothels and "blind pigs," as the illegal bars were called, or in dark alleys near the harbour, or, more and more often these days, openly, on the main streets, in full view of women and children.

The staid old Board of Trade, as worried about the loss of business among its members as about the growing lack of decorum downtown, had set up a committee to lobby for a plebiscite on allowing restaurateurs to sell beer and wine by the glass. Its members included some of the city's most prominent merchants. There was even a woman, from a fine south-end family, on the group's executive committee—Edith Macneill, Janet's sister—and she'd already begun making plans with their sister Isabel and another woman, a vivacious Montrealer named Dolly McEuen, to set up a club where ordinary British sailors could get a drink.

Two days after the Board of Trade meeting, the president of the Halifax Social Services Council, a churchly temperance group, sternly rebuked the Board for its godless action, warning, "Many a man has become a confirmed drunkard by the use of beer and wine."

But the verdicts rendered by local juries in a series of recent rum-smuggling cases probably reflected public sentiment more accurately than either the Board or the Council. Eric had covered the result of one trial a few weeks earlier. Despite forty-five Crown witnesses and what seemed like an airtight case, the jury had taken less than three and a half hours to acquit four alleged co-conspirators of all smuggling charges. The spectators, who'd waited until midnight for the jury to return, cheered as the men were freed. Two weeks earlier, two others had been found not guilty in connection with the same so-called conspiracy to smuggle liquor into the country.

The booming trade in illegal liquor was just a symptom of a larger and more complex problem. Halifax was being inundated with newcomers—British sailors on convoy duty, new Canadian navy recruits, soldiers passing through on their way to the front, bureaucrats who had to process them before they left, and on and on—and there was nowhere to put them all. Worse, at least according to Frank Doyle, the managing editor of the *Mail*, was that no one in authority seemed to care. While city fathers were happy to see the war as a symbol of Halifax's renewed role as "the warden of the honour of the North," he wrote, they did little to find accommodation for the fighting men the war brought to the city.

In a front-page editorial at the end of November, Doyle had quoted a few lines from Rudyard Kipling's poetic 1890s tribute to Halifax that had helped cement its reputation as Britain's most valuable wartime port:

> Into the mist my guardian prows put forth,
> Behind the mist my virgin ramparts lie;
> the Warden of the honour of the North,
> Sleepless and veiled am I.

"What is Halifax doing today to vindicate this record of history?" Doyle thundered. "Is this the key city of the Empire overseas that quibbles and procrastinates while British sailors sleep in doorways or on floors of public buildings, and red tape clogs plans for comfortable and adequate hostel facilities? Cannot someone rescue Halifax—and the serviceman—from this abysmal stagnation?"

In the ballroom at the Nova Scotian, Eric Dennis wasn't worrying about the generic plight of the serviceman. His concern was how to become one himself. He tried his best to listen—over the sounds of the increasingly raucous swing music the band was now playing—to McNab as he babbled on about how the First Canadian Air Squadron was going to challenge the Germans in the skies and that he, Eric Dennis, could join them if he wished.

If he wished? He wished for little else. Within days of Canada's declaration of war he and Colin Campbell, his boarding-house mate, had decided they would join the navy. When they arrived at the navy's so-called enlistment centre, however, the one person manning the office seemed totally uninterested in what they had to offer.

"What you fellows lookin' for?" he asked.

"We want to join the navy," Dennis told him.

"We haven't got any ships," the man replied dismissively. "Come back in a year or so."

The *Herald*'s waterfront reporter, who had been a ship's captain during the Great War and been called back into service earlier in the fall, had promised to help Eric get on with the navy, but nothing came of that either.

If it was up to him, Eric would have preferred the air force to the navy anyway. Before the war, his uncle had begun using airplanes to distribute the newspaper across the Maritimes. Partly as a result, the paper had started a flying club for members of the staff. Eric had been among the most enthusiastic of those who'd taken lessons. He loved the sensation of power he felt up in the sky. He'd got as far as taking the dual controls in one of the club's rickety old aircraft, but before the instructor would allow him to make the solo flight required to get a licence, he told Eric he would need to have a medical checkup. The doctor's report: Dennis had only 20 percent vision in his right eye, not good enough to pilot even a small single-engine plane.

Eric was disappointed but not surprised. When he was younger, he had spent a summer caddying at the Harrison Hot Springs golf resort. One day he and another caddy played a round of golf between assignments, and the other caddy's club clipped Eric under the eye as he pulled back for a swing. The country doctor who treated him told Eric he would need to wear a patch for a while, but that his eye would eventually get better. It didn't.

"Five-four-three-two-one . . . Happy New Year!"

Nineteen forty! Would the war go on for another year? Would it last long enough for Eric Dennis to get in on the action? Would anyone want him? He reached into his jacket's inside breast pocket for his own flask.

CHAPTER 2

1940
– Lineups and Loneliness –

Eaton's? Simpson's? Morgan's? The Hudson's Bay? In which department store should she spend her lunch hour today? Not that it really mattered. Marjory Whitelaw knew she couldn't afford to do more than window shop anyway. She had just about settled on Morgan's as her choice du jour when she heard shouting and clapping wafting towards her from down the street. She looked to where the noise seemed to be originating. Another platoon of fresh recruits for the war overseas were rounding a corner and marching, sort of smartly, along Ste-Catherine Street.

Yesterday, Germany had invaded France. Today in Montreal— a city where many, especially young francophones, had previously regarded the war as yet another Anglo plot to force young Quebecers to sacrifice their lives for the greater glory of the British Empire—the conflict overseas had suddenly become theirs too.

Marjory found it exhilarating. She could see the same sentiment in the faces of all the determined but smiling young men who paraded past her. They seemed so full of beans, she thought.

Her life? Well, it was not nearly so exciting. Her father, whom she adored, had just died, and her stepmother was dying. Although she was twenty-six now, Marjory continued to live in the family home in St-Lambert, a dull Montreal suburb she hated, taking care of her stepmother by night and commuting downtown each day to her "dull, dull, dull job" as a file clerk for an insurance company.

Marjory Whitelaw wanted something more exciting out of life. But what?

She thought again of the condolence letter she'd received from Uncle Alex and Aunt Tina. Alex and Tina Scott weren't actually blood relatives; Alex was a close friend of her father's who had recently been transferred to Halifax as the CNR's supervisor of engineering for eastern Canada. Alex's new job came with "a great big house" on Young Avenue in the south end of the city. Marjory was more than welcome to live with them for a while, Tina wrote, perhaps get away from Montreal's bad memories. Alex even offered to help her find a job.

Halifax? Marjory had heard Marion Watson, a friend of her parents and the wife of another CNR man, talk wistfully about what the city had been like during World War I. "It was wonderfully exciting," she gushed. "I danced every night until dawn."

Marjory glanced again at the platoon of fresh-faced Black Watch recruits passing in review. There were sophisticated young WASPs from Anglo Westmount marching side by side with poor pepsis, as they were called, from French Montreal, marching side by side with—Then she saw a face she recognized. He was a runner for the local bootlegger. She'd always thought of him as a shabbily dressed low-life with few prospects and of little interest. But now, marching by in his brand new uniform, an ear-to-ear grin splitting his face, he looked almost handsome. He seemed so cheerful, like he was heading off on an adventure.

Marjory decided she was ready for an adventure too. She would take Alex and Tina up on their offer. She would move to Halifax. She would dance until dawn.

"WE'LL TRY THIS ONE FIRST," Arne Benson declared to no one in particular, pointing a finger at another closed doorway on his right.

"If we don't find anything here, we'll try next door." The din of clashing conversations and raucous laughter that spilled out into the summer night air seemed to be coming from behind almost every door they passed along Hollis Street. How was he supposed to know which housed a bootlegger?

Arne Benson didn't want to be here tonight, leading this ragtag delegation of too eager Norwegian sailors. Somehow they'd managed to transform his wife's kindly offer of coffee at their apartment into a promise to lead them on their nocturnal quest for alcohol. But they were, after all, fellow countrymen. If he didn't help them find their way in this unfamiliar, inhospitable city, who would?

Benson, a slight, dapper man whose own drinking tended to little more than an occasional glass of wine with a meal, rapped hard on the door. He glanced up to see a heavy-set woman looking down on them appraisingly from a second-floor window. Satisfied that they were not cops (she knew most of the city's police force by face, name and sometimes even alcoholic preference), the woman signalled to someone across the room. He reached over and gave a quick tug on a chain at the top of the stairs. The chain snaked down the staircase along the wall to a spring lock on the main-floor door, which flipped open to allow Benson and his half-dozen thirsty Norwegians to enter.

Just as Marjory Whitelaw was planning to do, Arne Benson had come to Halifax from Montreal two years before in search of a better life. However, *this* was not quite the better life he had in mind.

When he immigrated to North America from Norway in 1930, Benson, whose training was in physical therapy but whose passion was music, had hoped to find fame and fortune as a musician in New York. Instead, he'd ended up managing the Turkish bath at the Mount Royal Hotel in Montreal, where his customers included some particularly enthusiastic travelling businessmen from a city called Halifax. They told him there was nothing in their city to compare with his steam baths and massages, and urged him to relocate to the east coast and set up his own business.

He might not have considered the idea at all, but his wife, Molly, another Norwegian who'd grown up in one of their country's largest port cities, had become homesick for an ocean. She told him they had to move to either Vancouver or Halifax.

Halifax was, at first, a disappointment. But they set up shop— The Arne Benson Health Studio: Swedish Massage and Physio Therapy—on the second floor of a Sackville Street barber shop and began to build a successful business, attracting the cream of Halifax's social elite. By the time war broke out, Arne had even begun to sit in with some of the bands that played the weekly supper dances at the Nova Scotian Hotel. In fact, his first thought about the war was that it would result in more dances at which he could play. Then, on April 9, 1940, the Nazis overran Norway, his homeland.

Norway's whaling fleet, on its way home from the South Atlantic, received mysterious messages from someone in England ordering all its ships to proceed so many degrees north and so many degrees west, to a safe harbour. The three-hundred-man crew of the *Sir James Clark Ross*, a whaling mother ship from Sandefjord, Norway, was so suspicious that it forced its captain to put into harbour in Bermuda so he could telegraph trusted contacts in England to make sure the message was genuine. It was. It came from the new Norwegian government-in-exile. The safe harbour it was directing the fleet to was Halifax. Within a few months, seven factory ships and twenty-two smaller whale catchers lay at anchor in Bedford Basin.

The whaling fleet's two thousand sailors were not popular among suspicious Haligonians, who questioned their loyalties, and with local authorities, who considered the noisy, swaggering newcomers such a menace that they initially refused to allow them to leave their ships. They finally relented only after Norwegian authorities agreed to build and pay for a special camp for the displaced sailors outside Halifax. "There are no Sunday school teachers among them," Halifax police chief Judson Conrod would warn his counterpart in Lunenburg after the Norwegians announced they would locate their permanent military camp and training base in the south shore community. "They are heavy drinkers and some have arms as big as my legs. On payday, the sky's the limit." Conrod suggested the Lunenburg chief consider hiring three or four extra policemen just to keep the whaling fleet in check. The Norwegians' reputation among Haligonians wasn't helped any when, later that fall, local newspapers reported that three prisoners had died and the entire population of the local lock-up had come down with diphtheria that was ostensibly spread by a Norse sailor who had been jailed for a minor offence.

The initial distrust—even disdain—was mutual. After they were allowed ashore, it was the Norwegians' turn to be appalled. There weren't enough hotel rooms to accommodate all of them, so some had to continue sleeping in cramped quarters on their dank ships in the middle of the Basin. Worse, they discovered that when they did get ashore, there was nowhere they could legally go to have a drink.

Walking along Barrington Street with Molly in the early evenings that summer, Arne Benson would sometimes feel an eerie sense of displacement, hearing nothing but Norwegian spoken on the streets. He was relieved none of the locals could understand what the sailors were saying. "This fucking town" seemed to be their favourite expression. Benson and his wife would occasionally try to placate them by inviting a few back to their apartment for a coffee. But what they really wanted was something to drink— something *alcoholic*.

Until tonight Arne Benson had never visited a bootlegger or been inside a blind pig. Like everyone, though, he couldn't help but know where to find them. The real action these days was along Hollis and Water streets, south of the downtown and close to the docks and the railway station, the main staging areas for troop convoys heading overseas. Arne Benson would often bicycle along Hollis on his way to and from the Nova Scotian Hotel, where he played his clarinet, saxophone and mandolin for supper dances at least once or twice a week. Inevitably, he'd see a lineup of men outside Germaine Pelletier's red brick house just across from the lieutenant-governor's mansion. The brothel had become so well known that its street address—51 Hollis—was incorporated into a sly saying popular among young sailors, soldiers and merchant mariners. "I'm going to die at fifty-one," one would say with a nod and a wink, and all his friends would know where he was headed. Tonight, as Benson and the Norse sailors walked along Hollis Street in search of liquor, he couldn't help but notice that the lineups at 51 Hollis included many more men in uniform: Canadian, French, British . . .

Halifax had become an international city. At any given moment there might be two thousand or more British sailors wandering the streets. The British had been here in force almost from the day last September when the first convoy assembled in Bedford Basin. Hulking British battleships steamed in and out of the harbour, playing mother hen to convoys bound for the mother country. They were joined by an ever-changing flotilla of British cruisers, destroyers, corvettes, submarines and cutters, not to mention the occasional aircraft carrier. And on top of all that there was the fleet of about two dozen former British passenger liners, like the *Rajputana*, *Jervis Bay* and *Ranpura*, that the Admiralty had conscripted into service and then hastily converted into ill-armed so-called Armed Merchant Cruisers to help escort convoys across the North Atlantic.

The Royal Navy was really running the convoy operation at this point, though the Canadians were loath, at least officially, to concede the point. The fact that Stuart Bonham-Carter, the British admiral in charge of Britain's Halifax-based Third Battle Squadron, outranked the senior Canadian naval officer in his own base had created such a delicate diplomatic problem that Bonham-Carter had been forced to move his headquarters and staff from shore onto a converted yacht in the harbour. The HMS *Seaborn* was small, so the ratings assigned to HQ duties had to bunk on yet another converted yacht beside it. There were no accommodations for them ashore—or for the British submarine crews, who had to be shuffled off to find a place to sleep on whatever Armed Merchant Cruiser happened to be in port at the time.

The French, who had also made Halifax their western headquarters for submarines assigned to convoy escort duty, were encountering similar problems accommodating their crews. When four French submarines arrived in port in the late fall of 1939, their 241 officers and men ended up sleeping on a disused Canadian National Railways liner that happened to be sitting idle in the harbour.

Housing had become a critical problem for everyone, but especially for the Royal Canadian Navy, whose numbers were increasing exponentially each month. More than eight hundred sailors had been sent out to find their own accommodations while the navy and the city tried to figure out how to cope with the influx.

The operators of bootleg establishments and blind pigs were learning how to cope with the crowds of servicemen, and they weren't complaining. Arne Benson looked around him. This building's second-floor kitchen, which did double duty as a barroom, was filled with men of every size and shape and hue and age and language, many in uniforms of one country or another. The barkeep served her alcohol—most of it moonshine made by suppliers in Terence Bay, a nearby fishing village—out of a gallon metal container that looked like, and may once have been, a gas can. She kept the bulk of her supply ingeniously hidden beneath the big kitchen stove in a corner of the room. In order to reveal it, you had to know enough to remove one of the stove's front legs, then lift up some of the floorboards underneath to reveal the hidden locker filled with its treasure trove of contraband alcohol and moonshine.

One of the Norwegians smiled at Benson from across the room as he raised his cup and downed the contents in a single swallow. How long, Benson wondered, before he could slip away, unnoticed?

JANET MACNEILL WATCHED in awe as the young men at the long tables in front of her wolfed down one heaping portion of ham and scalloped potatoes after another, and then called out for more. Janet had been volunteering as a server at the North End Services Canteen since it opened its doors in a converted church hall last fall, but she hadn't seen anything quite like this before. It's obvious, she thought to herself, that these Dutch sailor boys haven't had a decent meal in a long, long time.

The sailors had arrived from Britain shortly before noon today, aboard a Dutch warship carrying a pregnant Princess Juliana, the heiress to the Dutch throne, and her two daughters, Beatrix, two and a half, and Irene, ten months. They were on their way into exile in Ottawa, "driven," as one local newspaper reporter would have it, "from the land of tulips and windmills by the scourge of the swastika." The month before, in May, Hitler had invaded the Netherlands and Belgium, forcing the Dutch royal family to flee and provoking a political crisis in Britain as well. As far as Janet was concerned, the only good news to come out of all of that was that Chamberlain, the British prime minister, had resigned and been replaced by Winston Churchill. With Winnie at the helm, Janet believed, the Brits would soon put the boot to Hitler and his Nazis.

She certainly hoped so. She and Debby Piers were officially an item again, but they rarely got to be together because he was almost always at sea. Janet never knew from one day to the next when his ship would be back in port or, if it was, when it would leave again. Debby couldn't tell her, of course, even when he knew. So whenever a convoy left port, Janet and her daughter, Anne, would walk down to the breakwater near Point Pleasant Park to watch the ships make their way out of the harbour. Would the *Restigouche* be among them? If it was, she and Anne would wave at its passing grey hulk, just in case Debby could see them.

So much had happened in the three weeks since Debby's last departure, in Halifax and in the wider world. Belgium and the Netherlands were both now under Nazi control. And Italy had joined the Germans, declaring war on Britain and France. The day before France fell, Haligonians had been mesmerized by the incongruous sight of close to a hundred small airplanes, in a rainbow of colours, parading through city streets from the airport in Halifax's west end to the docks near the train station. The French government had purchased the American-made planes—Piper Cubs, Stinsons, etc.—for its war effort. The aircraft carrier *Bearne* had come to Halifax to pick them up. But with the collapse of the French government imminent, things had become complicated. Marshal Pétain, the eighty-four-year-old French general who'd been recalled into service after the Germans invaded, cabled orders to rush the planes aboard and leave Halifax as quickly as possible. But to where, and for what purpose? No one seemed to know.

The newspapers said nothing about the matter, just as they'd kept mum about the pro-German crew of another French ship in port at the time, the *Pasteur*, who had tried to sabotage their vessel to prevent the Allies from commandeering it. They would have succeeded, too, if not for the quick intervention of a Canadian naval boarding party. But even if the newspapers didn't print a word about it, everyone knew. Halifax was that kind of small, gossipy city where it was possible to know most of the news the papers, or the censor, had decided was not fit to print. Rumour had it that the *Bearne* was now somewhere in the Caribbean, though doing what, and for which side, no one could say.

The North End Services Canteen, located a few blocks from the dockyard, was as good a place as any to find out what was really happening. The canteen had been the first, but far from the last, set up after the war began to provide meals, dances and concerts—a kind of home away from home—for the men of the three military services, as well as for the merchant navy sailors from the convoys. Last Christmas the North End canteen had played host to five thousand French sailors and four thousand British.

Each evening after supper at home, Janet would take an always overcrowded tramcar up to the canteen at St. Mark's Church Hall, spend a few hours dishing up meals for hungry men and then return home again around 10 p.m. Though she found it difficult to think of the Halifax she'd grown up in as a dangerous place for a young woman alone at night, she wasn't taking any chances. There were empty bottles and used condoms even along Young Avenue. When she got off the tram at the corner of Inglis and Young, Janet would make sure to walk the rest of the way to her parents' home under the street lamps that lined the centre of the boulevard. And her hand was never far from the hatpin she kept in her purse, just in case.

HAROLD MASTERMAN SHOULD HAVE BEEN FRIGHTENED, but he wasn't. He was five years old, and he wasn't afraid of anything. Except, perhaps, that big old woman in the army uniform who strutted around the ship's deck like a witch, ordering all the children to do this or—more often—*not* to do that. But even she had turned out to be kinder than he'd expected. After discovering him roaming the SS *Anselm*'s decks by himself one day, the woman, who was in truth Edith Cowans, a veteran nurse who'd been a welfare supervisor in the Great War and had plenty of experience working with groups of children, invited Harold to her cabin and let him play with a Dinky car. Harold had liked that. In spite of himself, he'd liked her too. He'd even, strangely enough, liked the "de-fleaing" shower, cold though it was, that he and the rest of the children had been instructed to take yesterday in preparation for—

In preparation for what?

Harold still wasn't sure. But he had stopped asking so many questions. No one would give him any answers anyway. Not even Jack. Jack was his big brother. He was twelve, seven years older than Harold, and he knew everything. But he wasn't talking—not this time. Neither were his two sisters, Elizabeth, ten, and Marion, eight. Harold was the baby of the family. Maybe that's why nobody told him anything.

But that was all right. While he may have been too young to fully comprehend or appreciate everything that was happening,

Harold did know it was all very exciting. In fact, it sometimes seemed to him that everything that had happened during the past two weeks was just one more chapter in an unpredictable, unknowable, ongoing adventure story he was living.

By now, of course, Harold knew he wasn't—as his mother had told him when she packed his suitcase—going to visit his relatives in Kirby Moorside. He'd been there once before, and he knew you didn't have to get on a boat to travel the hundred or so miles from his home in Middlesbrough, North Yorkshire, to Moorside in East Yorkshire.

Harold had been surprised when so many other children boarded the train with them in York. All were older than him, and many cried as they hugged and kissed their parents goodbye. Harold's mother had cried too, while his father had tried not to. Harold didn't cry, and he couldn't understand why everyone else was. Kirby Moorside was where Robin Hood lived. Is that why all these other children were going to Kirby Moorside too? he wondered.

They weren't. Neither was he. It turned out the train was bound for Liverpool, half a day's journey away, on the other side of England. At the station there, solicitous adults he'd never seen before were waiting on the platform to greet them, whisk them off to a local orphanage, and then shepherd them through their medical checkups, interviews, luggage checks and even more endless rounds of waiting. But what were they waiting *for*? No one would tell him. Loose lips sink ships, his brother said, repeating a slogan even Harold knew by heart. Harold knew the Germans were bad, and that they dropped bombs on English schoolchildren. Back home he'd known exactly what to do when he heard the siren. He would go immediately to the Anderson shelter his father had dug into the ground in their backyard. The shelter was covered with a corrugated metal roof his father had piled with earth and sod.

The air-raid sirens sounded frequently while they waited in Liverpool, so he and the other children spent their nights in the cellar of the orphanage, trying to fall asleep amid the staccato bursts of anti-aircraft fire and the occasional rumbling thunder of exploding bombs. In the mornings the older boys would sneak out into the streets around the orphanage to collect souvenir shell fragments from the previous night's battles.

Harold wasn't sure how many days they'd stayed in Liverpool, but one day the children heard that their ship had arrived. They were going on a trip. Another one! To Canada. Canada? What's that? he wondered.

One of the adults gave him a little plastic disc with the number *12* written on a piece of adhesive taped to the front. "Don't take it off," she'd said as she tied it around his neck with a length of shoelace and pinned a matching name tag with the same number to his jacket. His sisters were *13* and *14*, Jack was *15*. They were each issued their own gas mask and an extra coat, which they carried as they walked, in groups of twelve, up the ship's gangplank. They were led aboard by gun crews—sailors in steel helmets—marching in formation. One gunner put his helmet on Harold's head. "You're in the bloomin' navy now, me lad," he said. As the *Anselm* slipped out of Liverpool harbour, the children and their escorts—the nurse Cowans, her five assistants, a Salvation Army officer, an Anglican padre and a Canadian Roman Catholic priest—stood on the deck singing "There'll Always Be an England."

Harold and Jack, together with four other boys they didn't know, were assigned to sleep in a cabin in the ship's third-class section, which had been transformed into dormitories for the children and their escorts. Harold's sisters were in a cabin on the other side of the ship with four other girls. Harold didn't see them very often, except during the daily life-jacket drills that were part of their shipboard routine.

When they weren't eating, sleeping or doing their drills, the children had the run of the ship. Harold would spend hours watching the dots of the ships in their convoy, their stacks belching black smoke into the grey sky. The vessels seemed to stretch off in every direction as far as the eye could see.

One day he was playing on deck when he heard a loud noise off the stern. Looking back, he saw smoke and then heard everyone yelling. People on the burning ship had had to jump into the water or get into life rafts.

It all seemed so long ago now. But the voyage was almost over, or at least that's what the escorts had said this morning as they hurried everyone out on deck to watch the *Anselm* enter Halifax harbour. So this is Canada, Harold thought, staring out at the jumble of fog-shrouded granite-cliff hills, and the boulders and stunted spruce trees that dotted the shoreline. It didn't look all that much different—certainly no better—than home. But then, as the *Anselm* passed through the submarine gates at the entrance to the harbour, Harold could see off in the distance to his left Halifax's impressive skyline of downtown office buildings, and to the right, across the expanse of harbour, a long line of heavy-laden, grey-hulled merchant ships waiting at anchor for the all-clear to begin their eastward journey across the Atlantic to England.

In mid-harbour the *Anselm*'s captain finally split off from the convoy's parade of incoming vessels, executed a smooth 180-degree turn to port and slipped gently into the jetty at Pier 21.

More than half of the children already knew where they were going and who was going to take care of them in Canada. Their parents had relatives or friends in places with strange names like Saskatoon or Regina or Vancouver who'd promised to take them. The rest were, as one of the children had explained it to a Canadian Press reporter back in Liverpool before the *Anselm* sailed, "prize packages" waiting to be won by some lucky Canadian family.

Until now, Harold hadn't been frightened. But as he looked down—way down—from the upper deck of the SS *Anselm* on the anxious knot of strangers staring up at him from the Halifax dock, he couldn't help but be at least a tiny bit apprehensive. Who would win him as their prize package?

STANDING IN THE SHADOW of the hulking eight-thousand-ton passenger liner now being secured to the wharf at Pier 21, Fred MacKinnon stared back up into the sea of smiling, eager, apprehensive children's faces that pressed against the ship's railings three and four deep.

In early June his bosses—Dr. Frank Davis, the Nova Scotia minister of health, and Ernest Blois, the head of his department's child welfare agency—had assigned MacKinnon the job of determining how Nova Scotia should cope with a sudden influx of British schoolchildren. The British authorities had decided to ship thousands of children off to the quieter corners of the Empire to keep them out of the way of German bombs or even a possible German occupation. The program, set up by the British Children's Overseas Reception Board (CORB), caught the public imagination not only in Britain, where the German bombing campaign was becoming more intense by the day, but also—and perhaps especially—in patriotic corners of the Empire like Nova Scotia, where taking in a child seemed like an ideal opportunity for families to make a contribution to the war effort while meeting a humanitarian need. By the summer of 1940 the parents of close to seventy thousand British children—most from the south and east coasts, where the bombing campaign was most intense—had applied to have their kids sent to live abroad. The first of what was expected to be dozens of convoys bound for Canada—the one in which Harold Masterman and his brother and sisters sailed—left Liverpool on July 21, 1940.

By that point, planning for their arrival in Canada was well advanced. In June the province had published a pamphlet and taken out newspaper advertisements urging Nova Scotians to open their homes and arms to endangered children from overseas. Hundreds responded. Health department nurses visited each of the would-be guardians, checking out everything from their physical health to the state of the emotional relationship between husband and wife. They also asked practical questions about the family's finances, and tried to determine just what the family itself could—and would—provide for the children, whom the pamphlet loftily described as "honoured guests." Not everyone's motives were altruistic. "How much is the allowance per week for each child?" was the first question a man from Richmond County asked. Another noted that she lived alone and a child could be "some help to me." Still another expressed a preference for "children who could be easily adopted if there are any such."

Even after he had weeded out the obvious undesirables and those looking to turn the program to their own purposes, MacKinnon realized that far more families would be lining up to take children than anyone had expected. Who should get these children? While MacKinnon's own inclination was to match children with families close in background to their own, he already understood that there were other, almost inevitably political or class considerations he had to take into account in Nova Scotia. Taking in a "guest child," as they had become known, was a status symbol in certain social circles. But many of the doctors, lawyers and prominent businessmen angling to be the first in their circle to have a guest child wanted to pick and choose which child they would take.

One man, a Rotarian from Yarmouth, had written to Blois asking him to please send him the child of a Rotarian. Blois replied dryly that he didn't expect many Rotarians among the evacuees. "They are from humble homes," he explained, adding carefully, so as not to put the man off, "but not by any means from slum homes, or the very poor districts. In fact, we have been very much impressed by the fine type of child that is coming."

The vice-president of Thompson & Sutherland, a well-known New Glasgow–based hardware store chain, wrote Blois to ask, "Would it be possible for Mrs. Sutherland to go to Halifax and make her own selection?" Blois wrote back that it wasn't "feasible." "We do not know the day or the hour when these children arrive. We do not know their ages, sex or religious affiliation until they arrive and have been checked and questioned." In muted admonishment he added, "These children are coming here as guests of the Canadian people and every child must be placed, irrespective of its looks or characteristics."

"I think your stand is ridiculous," Sutherland fired back in a return letter. Still, perhaps mindful of just how many of his friends also wanted guest children, Sutherland was quick to add that he and his wife weren't withdrawing their offer. "You are the boss and go to it," he noted, then added in a handwritten scrawl on the company letterhead, "We will do as you see best."

Blois, of course, had the final say on all these important questions. MacKinnon didn't envy him that responsibility.

Thankfully, there were only thirty-nine boys—one of them five years old, for heaven's sake—and forty-three girls aboard the *Anselm*, the only vessel in Convoy OB189 carrying guest children. Better still, MacKinnon thought, just thirty of them were destined for families in Nova Scotia. The rest, along with a nurse and a special conductress, would leave on the next train and soon be someone else's concern.

HALIFAX WAS . . . well, it certainly wasn't Montreal. Not that Marjory Whitelaw regretted for a second her impetuous decision just two months before to quit her job, pack her battered suitcase and try on for size a new—and hopefully more romantic and exciting—life in wartime Halifax. It was just that Halifax had turned out to be so much smaller, more crowded and, well, more *provincial* than she'd expected. There were few fine downtown stores in which to window shop, and even fewer good restaurants in which to imagine herself dining. And the roads! The weekend she'd arrived in town, Alex and Tina had taken her for a drive as far as Herring Cove, a fishing village on the outskirts of the city. What passed for a main "highway" seemed to be constructed of boulders, and was so rutted and washboarded that Marjory still felt nauseous just remembering the ride.

On the other hand, Marjory had got her wish. She was now living in a city that was alive with the sights, sounds, smells, tastes, loves, lusts and fears of war.

That Halifax was in the grip of war fever had been made abundantly clear to Marjory even before she set foot in the city itself. Just as her train began the final leg of its journey along the lip of Bedford Basin and onto the peninsula, the conductor passed through the coach, carefully pulling down all the blinds "so we couldn't see the ships in Bedford Basin." Even at the time it seemed a trifle absurd. "People laughed. I mean, all you had to do was walk down the corridor to where the cars coupled together and you could see everything there was to see of the Basin anyway."

The security measures seemed even sillier after she got to know the city better. There were an incredible number of vantage points from which anyone could easily observe virtually anything that was going on in the port. The main highway into Halifax snaked alongside Bedford Basin parallel to and just above the railway tracks, offering a stunning panorama of the ships at anchor in the Basin. So there was no way to prevent anyone travelling in an automobile from seeing what the blinds in the railway cars were supposed to hide. And the very publicly accessible campus of Mount Saint Vincent, the Roman Catholic women's college, was set high on a hillside with a particularly strategic view of the entire Basin and the harbour beyond.

However, Marjory soon came to believe that the official paranoia about spies was not totally misplaced. She heard rumours that a Mount student, a mysterious cello-playing young woman from somewhere in South America, was feeding information on ships' movements in and out of Halifax to Lord Haw-Haw. The woman had brought to Halifax two cello cases, one of which contained her instrument, the other secret transmitting equipment for sending reports back to Germany. As far-fetched as that might have seemed in normal times, it couldn't be dismissed lightly in wartime.

It was easy enough in Halifax these days to become caught up in playing "Who's a Spy?" Marjory did it herself. For example, that elegant blonde in the black Persian lamb coat—was she really a spy? She lived in Montreal but knew enough about supposedly secret sailing schedules to reserve her regular room at the Nova Scotian Hotel whenever the *Rajputana* arrived back in port. Undoubtedly, she was having a fling with the ship's doctor. But most everyone, Marjory included, assumed she was probably spying too.

The *Raj* was in port right now, and its officers would be at the dance at the Nova Scotian tonight. So would Marjory. Thanks to Alex and Tina's friendship with its captain, Marjory had got to meet—and dance with—many of the *Raj*'s "impossibly handsome" young British officers. It was the *Raj*'s captain who had invited Marjory to her first Halifax social event, a weekly supper dance at the Nova Scotian Hotel that was better known among locals as the Rat Race.

Marjory was surprised at how quickly and completely she'd become immersed in her new life. Thanks to Alex, she landed a job with the federal fisheries department within a few days of arriving in Halifax. The job was far from the glamorous one she'd envisioned, but it paid sixty dollars a month.

When she wasn't working, Marjory tried to meet new people. She had joined a ladies' singing group organized by Ernesto Vinci, a charming Italian-born vocal teacher at the Halifax Conservatory of Music, which performed frequently at Uncle Mel's Concert Parties. Uncle Mel was actually Hugh Mills, the owner of Mills Brothers, the carriage trade ladies' clothing shop on Spring Garden Road. When war broke out, Mills, a big, passionate, take-charge kind of guy with a passion for amateur theatre, had taken on the job of organizing entertainments for the thousands of servicemen and merchant mariners stationed in, or passing through, Halifax. It quickly became a massive undertaking with a rotating cast of local musicians, singers and entertainers, supplemented by talented amateurs, professionals and would-be professionals from the ranks of the military. It even had its own donated station wagon to ferry performers to all the various shows each evening. The shows might take place anywhere from a downtown hostel to Admiralty House to a hospital ward to the deck of a ship in the middle of Bedford Basin. Those last were the worst. Trying to leap from the bow of a duty boat to an ice-covered ship's ladder and then clamber up the side in the dark in an evening dress was no laughing matter. Still, Marjory thought, it was all good fun and, of course, a chance to meet lots of men.

Marjory had also joined the south-end Gorsebrook golf club and the Baptist Young People's Society, which boasted its own badminton court where young people could meet. She'd already made friends with a woman there named Barbara Eaton, who worked as the secretary for some Norwegian shipping company that had just opened an office in Halifax. She and Marjory were talking about finding an apartment together.

When she wasn't working at the fisheries department or singing for the sailors or socializing at the golf club or badminton court, Marjory volunteered at the Allied Servicemen's Canteen on Barrington Street. The canteen was a home away from home for merchant seamen whose vessels didn't provide them with meals while they were in port.

"What'll you have?" she asked one young sailor who she was sure wasn't even a teenager yet.

"Six eggs," he replied.

He ate every one of them and came back for more. Marjory soon became as adept at simultaneously cooking up a dozen eggs and a pound of bacon as she was in fending off the advances of lonely men. "I haven't seen my wife in two years," one forthright sailor declared. "Can I come home with you?"

Not all the lonely men were interested in her attentions, however. One night she overheard a man from France telling his companion how he'd lost his wife and six children to a German attack. Life in a military town, she was beginning to realize, was not all about dancing till dawn.

"C'MON. I'LL GIVE YOU some chocolate. Just say something. Anything. Please. C'mon."

The local teenagers on the other side of the chain-link fence were fascinated by Harold Masterman's English accent.

"Wot you wont me t'say?" Harold asked. The knot of older boys erupted into more gales of laughter.

One broke off a piece of chocolate and handed it to the five-year-old. "Say some more," he implored.

Everyone, even the teenagers, was very nice to him. Soon after the buses brought the thirty children from Pier 21 to the School for the Blind on South Park Street, across from the Victoria General Hospital, doctors and nurses swooped down on them. Their job was to answer the question: "In your opinion, is this child safe for foster-home care?" To do that, they had to examine each child carefully, listing his or her height, weight, medical history, current nutritional state and any physical deformities. They noted the condition of the teeth, throat, lungs, nervous system and heart. Every child was X-rayed and put through a battery of physical and psychological tests. Between pokings and proddings they were photographed for identification purposes, and psychologists interviewed them to determine academic potential as well as any behavioural problems that might affect placement.

That was the problem with Harold and his siblings. Harold was the youngest in his family group, so MacKinnon was eager to place him. But as he looked at the file containing the family history that had accompanied the Mastermans from England, as well as the notations added by his staff, he knew it would not be an easy placement.

"The four Masterman children undoubtedly came from one of the most inferior homes of any of the children," the report noted. "They were all below the average mentality of the other children. The boys were less mannerly and the girls less attractive and less placeable; consequently more difficulty may be expected from the placements of the Masterman children than from any others." After describing Harold's older brother John as "an aggressive, self-confident lad" who had been regularly caught begging for Canadian money from passersby at the Blind School, the report noted that "Harold Joseph was called Gobbler at the School because of the fact that he ate continually and never appeared to be satisfied."

MacKinnon put down the file and picked up the list of potential foster parents. He quickly found what he was looking for. Hugh and Gladys O'Byrne from Quinpool Road had lost their only son in a bicycle accident a year ago and were looking to fill the void in their lives by taking in one of the guest children. Perhaps they would be able to give young Harold the love and attention he needed. Perhaps . . .

"I ACKNOWLEDGE WITH THANKS your offer of service," began the letter dated July 1, 1940, from Naval Secretary J.O. Cossette. Eric Dennis scanned it quickly: ". . . regret not immediate entry . . . Naval service, of necessity, grows slowly . . . May not be called on for a considerable period . . ." He didn't need to read the rest. His appeal had been denied.

Eric's desire to join the navy had not abated. In fact, it had become more intense since the navy had accepted his buddy, Colin Campbell, for training. The navy turned Eric down, but not, as he'd initially feared, because he was practically blind in his right eye. Eric and a friend had concocted a complex scheme to help him get through the required eye examination. They got another friend, who was already in the navy, to teach them Morse code. On the day of his physical, Eric's friend stood behind him in line and tapped his fingers in code on Eric's back to indicate the letters he was supposed to be seeing on the eye chart. It worked—Eric passed the eye test. But the doctor turned him down anyway.

"You have a heart murmur," he said.

His own doctor said Eric's heart was fine and agreed to support his appeal. He was then sent to five different navy doctors, two of whom supported him and three of whom—"including the guy who turned me down in the first place"—opposed him. "They were very strict about medicals then, especially in the navy," he would later recall. But it wasn't just the navy. The air force turned him down as well, in spite of the support and encouragement of McNab, the young officer he'd met at the Nova Scotian Hotel last New Year's Eve.

Which left the army. He would try to enlist there next.

AS SOON AS HE HEARD the news, Fred MacKinnon knew there would be no more guest children for him to place. On September 17, 1940, a German submarine torpedoed and sank the *City of Benares*, a converted luxury liner carrying four hundred passengers, including ninety guest children and eight escorts. It wasn't the first time a vessel carrying evacuees had been torpedoed. Less than a month before, the Germans had hit the *Volendam*, but its 320 youngsters had all been rescued. The children aboard the *Benares* were not so lucky: only thirteen survived.

Although everyone involved had known and weighed the risks—the risk of the children being killed during the brief ocean crossing versus the risk of their remaining in England and perhaps being bombed by the Germans—no one had the stomach to cope with the possibility that more children would die this way. The Children's Overseas Reception Board suspended further evacuations by ship indefinitely, meaning no new children would be coming to Canada.

MacKinnon was relieved, but disappointed too. It had turned out to be a far more complex undertaking than anyone had guessed to find homes for even the 120 children who'd arrived so far. Although many families had offered to take children, they were frequently "extraordinarily fussy" about which children they wanted. As he'd put it in a plaintive letter to the head of the Sydney Children's Aid Society just a few days before the *Benares* went down, "Few applicants want more than one child . . . Of what value then are requests for one girl under 10 when there are not any children to fill them. As it stands now, we have to have many applications before we can place one child, and if a group of 100 children come within the next few weeks, I can assure you that we are going to run into grave difficulties."

The day before the *Benares* sank, MacKinnon spoke to a local Kiwanis Club, exhorting its members to volunteer to take in more children. He played on their heartstrings. He told them about another five-year-old boy who'd arrived in one of the convoys after Harold's. "George was an only child, and when I went through his luggage, I found tucked in the leaves of a New Testament, which his mother had given him when he left England, a picture of his mother and George taken when he was three and a half years old, and in much happier circumstances. On the back were these words: 'To wee George from Mother.'"

MacKinnon's sterner message was that it was Nova Scotians' patriotic duty to help out. "The people of England . . . are going through a veritable hell and the very least that we can do here is to receive their children and give them a haven for the duration . . . Canadians should receive these children regardless of whether they have blond hair or blue eyes, or any other minor specification that may appeal to the whim of some person who may wish to receive them."

Now, MacKinnon was relieved that he probably wouldn't have to make any more of those hectoring speeches. As tragic as it was, the sinking of the *Benares* meant he'd be able to concentrate his energies on the other part of his job: monitoring how the children were cared for in their new homes.

THE YOUNG WOMAN seated beside Jeff Jefferson this afternoon was in no mood for giving thanks. If she wasn't complaining about having to work Thanksgiving—"The only holiday they give us all year is Christmas Day"—she was bemoaning that yet another new, untrained girl had begun working in her office that very morning.

Jefferson was only thankful she wasn't talking directly to him. He and an acquaintance, an RCAF officer stationed in Halifax, had decided to have their Thanksgiving dinner together at Norman's.

After an even longer than usual wait because of the holiday, they'd managed to find two seats together. But they'd barely begun their meal—turkey with all the trimmings—when the unsmiling young woman plunked herself down at their table. She knew Jefferson's companion and proceeded to bend his ear relentlessly with all her woes.

"I don't see why I should have to train every new girl that comes along," she grumbled.

"This new girl," the air force man asked, apparently trying to elicit something positive from the conversation, "is she easy to get along with?"

"How should I know?" the woman replied sourly. "She hasn't opened her mouth yet."

No wonder, Jefferson thought to himself. No wonder.

Perhaps they should have gone uptown to Lohnes's or the Green Lantern, the only other restaurants in the whole city that Jefferson thought worth considering. But it would have been the same story at either of them, he knew. Lineups, shared tables, conversations with strangers—it was just the way it was. And not just at the better restaurants. There were more than fifty establishments in Halifax claiming to be "restaurants and lunchrooms," according to the latest *Might City Directory*. Even the worst dives— where the dishes "showed plainly what had been served earlier" and where you'd see "half-finished mashed potatoes from one order. being scooped onto the plate" for the next customer—were crammed to capacity, and often beyond, from opening to closing, every day, Sundays and holidays included.

Jefferson preferred Norman's. It was conveniently located at the corner of Hollis and Morris, just a block north of the Nova Scotian Hotel, where he and his wife, Lennie, had decided to live for the duration. Jefferson would often stop in on his way to or from his office, and he and Lennie ate supper there regularly. Because overcrowding often made it necessary to share a table with strangers, you could usually depend on finding an interesting companion or two for dinner—the tiresome complainer now beside him being the exception to the rule.

Yesterday, in fact, Jefferson had had dinner at a table with a soldier from his old hometown of Moncton, and then supper with an RCAF intelligence officer from Hamilton, Ontario, who'd recently arrived in Halifax after spending six months in Moncton. "Great town," he told Jefferson. "Stayed in a place where I paid six dollars a week for room, board and good meals. And they treated me like one of the family. I had the run of the place. They even took me out for drives with them." He paused. Halifax, he confided, was not nearly as welcoming. He didn't elaborate, except to tell Jefferson that his experience so far had been that Haligonians were all "out to trim you."

Jefferson wondered if the Kiwis—two New Zealand airmen he'd shared a table with earlier today—would say the same a few weeks from now. They'd arrived for flight training by ship yesterday, four and a half weeks after sailing from Wellington. Understandably, they were just happy to have their feet on dry land again. They weren't complaining about lineups, or the lack of good restaurants and places to have a drink. How long would that last, Jefferson wondered?

The woman beside him droned on.

HAROLD MASTERMAN TRIED to force himself to call Mr. and Mrs. O'Byrne Mum and Dad. But it just didn't feel right. Not that he missed his natural parents that much. Not yet, anyway. Everything was still too new.

The O'Byrnes lived in a nice house on Quinpool Road, much nicer than the cramped government-owned "corporation house" back in Whinney Banks, Middlesbrough, that Harold had shared with his parents, brother and sisters. The O'Byrnes' house had originally been a bungalow, but Mr. O'Byrne had raised the roof and added extra bedrooms. Harold had his own room, which used to be the room of the son who died. His name was Hugh, but everyone referred to him as Junior. Harold didn't know much about him other than that there was a train set in the basement that had been his. Mrs. O'Byrne didn't like to talk about him all that much, although she would sometimes take Harold with her when she went out to mow the grass on his grave in the Mount Olivet Cemetery.

Mr. O'Byrne was away a lot. He was a salesman for a Toronto stationery firm, so he spent a lot of his time travelling the Maritimes and Newfoundland visiting lawyers' and doctors' offices and taking orders for letterhead, invoice forms and so on. Harold's father back in England had been a guard with the London North Eastern Railway, but he was often out of work. Mr. O'Byrne, Harold figured, made more money than his father. Besides owning his own house, Mr. O'Byrne had a motor car. Sometimes they'd all go for rides in it.

The O'Byrnes also had a daughter. Her name was Mary, and she was five or six years older than Harold. Harold didn't think she liked him. Still, he didn't miss his own sisters or brother very much. The Mastermans had been among the family groups Fred MacKinnon had had to split up because no one wanted to take on so many children together. Elizabeth and Marion had gone to live with a Mrs. Scott in Enfield, about forty miles outside of Halifax. Jack was staying with the MacAdam family on Gottingen Street, on the other side of town. Mrs. O'Byrne had promised Harold she'd take him to see his brother soon.

That would be nice, but Harold had already made some friends. There were lots of kids his own age in the neighbourhood, and even more at Sir John Thompson School on Mumford Road, where the O'Byrnes had registered him in Grade Primary. The first time the air-raid siren went off, Harold crawled under his desk. The other kids laughed. It was just a test, they told him; it happened every Wednesday at noon. But back in England, when you heard the siren, you took cover. Some of the boys teased him, called him Limey, but just in fun. And the older girls were nice to him. They thought it was sad that he was all alone.

Funny, but it didn't seem that way at all to Harold.

IT SOMETIMES AMAZED Jeff Jefferson to realize just how many interesting stories the gossips at the local newspapers missed completely. Like the one Stanley Wetmore, the wire censor down at the cable office, had told him this morning. There'd been a mutiny aboard the *Nieuw Amsterdam* after she'd arrived from New York recently. Whatever happened during that leg of their journey had convinced the sailors they wanted no part of the North Atlantic war zone. They weren't alone. And who could blame them for their lack of enthusiasm? Jefferson had heard many stories about merchant seamen who'd had to cross the ocean in ships that weren't built to withstand the brutal North Atlantic storms or who'd been left to defend themselves against enemy attack. Many had not made it to the other side. No wonder the authorities had moved the *Amsterdam* from an anchorage in the Basin to Pier 20; that way, a destroyer crew could keep an eye on its unhappy sailors.

"Got a cable you should see," Wetmore said after telling Jefferson his *Nieuw Amsterdam* story. He handed the message to Jefferson. "Came in last night around eleven. We tried to find you, but we couldn't track you down."

Jefferson read the message once and then again, more slowly. It had come from the coast guard station at Cape Race, Newfoundland. A Swedish freighter wanted the coast guard to relay a message to authorities in Halifax that it was carrying sixty-five survivors from the HMS *Jervis Bay* and was proceeding to the point designated.

The *Jervis Bay*! How long ago had that been? A week? Two weeks? Jefferson had visited the Armed Merchant Cruiser the last time it was in port. He could picture the vessel in his mind. The old Aberdeen & Commonwealth liner was one of dozens of passenger ships the British Admiralty had taken over. She'd been repainted grey and equipped with seven six-inch guns dating from the turn of the century. The captain, a Royal Navy veteran named Fogarty Fegan, commanded its 254-man crew, a motley collection of Royal Navy sailors, reservists and merchant seamen.

The vessel, which was based at Halifax, escorted convoys as far as the east coast of Newfoundland, where they were met by the mid-Atlantic protection force for the next leg of their crossing. In September, just after the *Jervis Bay* handed over Convoy HX72 and was returning to Halifax for its next assignment, a wolf pack of German U-boats attacked and sank eleven of its forty-one ships. Such disasters were becoming far more frequent, Jefferson realized, now that the German subs seemed to be travelling in groups and attacking in concert. Last month, two other Halifax convoys had been attacked, with the loss of thirty-one more ships. Had the *Jervis Bay* been sunk by a wolf pack too? The cable didn't elaborate. He would have to wait for the rescue vessel, the SS *Stureholm*, to dock to find out more.

Back in his office, Jefferson called Commodore George Jones, the Royal Canadian Navy's commanding officer in Halifax, who hadn't heard anything from Ottawa concerning survivors. But he agreed to arrange newspaper interviews with some of the survivors once the navy had finished questioning them. This was one story the newspaper reporters were unlikely to miss.

The next morning, Jefferson did get a call from Mike Ryan at the *Herald*, who said the Admiralty had released a statement saying that most of Convoy HX84 had escaped unscathed from a German U-boat attack. But Ryan still didn't know that the *Stureholm* was headed to Halifax with survivors, and Jefferson wasn't about to tell him. Not yet, anyway.

Though he'd spoken to Jones, Jefferson now had second thoughts about whether that was really sufficient, given the delicate state of relations between the Canadian and British navies in Halifax. Jefferson wasn't keen to get into a "tangle" with the Brits over any decision to let the newspapers interview survivors. He decided to call on Stuart Bonham-Carter, the British admiral. It was Jefferson's first visit to his *Seaborn* headquarters, which weren't nearly as palatial as some had suggested. In fact, Bonham-Carter's office amidships in the *Seaborn* seemed decidedly dark and dingy. More local jealousy, Jefferson thought.

Given that the BBC was already broadcasting accounts of the attack based on interviews with officers from vessels that had made it to Britain, Jefferson and Bonham-Carter quickly agreed that it made sense to let the newspapers here have their chance to interview the *Jervis Bay* survivors too.

Jefferson called Gerry Gillespie at the *Herald*, Dal Warrington at the *Chronicle* and John LeBlanc at Canadian Press. "Meet me at nine o'clock at the *Comorin*'s gangplank," he told them cryptically. The *Stureholm* had tied up beside the British cruiser. Even though the Admiral had called ahead to let everyone know the pressmen were coming, the *Comorin*'s midshipman of the watch, "a typical English dumbunny . . . had great difficulty in understanding what a press party might be. He evidently had it confused with the press gang." Eventually, he had to call the lieutenant of the watch, a man named Bell, who finally straightened things out, bringing Jefferson and the reporters to the port lounge and sending someone to fetch the *Jervis Bay*'s senior surviving officer and the captain of the *Stureholm* for their interviews.

While a steward prepared drinks for the visitors, Bell, who "seemed to be slightly ginned up" and in what Jefferson regarded as a "jovial, more or less mischievous mood," confided to the reporters that the real hero of the affair was the captain of the *Stureholm*, Sven Olander. He had witnessed the valiant fight the under-gunned *Jervis Bay* had waged against the *Admiral Scheer*, a pocket battleship, Bell told the reporters, and had been so impressed that he assembled his men and "put it to them. 'Are you willing to go back and try to rescue the survivors?'" Despite the danger that the German surface raider would return to sink their vessel too, the crew's answer, Bell claimed, was a resounding yes.

Jefferson wasn't convinced. He'd heard so many of these damn-the-consequences tales of bravery recently, he didn't accept any of them at face value. The reporters, it was clear, were less skeptical—or perhaps just more hopeful. One even mused that the local newspapers should have their regular waterfront reporters visit merchant cruisers like the *Comorin* every time they came back to port, to see if there were any stories worth telling.

"Oh, that wouldn't be possible, sir," Bell said, a little too self-importantly for Jefferson's liking. "We're under strict instructions not to allow newspapermen on the ship."

Jefferson, who'd just about finished his glass of port, saw his opportunity. "In that case," he said, turning to Gillespie but directing his remarks straight at Bell, "perhaps you had better send some of your newspaper *girls*."

Bell laughed along with the others, but Jefferson noticed he didn't say anything more. Jefferson had subtly let the young officer know he was "wise" to the fact that ships' crews smuggled girls aboard for parties whenever they were in port. Bell got the message and toned down his ginned-up rhetoric about heroes and bravery. It was probably too late, though, Jefferson knew. The reporters had taken down every word.

Not that the story told by Olander and Lieutenant N.E. Wood, the senior officer of the *Jervis Bay*, needed much embellishing. According to Wood, whom Jefferson took to be an Australian or a Kiwi based on his accent, the *Jervis Bay* had been performing routine convoy escort duties when a large German warship suddenly appeared on its port bow at—

Wood was about to give the exact location in degrees where the German ship had been sighted, but the *Comorin*'s first lieutenant, who'd been delegated by Bonham-Carter to make sure none of the technical details got out, interrupted and drowned him out.

As soon as Captain Fegan realized he was facing a German battleship, Wood continued more carefully, he ordered the rest of the convoy to scatter and, laying a dense trail of smoke floats to mask their retreat, made straight for the much better armed enemy vessel. It was a suicidal attack. The *Jervis Bay*'s puny guns were far out of range of their target, while German return fire easily found its mark. The first shell exploded on the *Jervis Bay*'s foredeck. The next hit the bridge, taking out its forward guns. The force of the next explosion ripped off one of Fegan's arms, Wood said in a voice so soft Jefferson had to strain to hear him. The ship, now almost totally engulfed in flames, continued full speed ahead towards the German battleship. But finally the *Jervis Bay* took one last hit, rolled on its side and began to sink bow first. Those who could abandoned ship. When someone asked Wood if the *Jervis Bay* had landed any hits of its own, the *Comorin*'s minder jumped in, refusing to let him answer. That alone made Jefferson certain it hadn't.

Nevertheless, Fegan had accomplished his mission. He had held off the German battleship for a critical twenty-two minutes. That allowed most of the rest of the convoy, which otherwise would have been easy pickings for the Germans, to disappear into the enveloping darkness.

Sven Olander agreed. A burly, blue-eyed Swede who was probably in his sixties but looked younger, the *Stureholm*'s captain spoke in an accent so thick Jefferson found it difficult to understand what he was saying. He told the reporters he'd been on the bridge when the battle started and had seen the *Jervis Bay* go down. Even though his vessel followed instructions to head away from the fight, Olander said he decided to double back and see if there were any survivors in the area where the *Jervis Bay* had sunk. Although the merchant vessels were under strict orders not to try to pick up survivors, to avoid becoming targets themselves, Olander said his own experiences in the First War had convinced him that the safest place to be in such situations was close to the scene of the original attack, because the raider would almost certainly go looking for other ships to sink rather than hanging around at the scene of a kill.

Despite what Bell had claimed, Olander insisted he hadn't consulted his crew before he decided to go back. In fact, he seemed to say—Jefferson couldn't quite make him out—that some of the officers and crew were against returning. Jefferson looked around the small lounge at the reporters. Had they caught his clear denial? Or were they already writing the better story in their heads?

Too often, Jefferson knew, reporters did just that. One Toronto newspaper, for example, had recently published a dramatic tale of a sailor whose ship had been sunk by a German submarine. As he drifted helplessly in a lifeboat in the North Atlantic, the paper reported, the sailor decided to keep a diary of his thoughts. Since he had no pencil or pen, he took a sharp piece of wood and punctured a hole in his skin, and wrote his diary with his own blood. The problem was that none of this story was true. The reporter and his colleagues had been bewailing the fact that it was almost impossible to find a fresh angle on a recent spate of ship-sinking survivor stories, so the reporter simply invented one.

Thus, Jefferson was not surprised by the stories the next morning, which were all, as required, datelined "An East Coast Canadian Port." The focus was, naturally, on the heroically doomed merchant cruiser's last stand. The *Herald*'s headline writer outdid himself with three separate full-width headlines beneath the paper's masthead:

JERVIS BAY'S GALLANTRY WINS
Heroic Armed Merchant Cruiser Holds Off Pocket Battleship
SAVES CONVOY FROM DESTRUCTION

Describing the battle, Gillespie claimed the *Jervis Bay* had written "another glorious chapter in the Empire's naval history. The *Jervis Bay*, her duty done, her colours shot away in battle but swiftly replaced, went to the bottom, seas blacking out flames which had swept her from stem to stern without silencing her guns until the decks were awash . . . Probably never since Sir Richard Grenville and his little ship *Revenge* went to their deaths beneath the guns of mighty ships of Spain has such heroism been shown."

The daring rescue of the *Jervis Bay*'s survivors—and how it supposedly came about—was, of course, an important subplot to most of the stories. Gillespie's account in the *Herald* was typical. The *Stureholm*, he wrote, had "stayed near the battle during the gathering dusk and early evening, moving slowly. Theirs was the choice—steam full speed ahead away to safety [or] turn back into the unknown where the raider might be lurking still and save those of the *Jervis Bay*'s complement who might still be living in the rising seas. All hands were mustered on deck. The captain put the question. To a man, they ruled—back to the spot where the armed merchantman had foundered."

Jefferson had to remind himself that his job was simply to censor the dangerous bits, not to be a one-man truth squad. Or even an editor.

The *Stureholm*'s crew, which had supposedly voted "to a man" to look for survivors, was now mutinous and refusing to sail under Olander again because he'd risked their lives with his foolhardy rescue mission. According to a message the Commanding Officer Atlantic Coast sent to the British Admiralty, "all officers except the second officer refused to sail, stating they would prefer to be shot. Their example was followed by 14 of the crew."

Jefferson couldn't help but be amused. As he wrote in his journal, "This seems to illustrate Napoleon's old quip. What is history but a fable agreed upon?"

"WELL, WHAT DO YOU THINK?" the Admiral asked again. "Can you handle it?"

Dolly McEuen knew she should say no. The club wasn't anywhere near ready. The problem, she had discovered to her chagrin, was that she was totally dependent on volunteers to do the renovations and on generous donors to provide all the equipment and decorations. Dolly McEuen didn't like being dependent on the goodness of others.

In April, when she'd registered the Interallied Hospitality and Food Fund under the War Charities Act, it had all seemed so simple. In September, after she'd talked the trustees of the Odell estate, an unused twenty-five-room mansion off Tobin Street in the south end, into leasing her the property rent-free for the duration of the war to use as a private club for naval ratings, she thought she was home free. She announced grandly that the Ajax Club, named after the HMS *Ajax*, a Royal Navy cruiser, would officially open its doors in October. She had been wildly optimistic, she realized now, as she looked around at the very much in-progress renovations. It was now almost the middle of November, and plumbers, electricians and paperhangers were working diligently to transform what had once been a family residence into a modern private club. She was still waiting for the urinals to arrive. Dolly knew it would be at least another month before the club was ready to cope with paying customers, and then only if she could enlist the aid of more volunteer work parties from the Royal and Canadian navies.

This may have been one reason why McEuen hesitated only briefly when Admiral Bonham-Carter telephoned to ask her if the Ajax Club would be willing to host a reception for the *Jervis Bay*'s survivors and their rescuers.

"Of course," she told the Admiral. "We can handle it."

There wasn't much that Janet McEuen—"Dolly" to everyone who knew her—couldn't handle. She was the middle-aged wife of HMCS *Stadacona* medical officer Lieutenant Commander Stuart McEuen. Shortly after they'd arrived in Halifax from Montreal in the fall of 1939 and set up housekeeping in a suite at the Lord Nelson Hotel, Dolly volunteered at the North End Services Canteen. There she met the Macneill sisters, Janet, Isabel and Edith. While she understood the canteen was meeting an important need for many sailors—they could go there to get a hot meal, even to attend the occasional dance—Dolly believed that neither the canteen nor any other respectable organization in the city was currently satisfying another equally important need. Sailors had to have a place outside their barracks where they could go to have a drink and relax in comfort. The absence of such a spot not only left the market to the blind pigs and the bootleggers, but it increased the already booming business among prostitutes, who often operated in concert with the illegal liquor sellers. Her husband had told her venereal disease was already rampant among young sailors.

Dolly McEuen decided the solution was to open a licensed private club catering exclusively to naval ratings and offering "beer in decent surroundings." Since no one else seemed prepared to do it, she would. She enlisted the Macneill sisters—Edith became the secretary of the Interallied Hospitality and Food Fund, Isabel the treasurer—and set about looking for a suitable location for the club.

The Odell estate, located at the top of a hill a few blocks west of the Nova Scotian Hotel, was almost ideal: physically close to the waterfront but psychically far removed from the blind pigs, bootleggers and prostitutes flourishing on Hollis Street. *Almost* ideal. The problem was that the new club would be directly across from Fort Massey United Church.

The war—and the concomitant problem of public drunkenness—had revived interest among conservative Haligonians, including many church leaders, in the temperance movement. Dr. A.E. Kerr, the principal of Pine Hill Divinity College, suggested in one speech that France had fallen because "the moral fibre of her people had been rotted by drink." The Women's Christian Temperance Union even launched a campaign calling for total abstinence until the war ended, and enlisted local clergymen to circulate temperance pledge cards to their congregations.

While the Nova Scotia Liquor Commission did eventually grant McEuen a licence to sell beer, it was so nervous that it asked her not to publicize the fact. McEuen made a special effort to placate the elders at Fort Massey, prevailing on Bonham-Carter to approach the church's minister to make sure he didn't plan to raise a public fuss. Whatever Bonham-Carter said apparently worked. So did McEuen's decision to host the dinner in honour of the *Jervis Bay* survivors.

THEREAFTER, NOT EVERYTHING went so smoothly. Dolly invited Sir Gerald Campbell, the British High Commissioner in Ottawa, to officiate at the club's opening on December 14. Only days before

SAILORS, SLACKERS, AND BLIND PIGS

the ceremony, however, Nova Scotia's former premier and now Minister for Naval Services Angus L. Macdonald tried to talk him out of attending at all. Macdonald's call was prompted by a letter he'd received from his successor, Premier Stirling MacMillan, who not only warned that the Ajax Club would "accentuate" alcohol-related problems in the city, but also claimed "the joint is not run according to the regulations." MacMillan and his family were members of Fort Massey's congregation.

In the end, Campbell, who also happened to be a personal friend of McEuen's, told Macdonald it was too late for him to cancel. He was in good company. The Bishop of Nova Scotia gave the invocation while two Royal Navy admirals, along with official representatives of the Royal Canadian Navy, attended. So did many local businessmen, notably beer company executives. That wasn't surprising, given that Oland's Brewery had donated the bar, complete with a brass rail, National Breweries provided $30,000 worth of furniture, and Labatt's had offered a station wagon to ferry beer and sailors.

The Ajax Club was a success with sailors from the day it opened. And why not? Where else in town could you get a full-course meal for just twenty-five cents and polish it off with a draft beer for a dime? Even with a strictly enforced limit of five beers per customer per night, and no spirits allowed, the club soon earned enough income selling off its empties to cover day-to-day operating costs. And the attractions included more than just beer. The club boasted a library with "over two thousand new books," along with a card room and Ping-Pong table. There was even a back garden with deck chairs, and outdoor barbecue pits to supplement the club's kitchen facilities.

McEuen herself would later describe the Ajax Club as "an experiment in social service . . . My contention was that if we created an atmosphere for the men to respect and live up to, they would do so." But not everyone agreed, either that the Ajax Club was creating such an atmosphere or that the men who frequented it were living up to Dolly's lofty-sounding claims.

BILLY MONT COULD ONLY watch in silence as nearly half of the eighty "inmates" at the Halifax Industrial School departed one by one, mostly in the company of their parents or other relatives. Six weeks earlier, Reverend Wilson, the superintendent, had written to the parents of each of the boys in his charge, notifying them that, as had become the custom at the school, their sons would be allowed to go home for three days over Christmas if the parents were willing to take them *and* if their boys remained on good behaviour until then.

Billy Mont had been good. With the exception of that one incident with the toilet more than a year ago, he had never got into any trouble of any kind at school. And he was doing so well with his classwork that the teacher had already advanced him a grade.

Still, no one came to fetch him for Christmas this year either.

Instead, he and the other boys who, for one reason or another, remained at the school for the holidays attended a Christmas concert there. A choir from the Band of Hope, a British-based temperance organization that preached the evils of alcohol to young people, sang Christmas carols, and the six members of the school's own harmonica band entertained with seasonal songs. Billy enjoyed that.

On Christmas Day they got a special dinner of turkey with all the trimmings. There were even hard candies for a treat. But Billy would have been even happier if he could have gone home like the others.

AS 1940 ENDED, it was clear this would not be the quick, easy war many had expected. The Germans had overrun most of Europe, leaving the British fighting alone on the edge of the continent. While Hitler's scheme to bring England to its knees quickly with relentless air attacks on its major cities had failed, he wasn't about to abandon his dream of total European conquest. He simply shifted tactics, ordering his ever-growing submarine fleet to redouble its efforts in the North Atlantic, thus cutting off England's only remaining supply line and ultimately starving it into submission.

Therefore, the Battle of the Atlantic—and Halifax—promised to be even more important in the months, and perhaps years, ahead. So far, 2,800 ships laden with men, material and essential foodstuffs had set out in convoy from Halifax. Over the next twelve months more than 3,100 would attempt the same crossing. Many would not make it. Most of the unlucky were destined to fall victim to German wolf packs, though some would come to their end in brutal winter storms. No sailor could know, when his ship slipped out of port, if he would make it across the ocean alive. Some crews refused to sail, while others sabotaged their vessels to make them unseaworthy. The situation became so bad that Ottawa eventually passed an Order-in-Council giving the government the power to jail any merchant sailor who refused to serve. However, many preferred the certainty of detention to the possibility of death.

And that possibility was no longer remote. Consider the fate of the *Stureholm*, the supposed hero ship of the *Jervis Bay* rescue. After the nearly two dozen officers and men who'd refused to sail in her again were paid off, they were replaced by new crew members, some of whom had served on the *Jervis Bay*. The *Stureholm* sailed out of Halifax in early December in Convoy HX91. On the evening of December 12, it was torpedoed by a German submarine. This time, no one survived.

Such continuing painful reminders of mortality, as well as the growing uncertainty as to how it would all end, began to take their toll, not only on the men in the convoys but also on the city itself. The easy patriotic fervour of the war's early days had long since faded. Locals now began to notice the empty store shelves— convoys had priority on scarce supplies—and the increasingly long lineups for everything. And then, of course, there were the condescending attitudes of the Upper Canadian outsiders, who compared Halifax unfavourably to Toronto or wherever it was they came from. They dismissed the city's streetcars as Toonerville Trolleys, the name given to a problem-prone train in a popular cartoon strip of the 1920s. One anonymous letter that circulated in the city during the war urged passengers to take their Motherill's Seasick Remedy before boarding one of the city's tramcars.

The newcomers began to resent the locals, too. Sailors sneeringly nicknamed Halifax "Slackers," as in "those who avoid military service in times of war." There was no place for servicemen to eat, drink or sleep, and everything cost far more than it should. By the end of 1940, military and civic officials were trying to figure out what to do about the reality that four hundred to five hundred men had no place to sleep each night. The situation became even more desperate after a Christmas Eve fire swept through a dockyard barracks block, putting even more sailors, quite literally, on the street.

But things would get worse—much worse—before they got better.

CHAPTER THREE

1941

– Romance and the *Raj* –

As he stared hard at the distant white light in the North Atlantic's inky blackness, Commodore Leonard Murray couldn't decide whether to laugh or cry. This was definitely not the navy he'd joined thirty years ago. W.A. Manfield, the *Assiniboine*'s young officer of the watch, had called him urgently to the ship's bridge tonight to point out an unidentified object on the horizon and to ask for further instructions. Murray looked at the earnest, freshly minted officer beside him and then again out to sea. He tried not to smile. "Manfield, that's serious," he said finally, as gravely as he could muster, then turned on his heel and headed back to his cabin without another word. Oh, what he would have given to watch the earnest young man as he sat there trying to figure it out for himself.

It wasn't Manfield's fault, he knew. But it wasn't Murray's either. The Canadian navy had grown far too big far too fast. If it wasn't so dangerous, it might have been comic. Murray laid the blame for the naval inexperience and occasional incompetence that Ottawa was reaping these days where he believed it belonged: with several generations of federal politicians who'd never accepted that Canada needed a navy. In 1910, Prime Minister Sir Wilfrid Laurier officially launched the Royal Canadian Navy with just two hand-me-down Royal Navy cruisers. By the time Murray signed on as a fourteen-year-old cadet a year later, Laurier's Liberals had been replaced by Sir Robert Borden's Tory government, which imposed cutbacks on the fledgling force. In fact, the navy brass had to send Murray and his fellow cadets home that first winter because they couldn't afford to supply them with uniforms. In 1922, the defence minister tried to cut Canada's naval budget from $2.5 million to $1.5 million and replace its fleet of five warships with two trawlers, which would be used to train a 1,500-member volunteer reserve for the unlikely event that they were required for the "protection of our shores." In 1933, army Major General A.L. McNaughton went so far as to suggest scrapping the navy altogether so the rest of the military could survive drastic cuts in the defence budget. The navy, it seemed, was expendable.

Despite everything, the navy had somehow managed to survive. Now that it was clear, thanks to the growing success of Hitler's murderous U-boat fleet, that the navy did have a vital role to play, not only in Canadian coastal defence but also in making sure all those soldiers and airmen got to the front to fight the good fight, the Royal Canadian Navy suddenly found itself with plenty to do and plenty of money to do it with. But after all those years of neglect, there were few experienced or trained officers to do everything that needed doing.

The problem wasn't only all those bright young landsmen like Manfield who suddenly found themselves at sea—literally and figuratively. Even as he sat in his cabin in the middle of the North Atlantic, wondering with a smile if the penny had dropped yet for Manfield, Murray had to ask himself if he was avoiding allowing his own penny to drop. He looked over at a recent photo of himself on his desk. It showed him standing on the *Assiniboine*'s bridge, dressed in his winter jacket, a woollen cap pulled down over his head, his jaw jutting forward towards the ship's bow. It was his favourite photograph of himself. After too many years as a deskbound commander, he desperately wanted to be in charge of a ship again, to be involved in real action. But was that selfish? Could he captain a ship and do everything else he was being asked to do?

He'd taken command of the *Assiniboine* in October. "Bones," as the sailors called it, was a cast-off British destroyer assigned to escort convoys from Halifax to Newfoundland. But Murray wasn't just the captain of Bones. He was also—concurrently—Commodore Commanding Halifax and a member of the Permanent Joint U.S.–Canada Defence Board. That last appointment meant he'd spent a good deal of time away from his ship.

In 1940, Murray had been part of a top secret Canadian military delegation that had met with General George C. Marshall, the U.S. Army Chief of Staff, and other top military leaders in Washington. Their goal was to figure out how neutral America could surreptitiously help Canada defend North America once, as seemed likely to the Americans, the Germans defeated Britain. After Mackenzie King and Franklin Roosevelt formalized the co-operative efforts, Murray was one of the first members appointed to the new joint board. That meant he'd had to travel to San Francisco, Seattle, Esquimalt and Alaska for meetings with his American counterparts.

Now the *Assiniboine* was on its way to Greenock, Scotland, to join other Canadian destroyers recently seconded to help Britain fight the German U-boat threat off the British Isles. With Canada's growing commitment to British naval operations, however, it would soon become clear that Canada needed a full-time experienced officer on the ground in London "to coordinate and draw the threads together of Canada's efforts overseas," as Chief of Staff Percy Nelles had put it in a January 7, 1940, memo to Defence Minister Angus L. Macdonald. Nelles had "no hesitation" in recommending Murray for the job.

Almost before it had fully begun, Leonard Murray's war at sea would soon be over.

Back up on the bridge, Manfield, the puzzled young duty officer, continued taking bearings. The mysterious light kept rising but seemed to get no closer. Then it hit him. Sirius! The unidentified object he had called Murray up to examine was, in fact, Sirius, one of the brightest stars in the heavens, rising in the east.

Manfield was embarrassed, but grateful that Murray had left him to puzzle it out for himself. "From that one little incident," Manfield, who went on to command his own ships, would explain years later, "a long-lasting lesson was learned—that all is not that which it first appears to be."

ANOTHER LETTER, another rejection. "Your patriotism is appreciated . . . If you join another armed service, please let us know . . ."

Eric Dennis refolded the letter, put it back in its envelope. He was getting used to this. He'd been turned down by all three armed services, and now again by the navy, this time for a job as a press liaison officer. He'd heard from one of his contacts in Angus L. Macdonald's office in Ottawa that the navy would be setting up a press release office in Halifax. It wasn't the front lines, of course, but it was active service. And who knew where it might lead?

So Dennis had gathered up a whole bagful of his newspaper clippings and sent them off to Ottawa, along with a carefully composed letter offering his services in the war effort. The Naval Information Officer who replied made it clear that, Dennis's well-connected sources in the Ministry of National Defence for Naval Services notwithstanding, the navy had no immediate intention of setting up any such office in Halifax, so there was no position to apply for. And besides, the navy already had a surplus of writers.

The problem—at least it seemed so to him—was that everyone else in their early twenties was on active service. Perhaps, he thought bitterly, he would join the militia. At least they got to wear uniforms.

"THREE HOURS, MATE," the sailor said, slipping Byron Himmelman two dollars and giving him a conspiratorial wink as he clambered out of the cab's back seat behind his girl. Byron watched as the sailor, unsteady from the alcohol, or the nervousness, or the excitement—

who could tell?—put his arm around the young woman who now guided him towards the main cabin, where the check-in was.

"I'll be here," Byron said, as much to the Plymouth's back seat as to the sailor and his girl. He'd done this before. Many times. Sailors, soldiers, airmen, merchant navy types—men from all over. The girls were mostly from town. They'd meet at Norman's, the Saturday-night rat-race dances down at the Nova Scotian, or one of the other dances at the Lord Nelson or the Roseland or the Silver Slipper. They'd exchange a furtive kiss or two, maybe neck a little during the slow dances. He'd tell her he loved her but his ship was leaving in the morning. She'd say how much she'd miss him. Things would progress quickly after that, and then, suddenly, urgently, they'd need a room for an hour or two. He couldn't take her back to his barracks, of course, and she was probably still living at home, so they'd call a cab. Sometimes they already knew where they wanted to go—"Johnson's Cabins, and quick"—and sometimes they'd ask if he knew a place where they could go "for a few hours . . ." Byron knew what they meant. Every cabbie did. Though there were plenty of places that were happy to cater to the less-than-a-full-night crowd, Johnson's Cabins was the most popular trysting spot. A cluster of cabins nestled in the woods just off the St. Margaret's Bay Road on the outskirts of town, it was close enough to Halifax to be an affordable cab ride but far enough from downtown to be discreet—if renting a cabin for a couple of hours on a spring afternoon could ever be considered discreet.

Byron Himmelman didn't care. Driving cab was a means to an end, and the end was becoming an electrician. Clean hands, well fed, well looked after. Byron was going to become an electrician and then go back to sea, where he belonged. He'd been born in Lahave on the province's south shore eighteen years ago but had spent most of his growing-up years in Halifax. His father was a sailmaker and sometime fisherman who'd been forced to move to the city to look for work during the Depression. There not being much call for sailmakers in the age of steam, he finally landed a job as an able seaman aboard Imperial Oil tankers.

When war broke out, Byron, like most of his fellow grade ten students at Halifax Academy, was eager to volunteer. In early October he got in line at the hastily organized navy recruiting office at the dockyard's North Gate and filled out an application.

"What branch do you want to be in?" the officer asked.

"What do you recommend?" Byron answered, not knowing what else to say.

"Victualling assistant," the man said, deadpan. "That's always a good place to start."

Victualling assistant? Byron didn't know what that meant, but he liked the sound of it. "Sure," he said.

It was only later that he learned it was a fancy way of saying mess boy, the lowest of the low in the navy's pecking order. Not that it mattered; he never got called back. When he returned in January to ask why he hadn't heard anything, he was told that they were going through the piles of applications they'd received, but not to expect anything quickly. The navy had so few ships, it had little need of sailors.

The army turned him down—he'd had pleurisy as a kid—and the air force recruiter laughed at him. He'd never even been on a plane.

At his father's urging, Byron had signed on the *Montrolite*, the oil tanker where his father was now the bosun. He became a mess boy; there were no fancy titles in the merchant navy. "My job was to serve the officers," he recalled years later. "I served them their meals, I cleaned their rooms, I got the stores for the meals for the cooks. And one guy I envied right off the bat was the electrician. I'd watch him. He was one of the few guys who never seemed to get his hands dirty. He was always dressed to the hilt. He had his meals served and someone—me—to clean up after him. I thought, 'Now that's for me.'"

So, in the summer of 1940, Byron quit the *Montrolite* and returned to Halifax, where he enrolled in a three-year night course in electrical engineering at the Nova Scotia Technical College. To make ends meet, he took a day job driving cab for Wade's. It was one of the city's biggest taxi companies with a fleet of ten cars and two seven-passenger limos, used mostly for weddings. One even had a horn that played "Here Comes the Bride."

Most of his customers were either sailors or visiting war workers. The locals who were wealthy enough had their own cars; the rest depended on the tramcar for basic transportation. But there were more than enough sailors to keep him busy. Byron couldn't get over how much the city had changed in the few months he'd been away. There were people everywhere now, and all sorts of activity. There'd also been a big influx of Norwegians. They drank a lot, Byron had noticed, a horny bunch, but nice guys, good tippers.

Unlike some of his fellow cabbies, who sold booze out of the trunks of their taxis or had special deals with madams like Germaine Pelletier to steer business their way, Byron was happy enough just to offer directions and advice. The truth was, he didn't intend to drive cab for long. He had his name in at the Halifax Shipyards. If he could get on there as an electrician's helper and combine that with his night school courses, he could be back at sea in no time, but this time in a cushy job.

He looked at his watch. Just after one. He had time to drive back downtown, maybe pick up a few after-lunch fares from Norman's, and then head back to Johnson's to pick up the sailor and his girl.

JEFF JEFFERSON SAT alone in his censor's office as the late afternoon sun dipped out of sight beyond the stone fortifications of Citadel Hill. His phone had stopped ringing, at least for a few welcome moments. Time to consider, to write down his thoughts in his journal. He took another look at the words he had just typed. Were things really as awful as they seemed, or was it just this nagging head cold he was battling that made the latest turn of events in Europe appear much worse than it actually was? Jefferson couldn't decide.

Back in his days as an editor at the *Chronicle*, Jefferson's fellow journalists had often marvelled at his uncanny ability to read between the lines of even the most innocuous "bush notes" from the paper's far-flung network of rural correspondents. He knew how to read the codes in the correspondents' copy, and to divine who was in and who was out—even who was sleeping with whom—in virtually any community in the province. But that was easy. Jefferson had put in nearly thirty years covering every event of even passing significance from Yarmouth to Sydney and back again. But what could he read between the lines of unknown reporters' dispatches from far-off battlefields?

He reread the bleak words he'd written. "This afternoon came news that the Germans are in Salonika." Jefferson knew that Salonika, the ancient city where St. Paul had founded the first Christian congregation nearly two thousand years before, was a key seaport in northern Greece. In October 1940, the British came to its rescue after Mussolini invaded Greece. The Italians had been beaten back, but the presence of British airplanes within striking distance of Germany's main source of oil, in Romania, made Hitler nervous. So on April 6, 1941, he launched his own attack on Greece. Greece's army of 430,000 soldiers, even bolstered by 62,000 British troops, proved no match for the Nazi invaders. Within three days the Germans had taken Salonika and forced half the Greek army to surrender.

"Maybe," Jefferson began typing again, "it is because I have a bad cold but this is the most depressing incident of the whole war; not even the capture of Paris, the collapse of France and the retreat from Dunkirk have caused so much disappointment . . ."

Perhaps, he thought, he should stop writing now, go home, get some rest. Maybe things would look better in the morning.

Maybe.

THE *RAJ?* NOT THE *RAJ!* Marjory Whitelaw couldn't believe it. She had danced with so many of them. They were so handsome, so young, so full of life. And now . . . She looked again at the story in the newspaper. Ten days ago, on Easter Sunday, April 13, 1941, the Armed Merchant Cruiser *Rajputana* had been torpedoed and sunk in the Denmark Strait between Greenland and Iceland, with the loss of forty-one crew members, including a Canadian midshipman. During its thirteen months of wartime service, the former P&O liner had safely escorted more than seven hundred ships across the Atlantic, never losing even one. It had, in fact, only recently left Halifax to escort yet another convoy across the Atlantic when it had been ordered to leave the convoy and take up patrol in the Denmark Strait instead.

It was the Saturday before the convoy left port, Marjory realized with a start, that she had been at a dance with many of the *Raj*'s officers. She'd sat at a table with some of them, danced with others. She'd hidden the flasks they'd smuggled into the ballroom in her overstuffed, oversized purse. She could see in her mind's eye the ship's doctor, smiling, his arm wrapped around that glamorous gal from Montreal. Had she really been a spy? Would she be heartbroken now? And the "Canadian midshipman"—could he be the one she saw at the top of the ballroom stairs that night, stretched out on a sofa in the foyer, passed out after drinking too much too quickly, sleeping like a baby?

She tried not to, but she couldn't stop herself from visualizing the scene in the Denmark Strait. The torpedo. The alarm. Did they die when the torpedo ripped through the ship's hull? Or did they drown when the *Raj* sank? Or did they survive the explosion and the fire—would there have been a fire?—and escape into the North Atlantic night—was it night?—in one of those mahogany lifeboats they were all so proud of, only to die a slow, painful death from exposure and starvation?

They were the first young men Marjory actually knew who'd been killed in the war.

JEFF JEFFERSON COULD ONLY SHAKE HIS HEAD in wonder. It was the morning after news of the *Rajputana*'s sinking had been released to the press, and Bert Wetmore from the Halifax *Mail* was calling to ask his advice about a follow-up story. A local girl named Margaret MacEachern had been due to wed a *Raj* stoker named Jenson after the ship returned to Halifax on April 28. Jenson had been among those killed, so Wetmore's story was focusing on how the young woman was dealing with her grief.

Jefferson tried to listen as Wetmore read him his draft, but he couldn't get past Wetmore's mention of the date the *Raj* had been expected back in port. You'd think by now the reporters would know the rules: they weren't allowed to publish any dates or place names that could possibly help the enemy figure out Allied war plans. If the stoker's bride-to-be was from Halifax, it only stood to reason that the *Raj* sailed out of here. And if the vessel was supposed to be in port April 28, it probably meant another convoy would be forming in Halifax harbour then. The Germans could be waiting for them at the harbour mouth, for heaven's sake.

Even though the *Raj* had been "1,900 miles at sea on a supposedly secret mission," Jefferson wrote in his journal, "the exact date of its projected return was known here and probably had been ever since its departure." What was the point of secrecy if everyone in town knew all the secrets?

Sometimes it seemed the best hope the Allies had was journalistic incompetence. Jefferson's favourite "ne plus ultra pooper" had been the newspaper photograph that some editor had "flipped" so that what was, in fact, a photo of a ship that had run aground coming into the harbour appeared to show the grounding happening on its way out of the harbour. That should confuse the Nazis. And then, of course, there were all the contradictory stories about ship sinkings.

"One of the things that helps to lighten our task of covering up and confusing ship identities," Jefferson noted in his journal, "is that when one is sunk, the CP [Canadian Press] will come through with 18 killed, 20 saved; the BUP [British United Press] with 20 killed, 18 saved; while the Toronto *Star*, *Telegram* and the two locals will each have some other different version. Not only that, but in successive stories about the same ship they will call her a freighter, tanker, etc. This of course is all to the good from a censorship standpoint, but don't tell the government—they might figure that the best method of confusing the enemy would be just to give the newspapers their heads and let them proceed by the light of nature in their own inimitable promulgation of Acurracy, Accuracy, Accureacy."

In the end, Jefferson OK'd Wetmore's story but advised him not to include the exact date and not to say that the woman was from Halifax.

MARJORY WHITELAW AND HER FRIEND Barbara Eaton had decided to stop at Norman's for tea after their badminton game to avoid having to walk home with Bradford Ellis, "the most unlikeable virgin" in their circle. As usual, there were no free tables, and only one with even two spare chairs.

"Mind if we join you?" Marjory asked the uniformed man who occupied the table's other chair. She'd had lots of practice at talking to strangers since she'd moved to Halifax. What choice did she have? And besides, many of those strangers were now, at the very least, acquaintances. Some had even become friends. Perhaps this man would too.

He was not conventionally handsome. Tall and slight, with thinning hair and a full beard, he was considerably older than she was, probably in his mid-thirties. But he had what she thought of as a kind face, and an easy smile. She noticed right away the two wavy gold stripes on his blue uniform sleeve that marked him as an officer in the Royal Naval Reserve. She and Barbara often joked that the first thing any girl looked at when she met a man in uniform were the gold stripes on his uniform. She did too, she had to admit. She also noticed—the second thing a girl looked at—that he wasn't wearing a wedding ring.

"Please do," the man replied pleasantly enough. His name was Thane Parker, and he was a lieutenant on the *Lady Somers*, one of CN's aging fleet of Lady Boats. He'd been in town four days, he explained, and theirs were the first friendly faces he'd seen.

They quickly fell into the intimate conversational mode that was almost the norm among strangers in wartime Halifax. Before long, Thane and Marjory—Barbara quickly became little more than an interested spectator of their mating game—were exchanging life stories.

Before the war he'd been the business manager for Sadler's Wells, a well-known London venue for opera, dance and musical theatre. That immediately piqued Marjory's interest. Since she'd moved to Halifax, she'd joined a local small theatre and become a member of a choral group that entertained the troops on ships in the harbour. She became even more enchanted when he began to tell her of his adventurous childhood. His father, it turned out, was a not very successful English painter who'd articled him to a merchant ship when he was still a boy. After some financial reverses, his father stopped paying Thane's fees, so he'd been forced to jump ship in Pensacola, Florida. There, he met a man who was heading up to Tennessee to travel through the hill country in a cart and horse, interviewing the locals and recording their songs. Thane went with him. Later, he returned to England and fell into his job in the theatre. When the war began, he decided he should do his bit. To Marjory it all seemed dreadfully romantic.

In return she told him about her less adventurous but not much more conventional upbringing. When she was only three, her mother had died after eating "bad" canned lobster. Her father, a Scottish-born engineer who'd immigrated to Moncton to work on the railway, packed Marjory back to Scotland to live with her mother's parents in Edinburgh, where she attended Sir James Gillespie's School for Girls (later to be the inspiration for Muriel Spark's novel *The Prime of Miss Jean Brodie*). Her father remarried when she was seven and Marjory moved to Montreal, where her father was working for the CNR. She told Thane about her father's death, and her stepmother's, and, of course, about her decision to come to Halifax the year before. Someday, she confided, she wanted to write novels and plays and poetry, and—oh yes—travel the world, too.

They talked and talked and talked. Finally, he walked them both home—Barbara first, Marjory noted with satisfaction, and then her. Outside Alex and Tina's house, he kissed her.

"If I call you tomorrow, would you go for a walk with me?"

She said yes. Yes, yes, yes. This was so unlike her. Usually, she thought too much—should she? shouldn't she? By the time she had worried her way through all the emotional combinations and permutations, she had wrung all the spontaneity, all the romance, out of everything.

Not this time.

The next afternoon, a Saturday, Marjory and Thane went for a long walk-and-talk through the still snow-covered trails in Point Pleasant Park. There seemed so much to talk about, and so little time for it. The *Lady Somers* would be sailing Monday.

"Would you like to come in for tea?" she asked when they'd got back to Alex and Tina's house.

"I'd like that very much." Like her, he didn't seem to want the day to end.

She'd already told Alex and Tina and old Angus, Tina's father, about her new young man. "You've been hoodwinked," Tina had concluded immediately. "What do you really know about him?"

More than enough, she'd thought but didn't say. No point in starting a row.

Now Angus appraised Thane carefully, then turned to Marjory. "Don't you think he's a little old for you, Marjory?"

If Thane was offended, he kept it to himself. Marjory steered him into the kitchen as quickly as possible. She'd use Tina's elegant tea set, she thought, the antique one with the flowered teapot. But when she went to pour the boiling water into the pot, it began to leak from every crack.

Thane laughed. He didn't seem to mind. And neither did she. Perhaps this was what it was to be in love.

If only he wasn't leaving tomorrow. If only there was no damn war. But of course, if there hadn't been a war, she'd never have ended up in Halifax, and most likely neither would he. Perhaps, she smiled to herself, the war wasn't so bad after all.

EVEN THOUGH THEY LIVED only a few miles across town from each other, Harold Masterman hadn't seen his brother, Jack, in nearly a year, not since they'd been sent to live with separate foster families last August. But Mrs. MacAdam, Jack's foster mother, had finally arranged for Harold to come and play with Jack. The MacAdams lived in a big house, even bigger than the O'Byrnes', on Gottingen Street, next to the naval base at Stadacona. Mr. MacAdam was the manager of the Casino Theatre, which meant that Jack got to see lots of movie matinees for free.

Jack seemed to be happy. Harold was too. Playing war with Jack's tin soldiers up in his bedroom reminded Harold, for the first time in months, that he hadn't always lived with the O'Byrnes.

Jack's memories were stronger. "Remember when we called shit *cack*?" he asked at one point, as Harold killed another Nazi soldier.

"No," Harold answered. The truth was, he didn't remember much any more about where they came from or what it was like. He even had trouble recalling what their parents looked like.

IT WAS JUST AFTER five o'clock and the downtown streets were in the middle of their daily changing of the guard. As the small army of exhausted secretaries and clerks spilled out of their offices and shops and onto tramcars heading to the northern and western sub-urbs, hundreds of laughing, talking, joking, prowling sailors, eager to begin another summer night on dry land, arrived on board duty boats at the downtown wharves from their ships' anchorages in the harbour or Basin.

Marjory Whitelaw was happy to fall in with the departing

throngs heading up Prince Street hill towards Barrington. After yet another day spent tallying up the total landed catch of each of the hundreds of different species of fish caught in the Maritimes, she would be happy to relax this evening with Barbara at their new apartment.

Unless, of course, Thane called. He'd told her when he left the last time that the *Somers* would be back in forty days. He should have arrived more than a week ago. Not that there was anything unusual about that. She knew as well as anyone that sailing schedules changed for all sorts of reasons, often at the last moment and almost always without warning. There was no way he could get in touch with her and no one she could call to find out when the *Lady Somers* was expected. She would just have to wait.

Though they'd met less than six months ago and had been together on only three occasions, for no more than a few days each time, Marjory already thought of them as a couple—for life. "If I could have," she would say later, "I'd have gone off and married him the next day."

When he was away, she replayed their time together over and over. The dinner at the Carleton Hotel. The movies. The day he'd called her at work and she'd giggled like a schoolgirl and then she'd met him after work at the Green Lantern. She told him its local nickname, the Green Latrine. He'd laughed. There were more walks in Point Pleasant Park. More talks too. They talked about everything and anything, and never managed to exhaust themselves. Not that she was taking any chances with that. She'd managed to buy a copy of Sheldon Cheney's *The Theatre: Three Thousand Years of Drama, Acting, and Stagecraft*, which was the only book about theatre she could find in Halifax, and was slowly working her way through its 592 dense pages of history in search of conversational bon mots to throw into their next discussion. "The *commedia dell'arte*— now there's a thing," she would say. "But I thought some of his ideas were a bit outdated, maybe . . ." Oh dear, she would have to work on that before Thane returned.

There were other things she was eager to share too. She couldn't wait to show Thane her new apartment. Though she was grateful to Alex and Tina for giving her a place to live when she first arrived in the city, Marjory had long been eager to strike out on her own. She and Barbara had finally found a wonderful apartment on the main floor of a converted old home on Queen Street near Morris, just a few blocks from downtown. It featured a triple drawing room that would be ideal for entertaining, and a double back room where they slept. The building was full of other young, single women like themselves. Marjory had got to know a few of them already. Eleanor Fairn and Rhoda Wright lived on the top floor. Their men were overseas. Rhoda's intended, a fellow named Alex Colville, was apparently a very good artist. Maybe he and Thane could meet someday, she thought.

The landlady, Helen Gough, lived across the hall from Marjory and Barbara, and would often favour them with her renditions of the arias from various operas. Thane would love that too, Marjory thought with a smile as she reached the corner of Prince and Barrington. So many people heading in all directions. Perhaps she would do a little browsing in the windows of Eaton's department store before she went home.

She had just turned the corner when she saw it. First, the newsboy hawking the latest edition of the Halifax *Mail*. Then, the headline. She couldn't breathe. She thought she was going to fall over, collapse right there in the street.

'LADY SOMERS' IS SUNK
Auxiliary Naval Vessel Goes Down With Loss of 37

She bought a copy, trying not to shake as she read and reread the too brief, too superficial account. Not known if any Canadians aboard . . . in peacetime a Canadian National Steamship vessel . . . Admiralty announcement "did not specify the manner of the sinking nor where it took place."

What about Thane, she wanted to scream?

But Marjory knew there was no one who could—or would—tell her what had happened to him.

No one told him anything. One day Billy Mont was halfway through serving a five-year sentence in the Halifax Industrial School for having played hooky from public school, and the next day he was free to go. He was twelve years old.

It hadn't been so bad, really. He'd discovered he was smarter than he or anyone else imagined. He'd squeezed three school years into the two and a half years he spent at the Industrial School, and would be going into grade five at Tower Road this fall. Better, he'd discovered he liked learning, if not school itself.

He had realized other things as well—like how to communicate using the sign language some of the other boys had taught him so they could pass messages back and forth in class without the teacher catching on. And that there was a world beyond the city. During the summers, the boys went on outings to a farm in nearby Sackville. The farm was near a racetrack and the boys got to watch the horses. Sometimes an adult would go around the track in a horse and wagon, throwing candies to the boys.

Occasionally, visitors would come to the school, often well-meaning religious groups like the Band of Hope, a temperance organization for working-class children. They'd lecture on the "evils of drink" and encourage the boys to sign pledges agreeing to abstain from liquor, tobacco and swearing. Billy had signed. And, except for the occasional swear word, he'd honoured his pledge. The fact was, the Band of Hope volunteers had been among his few contacts with the outside world since Alice, Billy's step-grandmother, had succeeded in having his mother, Mary, committed to the City Home for the mentally infirm. Neither Alice nor his grandfather came to visit often.

Still, when Billy was finally released from the Industrial School, his grandfather not only allowed him to rejoin them in the

Greenbank cottage, but he also helped Billy find a summer job at the Halifax Shipyards, where Mr. Mont worked.

Billy was a boiler chipper, the dirtiest job on the waterfront but one for which he was made, being small for his age. A boiler chipper squeezed into ships' cramped spaces—boilers, tanks, bilges—and used a wire brush to scrape the soot and rust and gunk off the inside walls. The oil tanks weren't so bad, Billy found, because at least he could stand up. The bilges were the worst. Billy would have to climb down a manhole into the crawlspace at the bottom of the ship's hull, then work his way through a labyrinth of steel beams and posts to the even more claustrophobic confines of the bow, cleaning as he went. It was definitely an advantage to be small, but it was so dark! Billy was always worried someone would close the manhole cover on him.

It was almost enough to make him look forward to September, when he'd have to quit to go back to school. Almost . . .

WHEN HMCS *RESTIGOUCHE* ARRIVED back in Halifax one afternoon in late August, Debby Piers decided to surprise Janet by showing up, unannounced, at her parents' home; but the surprise was on him. He knocked on the door just as Janet's sister Edith was exchanging marriage vows with her army sweetheart in a ceremony in the Macneill living room.

Debby and Janet were by now more than just an item. During a romantic dinner aboard the *Restigouche* in July, Debby had officially proposed. But they'd put off setting a wedding date because Debby never knew when, or for how long, he'd be in port. Now the *Restigouche* needed some minor repair work, and it would probably remain tied up at the jetty in the dockyard for two weeks. Time enough.

As the bride and groom said their I do's, Debby slipped into the seat beside Janet and kissed her on the cheek. "I've got ten days," he said simply. "How about it?"

During the reception they announced their plans to Janet's

parents. There followed a whirlwind week of hasty arrangements, decisions, compromises, more decisions, parties for family and friends, and still more decisions.

The Admiral gave his blessing for the wedding ceremony to be held aboard the *Restigouche*—where Debby was now the youngest destroyer captain in the Royal Canadian Navy—but he insisted that Ernie Foote, the navy's United Church chaplain, perform the ceremony to make it an "authentic" naval wedding.

The wedding was set for Tuesday, September 2—the day after Labour Day—at five in the afternoon. *Restigouche* shipwrights made a kneeling bench, a cross and candlesticks for the service. However, no one thought to factor in the reality that nine thousand sailors and civilians working the day shift at the dockyard would be spilling out through the gates just as they tried to enter, so Janet, her mother and father, and sister Isabel were almost late for the ceremony. After the wedding the crew had a party for the newlyweds on the deck and gave them a silver tray as a gift. The formal reception was at Janet's parents' home. Despite increasingly tight restrictions on liquor sales, there was no shortage of alcohol. "We'd saved up any booze we could get our hands on," Debby would explain simply. "It was a lovely party."

Later, Debby and Janet drove to Chester to spend their first night as a married couple at a Piers family cottage by the water. With fifty-two dollars that Debby had saved—he was then making five dollars a day as a lieutenant, plus a dollar a day extra for commanding the ship—he and Janet managed to take a three-day honeymoon in Cape Breton, camping out except for one night, when they treated themselves to a stay at the Keltic Lodge resort.

Then Debby was due back aboard ship. And then? Who knew how long it would be before they'd be together again?

MARJORY WHITELAW REREAD the words she had so carefully written. They seemed rambling, disconnected, incoherent. She wanted to explain herself to him. She tried again. "Dear Thane. I never mean to babble so much, but there is always such a lot I want to tell you."

It was November 4, 1941, nearly four months since the July afternoon a newspaper headline had turned her girlishly romantic dreams into a nightmare, and still she didn't know whether Thane Parker had survived or . . . So she continued to write to him at his home address in London, England. The most recent letter had come back unopened a few days ago. "It was a bitter blow," she wrote now, but "I still want you to have it and so I'm trying again." She would enclose the last letter with this one—just in case.

She had tried to put her thoughts into words, but they never seemed to come out right. "I feel as though I'm wandering in a horrible sort of desolate fog of circumstance, with every road leading to a dead end or a maze," she explained, then added more forcefully: "I'll be damned if I'll let you slip off in the fog; I simply must find out what has happened to you before I can go on to anything else. Oh, Thane, I know it could have been any of a dozen quite usual things—or usual in 1941—but my imagination plays me some foul scenes sometimes. Couldn't you send me a postcard saying, 'Of course I'm all right and don't be such a damn silly little fool'?"

Was she being too melodramatic? Keep the tone light, gossipy. "The Halifax *Herald* and *Mail* has a feature writer in Britain just now doing gooey stuff. She is a blonde bitch from Wolfville called Tufts, and Barbara knows her quite well . . . Michael Redgrave was here last week; I'd like to have met him because I liked his funny face in the pictures, but I didn't hear about it until he had left. He was an able seaman and on his way to join a ship—some of the men at the radio station were talking to him . . .

"Life here is getting more primitive. We are Learning To Do Without. No gas from Saturday noon to Monday morning, or from 7 p.m. till a.m. We went out in the woods and chopped our own firewood—there's no one to do that sort of work now. We could have robbed one of the woodpiles you admired so, but we felt there was virtue in honest toil. And pretty soon, damnit, I'll be wearing cotton stockings on my fine long legs. Taxes are flourishing and restrictions numerous.

"This is really your Christmas letter," she added, switching moods with the paragraphs. "It seems too early to say Merry Christmas, somehow, but may you have a merry one wherever you are, darling, and would you think of me? . . . Would you spend your leave with us? [Barbara's boyfriend] Tony and Barbara and I are going out to the woods to chop us a Christmas tree. I've never done this before, we always bought one at the grocer's, and this is much better. I love the woods in winter. Anyway, we will have a really good Christmas dinner with guests and a turkey and the best damask tablecloth and all possible trimmings. I would love to have a suckling pig and mulled something or other to drink, but it is now unpatriotic to eat pork; pork must go to Britain. A murrain on you pork eaters. And to ensure that we will not be tempted by our grosser appetites into unpatriotic ways, they jacked up the price so that we can't afford the damn stuff anyway. I want a party on Christmas Eve and a foot of snow falling softly, and on Christmas day a drive in the country behind two bloody fast horses harnessed with silver bells, like they have in Quebec. And I bet you it rains. We'll go skating on all the ponds and come home and make hot rum punch; you remember how icy it was here last winter? Please, sir, we would like to have you. We would make you welcome, darling."

Enough fantasizing. She missed their talks, the chance to tell Thane all the sundry thoughts going through her head. "My mental life is badly confused these days," she wrote. It was, and not just because of him. Barbara and her boyfriend, Tony Sheppard, were part of an informal group of young socialists. They had begun to include Marjory in their social gatherings. "My capitalistic education has been taking a terrific beating and I'm having a horrible time being worsted in argument about twice weekly," she confided. "I now feel as though I knew nothing and should start over—they tell me this is Step No. 1 in the realignment of one's ideas."

Work. She should tell him about her job prospects. "I may go to work for the navy—at the dockyard. I feel that if I have to write one more report for the fisheries saying that this month's catch of cod is umpteen hundred weights more than the same month last year, I shall expire. I nearly got a job with the Economic Council which would have been marvellous training and set me off beautifully on a career, but they gave it to a man with a degree in Economics instead. However, I feel it gives me a certain standing to have been considered for the thing at all . . . The dockyard will probably pay me as much as I can get in Halifax, and if it is interesting I think I'll take it and shake this stultifying air of dried codfish."

There was something else Marjory wanted to write, something she'd been avoiding. She'd hinted at it earlier in her letter: "It's a most tantalizing thing to know that England is only a few hours away by plane." What she really wanted to tell him was that she would drop everything and hop on the next transatlantic flight if only he would give her some signal, some sign to let her know he was alive and wanted her as much as she wanted him. But for some reason that she couldn't quite put her finger on, she was too shy to say so directly. Instead, she approached the issue elliptically. "I have a friend who wants me to go to England next spring if we can manage it," she wrote. "I want to do this so much that I can hardly bear to put it on paper; I've talked about it for years and suddenly such things as going to England seem possible. My heavens but I'm tired of talking about things I want to do and never doing. This is the beginning."

Was it? Or was she just kidding herself, pretending Thane was still out there somewhere, just waiting for her to find him again?

She should end this on an upbeat note, she thought. "If you do get this letter you get two batches at once, you lucky fellow, you."

If he didn't get the letter? Marjory wouldn't let herself think about that.

THE BRIDE WAITED nervously at the back of the church for a signal from the organist. She looked radiant in a simple white satin wedding gown set off by the bouquet of Joanna Hill roses she carried in her arms and the delicate blue Wedgwood locket around her neck. It had been a gift from her mother, who'd worn it on her own wedding day. The groom, equally nervous, was already standing in his place at the front of the church next to the minister. He was wearing a black tuxedo with a white carnation boutonniere in his lapel. His best man and the two ushers were resplendent in their dashing navy dress uniforms. That he was not wearing a uniform was Eric Dennis's only regret as he stole a quick glance back towards Maxine.

They'd met just over two years ago, during one of his brief visits home to Vancouver. That date had sparked a passionate long-distance romance, stoked by almost daily letters and fanned by occasional visits. During their one and only long-distance—and long-lasting—telephone call, earlier this summer, they'd decided it was time to at least live in the same city for a while. So Maxine had come east with a girlfriend, who was moving to Halifax to marry her boyfriend, a junior naval officer about to be posted to sea. Eric had arranged for Maxine to rent a room in the west-end home of Ron Shaw, the vice-president of a well-known brick-making firm. Now he and Maxine were about to begin their married life there.

Even before Maxine arrived, Eric's fortunes were looking up. After their phone call this summer the telephone company had felt the need to contact Dennis's landlord to reassure itself the young man could indeed afford the $76 charge he'd just run up. Surprisingly, he could. He was now earning $25 a week at the *Herald*, but he, like many of his fellow reporters, had begun supplementing his wages by freelancing war-related stories to big-city newspapers and magazines. Thanks to a seemingly insatiable public demand for war news, the fact that Halifax generated more than its fair share of such news, and—most importantly—Dennis's own growing reputation for ferreting out the most dramatic tales of rescue and survival at sea, freelancing had become a lucrative sideline for him. "I sent something to the Toronto *Star* almost every day, and *Time* magazine was after me whenever there was something that might interest Americans. The only problem was finding time to do it all," he would later recall.

Largely because of his impending nuptials, Bob Rankin, the paper's managing editor, had switched him from night-side reporting to a new job as city editor of the afternoon *Mail*, and his uncle had given him a $10-a-week raise. Eric had mixed feelings about what was certainly a promotion. He would now oversee the work of six reporters and two other editors, not to mention handling the editors who looked after the "bush notes" correspondents—the amateur reporters from rural communities who filed regular reports to the paper on local happenings. While Eric's new position meant he'd work fewer nights, and less often sleep on a table in the newsroom because he was too tired to walk home, it also meant fewer opportunities to do the kind of stories he could now freelance to others. (As it turned out, he need not have worried: the paper was so short-staffed, Eric would end up working most nights anyway. The only difference was that his day began at 7 a.m. instead of 4 p.m. When the *Mail* came out at 12:30 or 1 p.m., he simply switched to reporter mode, covering city council or the legislature, or the arrival of survivors from the latest torpedoed merchant ship. There were so many of them, "torpedo survivors" could have been a reporting beat of its own.)

As his best man, Colin Campbell, handed him the ring to place on Maxine's finger, Eric noticed the single sub-lieutenant's band around his uniform sleeve. Colin, who was the nephew of a naval commodore, was finishing up his training at HMCS King's on the former King's College campus in the city's south end. The navy had taken over the small university in April for the duration of the war as an officer training school. Though Eric hadn't yet resigned himself to the fact that he would not be joining his friends and colleagues to fight the Nazis, he had done the next best thing to enlisting: he'd recently joined the Non-Permanent Active Militia, a local volunteer group made up of men too old or too young or too sickly to fight. They spent their evenings marching at the armouries, and their weekends practising (for what, he wasn't quite sure) at a rifle range in Bedford. It was some consolation, of course, but no substitute for the real thing.

"I pronounce you man and wife," the minister said, snapping Dennis out of his reverie. "You may kiss the bride."

While the wedding party signed the register to make it all official, Austin Gough, the soloist, sang "Because."

After the ceremony, Eric's uncle and boss, Senator Dennis, and his wife, Hilda, hosted the wedding reception at their home on Jubilee Road, overlooking the Northwest Arm. The Senator helped out with the honeymoon too—an early winter trip to Niagara Falls.

After that, it would be back home to reality: a room in someone else's house and work that never seemed to end.

THIS COULD BE A SCENE from a Hollywood musical, Debby Piers thought to himself. Except it wasn't. Worse, he knew now that this trip would not have the happy holiday ending he'd been planning and dreaming about.

The roiling seas continued to wash over the *Restigouche*'s icy, wind-lashed deck. Looking down from his post in the bridge, Piers could see most of his ship's crew, now formed up into a huge bucket brigade to bail out the water-filled forward magazine compartment and keep their destroyer afloat. It was four in the morning and they'd been at it since six the evening before. As they bailed, they sang along to "Paper Doll," the new Mills Brothers tune that blasted out into the night from the ship's SRE. The Sound Reproduction Equipment was about the only thing still working on the *Restigouche*.

This should have been a routine trip. On December 7, 1941, the *Restigouche* left Iceland to meet up with a convoy of empty ships heading west from England to Canada. Piers hoped to escort the convoy as far as Halifax, where, with luck, *Restigouche* could tie up alongside over Christmas. He hadn't seen Janet since their honeymoon more than three months ago and he was eager to renew acquaintance.

They were just thirty miles from the convoy when the barometer began to fall faster and further than Debby had ever seen. Then the storm struck, suddenly and with a vengeance. The winds, gusting at eighty to ninety miles an hour, toppled the ship's foremast, taking out the wireless aerial and short-circuiting the ship's hooters, the noisemakers the ship used to indicate it was turning to port or starboard. "They both went off at once," Piers would recall, "creating the most awful, most diabolical noise." Just when the electrician had managed to disconnect those wires and Snakey Ellis, the ship's resourceful wireless operator, had juryrigged another aerial—"We barely missed a message"—a rogue wave knocked over the ship's funnel, flooding the boiler room. One of the ship's inflatable life rafts, a carlyfloat, was then blown off the afterdeck, was carried up into the air and came crashing down on the quarterdeck. That sheared off the hatch to the steering compartment, which began to fill up with water. This knocked out the ship's automatic steering gear. When one of his officers, Lieutenant Moore, went on deck to try to force the cover back on the hatch, another wave washed over him, slamming him into a store of depth charges and breaking his leg. To make matters even worse, the water leaking into the forward magazine was causing the ship to list ten to fifteen degrees. Piers called out all his crew members to begin bailing to keep the *Restigouche* from sinking. Finally, it seemed like they were gaining on the water.

When daylight came, the weather was "only awful," and the question for Debby Piers became, what now? The *Restigouche* hadn't linked up with the convoy, which was now heading west without an escort. Halifax for Christmas was out. Since there were no repair facilities in Iceland large enough to do what would need to be done to make the *Restigouche* shipshape again, Debby decided to alter course and head for Scotland's Clyde River.

As they limped up the Clyde and into dry dock at the Harland and Wolff shipyards on Christmas Day, 1941, Piers was surprised to hear cheers coming from the crews of the ships they passed. Then he realized that the battered *Restigouche*—her mast gone, her funnel destroyed—must look like she'd been in a sea battle rather than a storm. It felt that way to Piers too.

The only bright spot was the news they received when they docked: the Japanese had attacked Pearl Harbor, finally bringing the Americans into the war. Maybe the Yanks could change things.

IT WAS JUST GOSSIP and probably not even true, but it was good gossip nonetheless, and Marjory Whitelaw couldn't wait to share it with Barbara.

She'd heard it this afternoon during a holiday visit with Alex and Tina. Like many in her social circle, Tina was no fan of the Olands. Lieutenant Colonel Sidney Culverwell Oland, president of the S. Oland Sons & Co. brewery, was all right, Tina would say, but *his* father had been a bootlegger during Prohibition. And his wife, Guillermina Maria del Pilar Socorro Herlinda deBedia y Martel Oland—better known simply as Linda—who was the daughter of a Spanish colonel and had grown up in Cuba, was . . . well, she was a social climber who misused her position to puff up her own importance. Perhaps, Marjory sometimes thought but never said, Tina was just jealous.

The Olands owned one of the city's showiest homes, a gleaming white dolomite castle with its own tower and private family chapel. Sidney had named the four-storey, German-style castle, which was just down the street from Alex and Tina's railway-owned home on Young Avenue, "Lindola" in his wife's honour. The chapel had a name too: Santa Maria del Pilar.

Though few outside the select social circle known as the Halifax 400 had ever been inside Lindola—Tina was certainly not among those who'd had that privilege—rumour had it that the rooms were filled with ornate French provincial furniture and graceful Hepplewhite cabinets topped with Chinese vases and bowls, and that the walls were covered with sombre but valuable oil paintings, including at least one Rubens. The Olands, the gossips said, had no idea of the value of their collection or any appreciation of its artistic merit.

Since the war began, Sidney and Linda had done their patriotic bit by turning Lindola's walnut-panelled Tower Room into what one newspaper described as a "sort of club . . . [for] high-ranking officers of all three services . . . Here they could read, relax, have a drink and write letters." The emphasis, of course, was on "high-ranking."

The Olands' entertaining of the top brass formed the subject of the latest Oland story circulating in Tina's circle. It seems Linda Oland had telephoned naval headquarters to ask them to send over a few lonely servicemen to share Christmas dinner with her family. Unfortunately, the navy misunderstood the unspoken subtext of her request and, instead of officers, sent her three young ratings. At this point the stories Tina and her friends were telling diverged. Some said Mrs. Oland coldly banished them to the kitchen to eat with the maids, while others claimed she sent them back to their base unfed. There was disagreement too over the identity of the sailors in question. In one version, one of them was actually a member of the British royal family, but Mrs. Oland didn't recognize him. In another version, the one Marjory Whitelaw would choose to tell Barbara, the rating Mrs. Oland didn't recognize was in fact Michael Redgrave, the famous British stage and film actor.

Marjory didn't know which—if any—of the stories were true, just that they were worth retelling.

THE GOSSIP AMONG the wags in navy wardrooms that season centred on the brass's latest snub of Leonard Murray—who'd recently been appointed to head up Canadian naval operations in St. John's—and Murray's hasty, ill-considered response to it.

It certainly wasn't his first tiff with his bosses. A few months earlier Murray had written to Commodore H.E. Reid, Canada's

Vice Chief of Naval Staff, bitterly carping that his rival, George Jones, was being permitted to make appointments to ships under Murray's command. Reid replied that his letter seemed to be "about 90 per cent bleat." When Murray tried to take the sting out of Reid's criticism by suggesting "the Ottawa summer heat . . . appears to have got you down," Reid fired back that it wasn't Ottawa's heat that "made me sick. It was you!"

The tensions escalated on December 1 when Admiral Nelles elevated Jones to the rank of rear admiral. As in 1938, Nelles's plan was to do the same for Murray a day later. But, according to the gossip, Murray, who didn't know he too was about to be promoted, immediately fired off a message to Ottawa in which he took an oblique swipe at the Jones appointment. As ships at sea sometimes communicated with each other using biblical verses to confuse the enemy, Murray's message to Ottawa was similarly couched. The text came from Genesis 42:8: "Thus Joseph knew his brothers," it said simply, "but they did not know him."

Luckily for Murray, Nelles ignored the message and promoted him anyway.

"HAVE YOU HEARD what Lord Haw-Haw's been saying, Jannie dear?" her mother began tentatively.

Janet Piers had heard—over and over again all day, and now again tonight, this time from her own mother on the telephone from Halifax. So much for the official prohibition on listening to the Nazi propagandist's daily shortwave broadcasts.

After the wedding, Janet had decided she and her daughter would move out of her parents' Young Avenue house and spend the winter at the Piers family's cottage in Chester. Janet had hoped— but dared not expect—that Debby might be home so they could share their first Christmas together. Instead, Christmas had come and gone with no sign of the *Restigouche*, and no letter from Debby even hinting at where he was or when he'd be back.

Janet didn't believe Lord Haw-Haw's broadcast, not for a second.

He'd already claimed the same thing once before and had turned out to be completely wrong. Still, the phone calls were disconcerting. The gossip had spread like wildfire through the crew's wives and girlfriends, naturally enough, and they called the captain's wife to find out what she knew. "They were in a terrible state," Janet would remember. Was it true? they wanted to know. Had the Nazis really sunk the *Restigouche*? Janet did her best to reassure them. Remember the last time, she'd say. He was wrong then; he's wrong now.

But she couldn't be sure. That was the hell—the not knowing for certain. She had reassured the women who'd called, her mother too: everything is all right, otherwise we'd have heard. But now she was alone, and she couldn't help but worry.

IF NOTHING ELSE, the war had been a boon for what ailed Halifax's economy during the thirties, when six thousand locals had depended on government relief payments. Despite a dramatic increase in population—from 60,000 in 1939 to 100,000 by the end of 1941—officials could have shuttered the local unemployment office. In the first week of 1942 there would not be one new claim for unemployment insurance. On the contrary, many employers couldn't find enough qualified applicants to fill positions they had open. The Halifax Shipyards claimed it could use five times as many skilled workers as the 1,200 now working flat out in order to keep the yard from falling too far behind on repair work and new ship construction.

While the war generated more new jobs at better pay than Haligonians had ever known, it was a mixed blessing. The city still couldn't cope with all the newcomers. In April, the *Mail* published a photo showing servicemen sleeping on the floor of the local YMCA. DISGRACE TO CANADA harrumphed the headline, over a story that claimed overcrowding had forced "hundreds of men to walk the streets [or] resort to dives to escape the winter weather." By the time the Halifax Rentals Committee of the

Wartime Prices and Trade Board held its first meeting at the end of 1940, it was already facing a backlog of 140 complaints. The first to be heard was not untypical. In August 1939, just before the war began, the complainant had rented a one-room apartment for $21.70 a month. By June 1940, less than a year later, the rate had jumped nearly 30 percent, to $27.50. While government officials talked bravely of a crash construction program to build a thousand new houses in Halifax, the understandable truth was that housing was a low priority for a country in the throes of building a naval fleet almost from the keel up.

Civilian transportation was also overlooked. Of the city's 114 miles of streets, 51 miles were still unpaved. And there were no stoplights anywhere. Despite nearly tripling the number of tramcars to sixty, there were still not enough. For most people, private cars weren't an option.

To exacerbate the frustration, lineups for everything from necessities to necessary pleasures kept getting longer. The line outside Germaine Pelletier's brothel now began to form around noon. By late afternoon it would often stretch three city blocks south, as far as the Nova Scotian Hotel. Incredibly, whenever the police raided the establishment, they found no girls inside. That's because Pelletier had had false walls built into the structure; as soon as an informant tipped her off that the cops were about to raid, she would hustle the girls into the spaces between the walls.

The police had more luck clamping down on the illicit liquor sellers. In November the military police, in concert with the RCMP, began sending soldiers into local bootleg establishments to buy booze with marked money. They then arrested the operators and seized their booze.

Before this sting operation could have its desired result, however, military authorities were involved in inadvertently topping up the supply. While clearing the shoreline near the entrance to the harbour mouth, the navy attempted to float a rum-runner that had gone aground there years before. When they did, its previously undiscovered cargo—twenty-five kegs of rum—floated off into the harbour with it. Although the Mounties managed to corral some of the barrels, the rest soon found their way into the hands of bootleggers, just in time for the Christmas rush. There were rumours that the kegs, each of which held about thirty gallons, sold for $125 each on the black market.

It wasn't just booze that was in demand. The number of sailors and soldiers needing to be fed on a daily basis was staggering. In September, the North End Services Canteen moved out of its cramped quarters in a church hall into spacious new facilities on Barrington Street. The staff—eight women and more than a hundred volunteers, including Janet Piers—were now serving 30,000 meals a month compared with the 10,000 they'd been able to dish up in the old location. But still the servicemen kept coming. And coming.

The number of different groups, organizations and even countries providing services had also increased dramatically. The Norwegians had their own hospital, which was treating up to a thousand sailors a month, their own church, and even a Norwegian Sailors' House, an inn with accommodation for fifty guests and a small restaurant. In July, ANZAC, the Australian and New Zealand Servicemen's Club, opened at the corner of Barrington and Buckingham streets. In September, Princess Juliana of Holland came to town to officiate at ceremonies marking the launch of her countrymen's Seamen's Residence on Dresden Row. The princess was just one of many prominent foreign visitors to Halifax in 1941. From the February visit of Norwegian Crown Prince Olav and Princess Margaret to the December inspection tour of Vice Admiral Emile Muselier of the Free French Navy, Haligonians had become almost blasé about dignitaries in their midst.

Even before Pearl Harbor, the American presence in Halifax had become increasingly significant. U.S. naval vessels had taken over the Royal Navy's responsibility as the primary escort for merchant convoys from North America to Iceland; the Royal Navy's warships were more desperately needed back home. Despite the dramatic growth of the Canadian navy since the beginning of the Battle of the Atlantic, neither Churchill nor Roosevelt seemed anxious to turn complete responsibility for the convoys over to Canada just yet. Instead, Canada's new assignment—under the overall command of the Americans—was to provide convoy escorts for the Newfoundland-to-Iceland leg of the North Atlantic passage.

To take command of the new Canadian naval force in Newfoundland, Percy Nelles had brought Leonard Murray back from England. What Murray couldn't know was that the seeds of his ultimate undoing were already firmly planted in the fertile soil of Halifax.

Leonard Murray: hero of the Battle of the Atlantic, scapegoat for the riots that followed. (Courtesy Maritime Command Museum)

H. B. Jefferson, Halifax's wartime press censor, was an acerbic observer and inveterate diarist. (Courtesy PANS)

Billy Mont would remember the war as "fun." (Collection of William Mont)

Janet and Debby Piers were married aboard the HMCS *Restigouche* in September 1941. (Collection of Debby and Janet Piers)

Debby Piers leads King George as he inspects his crew prior to the D-Day invasion. (Collection of Debby and Janet Piers)

Dorothy Hendsbee, a "dark-eyed, dimple-cheeked . . . comely maid," in her welder's gear. (Collection of Dorothy Chisholm)

Harold Bowman instructs the "Electric Five," including Dorothy (second from left) in the finer points of arc welding. (Collection of Dorothy Chisholm)

ODAFOUNTAIN STAFF 1944-45
Front Row from D...E... AMY ERNST, PRUNA CARLTON, EVE...

When a returning male veteran claimed her welding job, Dorothy (third from right) ended up working in a department store soda fountain. (Collection of Dorothy Chisholm)

Harold Masterman, one of the British "guest children," talks with an immigration official at Pier 21. (Collection of Harold Masterman)

Marjory Whitelaw came to Halifax hoping to find romance, and the chance to "dance until dawn" at regular dances like this one. (Bollinger Collection. Courtesy PANS)

During the war years, the Green Lantern, popularly known as the "green latrine," was one of the few Halifax restaurants worthy of the name. (Courtesy PANS)

In Halifax during the war, you lined up for everything from movies to brothels. (Bollinger Collection. Courtesy PANS)

CHAPTER 4

1942
– Wolf Packs, War Weariness and Petty Crime –

"Can you get the next plane to St. John's?" Janet could barely make out Debby's voice through the telephone's static, but she heard enough to know what he was asking. She'd been praying he would call soon.

Janet Piers had not seen her husband since their honeymoon eight months earlier. Because they knew their letters were read by the censors, they tended to edit themselves in their correspondence. The result, too often, was an antiseptic listing of Anne's accomplishments, Janet's social engagements, Debby's days at sea. That might explain why, when Debby left last summer for his new posting in Newfoundland as the Escort Group Commander, Fourth Canadian Escort Group, they'd agreed that if he ended up in a port long enough for her to fly over and spend a little time with him, he would call. He didn't explain this over the phone— nor did she expect him to—but the *Restigouche* was in St. John's for a routine refit.

She made arrangements to leave Anne with her parents and then took advantage of their friendship with Angus L. Macdonald, the federal cabinet minister in charge of the navy, to get a seat on a plane leaving later that day for Moncton and then St. John's.

She and Debby spent a glorious week together in the Hotel Newfoundland. But, as quickly as it had begun, it was over. Boarding the plane for the return trip, Janet wondered how long it would be before she saw her husband again.

THE LETTER WAS BRIEF and to the point. "In view of the strong opposition from Fort Massey United Church," A.S. Mahon, Chief Commissioner of the Nova Scotia Liquor Commission, wrote to Janet "Dolly" McEuen on January 19, 1942, "your club licence will not be renewed for 1942."

It wasn't the first time the Ajax Club's future had been threatened. When the Royal Navy withdrew from Halifax in October 1941, the club had closed for two months. McEuen and Admiral Bonham-Carter had had an understanding by which he assigned three of his men—a chief petty officer and two leading seamen—to work full-time at the club as a contribution in kind to McEuen for making the facilities available to RN ratings. After the Royal Navy left, McEuen tried to strike a similar deal with the Royal Canadian Navy, but negotiations stalled over who would control the club. Commodore George Jones, himself a Haligonian with close connections to the city's business and political establishment, was concerned about how locals might react to associating the navy too closely with the club. Assigning naval personnel to work at the club, he noted in a report to his bosses in Ottawa, "lays the naval service open to the criticism that Canadians are being recruited for service in a wet canteen. This may appear trivial," he added, "but this reaction is prevalent among a portion of the community." When he demanded that the Navy League be put in overall charge of the facility, McEuen, who was just as headstrong as Jones and determined to run her own show, refused and closed down the club instead. Eventually, the Chief of Defence Staff, Admiral Nelles, had to step in and sort things out. He overruled Jones and approved a proposal that not only assigned Canadian sailors to staff the club full-time but also left Dolly in complete charge. Needless to say, that decision, together with the sense that Dolly had used her personal friendship with Nelles as a bargaining chip to get her way, did not endear her to Jones.

McEuen offered to buy the Odell house and property, which she had been leasing from the estate, and donate it to the navy "in grateful recognition of the services rendered by our navies in this war." There were two conditions attached to her offer: "that the property continue . . . as a club for the pleasure and benefit of ratings of His Majesties' Navies [and] that the name of this club continue to be the Ajax Club." Angus L. Macdonald, the minister for naval services, wrote back his "sincere appreciation . . . I am pleased to be able to inform you that this . . . gift is accepted upon the terms set out in your letter of Nov. 30."

To seal the deal, McEuen replied on December 20, enclosing two cheques for $4,000 each to cover the first half of the $16,000 total purchase price for the estate, and promised to send the rest at the beginning of January. Then, just two days before Christmas, she received a curious telegram from the defence department's Assistant Judge Advocate General:

CHEQUES RECEIVED BY MINISTER STOP
SHOULD YOU NOT TAKE PRECAUTIONS TO
CHECK WITH PROVINCIAL AUTHORITIES
MATTER OF RENEWAL OF LICENSE STOP
WHILE WAITING FURTHER WORD FROM YOU
CHEQUES NOT BEING PRESENTED.

This was the first McEuen had heard that renewing the club's licence to sell beer would be anything but a formality.

It wasn't that Dolly didn't realize there were plenty of people in Halifax—an unlikely mix of temperance groups, church leaders, bootleggers and prostitutes—who wanted the Ajax Club closed. One night a group of club patrons had had to escort Dolly home after neighbourhood bootleggers, upset that the Ajax was taking business they considered rightfully theirs, threatened her with physical harm. Local ladies of the night, dressed in their trademark white leather boots, were none too pleased with her either. They'd been delighted when the club first opened; some had even set up shop in the park across from the club and advertised their wares as the throngs of potential customers passed. But then some of them got bolder, climbing over the low wall that surrounded the property and wandering into the back garden, where they could make their solicitations more directly. McEuen countered with a barbed wire fence.

As it turned out, the prostitutes and bootleggers were easy foes compared with the Reverend Gerald Rogers, his church elders and, perhaps most dangerous of all, the wife of Premier MacMillan, who was also the head of Fort Massey's women's group. Mrs. MacMillan had been walking through the church one afternoon when a sailor, who'd been sleeping in one of the pews after a few too many drinks, woke up and, seeing a woman walking by, gave her a wolf whistle. Mrs. MacMillan was not amused. She assumed he'd got drunk across the street at the Ajax. This might explain why Premier MacMillan himself was less than sympathetic a few weeks later, when McEuen appealed to him to overturn the liquor commission's decision. The Ajax Club, he informed her curtly, would *never* get a beer licence.

That night, McEuen climbed atop the club's bar to announce to her unhappy customers that "we are unable to serve you beer. But," she added, "I now as a citizen intend to take up the cudgels on your behalf. All I ask of you is to continue your good behaviour so that I may be free to fight for you."

Dolly attended one meeting with church elders, representatives of the navy and liquor commission officials to seek a compromise, but no one, least of all Dolly, seemed in a compromising mood. Who among the church elders, Dolly demanded to know, was responsible for undermining the Ajax Club? A few weeks after that meeting the liquor commission wrote her to confirm its earlier decision:

"The continuance of the Ajax Club permit has been further considered and it has been decided that it will not be renewed for your present location."

The battle soon became public, when Fort Massey's elders issued a statement blaming the Ajax Club for a number of incidents in which drunken sailors had threatened church members, used unseemly language and otherwise disturbed the parishioners. Granting the club a new licence, the church elders argued, "might constitute a menace to the life and work of any church in the province."

The next day Dolly fired back with a statement of her own, castigating the church leaders for trying to blame the club for wartime social ills, noting that she had twice invited Reverend Rogers to visit the Ajax Club to "discuss social problems of interest to both of us," but that the clergyman had turned her down flat, arguing that he would "not cross the threshold as a Christian gentleman." Instead, McEuen said, he and other church leaders preferred to ignore the realities around them. "Let them indicate how many bootleggers' establishments and brothels are in the vicinity of the church."

The verbal battle was quickly joined by thirty-six thousand naval personnel, who signed a petition supporting the club. Hundreds wrote letters to the editor—and not just in Halifax. "Why have we no licence?" Dolly McEuen asked at one public meeting. "The question is being asked all over Canada." And it was.

The novelist and Halifax native Hugh MacLennan, who was now based in Montreal, wrote in one letter to the editor: "To alienate service men from the citizens they protect is the most serious breach of national discipline possible today . . . Let the majority in Halifax do their duty, for nobody else can do it for them." The Montreal *Gazette* weighed in with an editorial, criticizing Halifax as "one of those places, now luckily reduced in number, where people drink wet and vote dry . . . In peacetime, Haligonians might argue that the matter was strictly their own business. [But] war has

made Halifax a major Canadian centre . . . Halifax should, therefore, heed the views of other Canadians, few of whom share the
Haligonian attitude toward liquid refreshment."

If the *Gazette*'s views appeared to reflect the national mood,
opinion in Halifax was more sharply divided. "Judging solely by
the letters," one correspondent wrote to the *Star*, "it is clear that
the present case is one where the great majority of opinion is
against the club, and the spokesmen for it are made up entirely of
its members and their personal friends who, for personal aggran-
dizement or other reasons, wish to force their own interest down
the throat of the community."

In fact, opinion was anything but unanimous even within the
congregation at Fort Massey. Ironically, some prominent members
of Fort Massey had been among the key volunteers at the Ajax
Club. Though not a member of the Fort Massey Church himself,
prominent Halifax lawyer Harry MacKeen became so upset with
the church's campaign against the Ajax Club that he forbade his
teenaged daughter Judy, who often went to services at the church
with a girlfriend, from attending again. And he made his younger
son David quit the Boy Scout troop he was in, simply because it
met at Fort Massey.

None of this changed the outcome, which had seemed almost
preordained after the Premier dismissed McEuen's plea for assistance in early February. In March, Ottawa announced plans to
build its own club for naval ratings at the Wanderers Amateur
Athletic Club field near Citadel Hill. It would include separate
wet and dry canteen facilities. On March 21, the Department of
War Services froze the Ajax Club's assets. Two weeks later it
revoked its charter under the War Charities Act because of "the
changing circumstances."

Though the navy tried to convince McEuen to follow through
on her offer to turn over the Odell estate, she was so resentful at
Ottawa's handling of the whole affair that she announced on May 1
she had sold the club and property, including furnishings, to the

Royal Norwegian Government for use as a hostel. However, she had no plans to disappear. She immediately announced she was setting up a new committee, the Ajax Hospitality Fund, to arrange for visiting sailors to spend time *outside the city*, mostly in private homes.

The Ajax Club was dead, but it would not be forgotten. That Haligonians had conspired to close down the one establishment that seemed to have as its main purpose the comfort and convenience of ordinary sailors became one more resentment that would fester through the rest of the war years.

"HAROLD'S ON YOUR TEAM."

"No he's not. He's on your team."

As soon as it got cold enough, usually after the first big storm of the winter, the older boys would carve a makeshift rink out of the snow covering the frozen Northwest Arm. Then, every day for as long as the temperature stayed below freezing, the neighbourhood boys would hurry down to the Arm with their skates and sticks as soon as school let out. Two of the older boys would name themselves captains of their respective teams and choose who would be on whose side.

"You take Harold, he's your friend."

"No he's not. He's yours. You take him."

Harold Masterman understood why he was always the last one picked for ice hockey. It wasn't just that he was the youngest kid in the group; he could barely stand up on his skates. The team that got him usually positioned him in front of his own net so he wouldn't get in their way and, with luck, might happen to block one or two of the other team's shots.

When he did stop the puck, Harold imagined he was Turk Broda, the goaltender for the Toronto Maple Leafs. Mr. O'Byrne, who was originally from Toronto, was a Maple Leafs fan. So, of course, was Harold. On Saturday nights when the Leafs were playing, Mr. O'Byrne would let him stay up and listen to the first period of the game on the big table radio in the den. Harold liked to listen to the play-by-play announcer, Foster Hewitt, who would get so excited when the Leafs scored. So would Mr. O'Byrne. He'd clinch his hands together anxiously if the team was losing, but he'd jump out of his seat and clap when they scored.

There had been plenty to clap about this season. Finally, said Mr. O'Byrne. The Leafs hadn't won the Stanley Cup since 1932, even though they'd been in the finals on six different occasions. This year had looked to be more of the same. They'd fallen behind three games to none to the hated Red Wings from Detroit, and were behind 2–0 in the fourth and possibly deciding game when the Blue and White began their comeback. They won that game 4–3 in Detroit, and then the next game in Toronto and the next back in Detroit. Turk Broda had a shutout that night to even up the series. No one had ever come back from being down three games to none and won the Cup. In the seventh and deciding game, the Leafs were trailing 1–0 going into the third period, but then Sweeney Schriner scored on the power play, and a few minutes later Pete Langelle put the puck in the net too. The Leafs had won the Cup with the greatest comeback in NHL history.

The adults might argue over whether you could even count it as a victory, considering that so many of the league's best players were serving overseas, but that didn't bother Harold. He wore the Maple Leafs sweater Mr. O'Byrne had bought for him, and now waited patiently for someone to pick him.

"Oh, OK, we'll take Harold—but we get first puck."

JEFFERSON PUT HIS NIGHT GLASSES up to his eyes and looked again at the scene unfolding in the harbour before him. It was such an eerie coincidence, he thought to himself. Twenty-five years ago, when he was a young reporter, he'd covered the official inquiry into the causes of the Halifax Explosion. For some reason the authors of the report had decided to take a Pollyannaish view of the infamous disaster. As bad as it was, they noted, it could have been much worse. If, for example, instead of coming together in the harbour's

Narrows, the *Imo* and *Mont Blanc* had collided, say, near the ferry slip downtown, the whole city would have been levelled.

Jefferson thought of that line as he watched the burning hulk of the British steamship *Trongate* drift helplessly in mid-harbour, half a mile from the ferry slip at King's Wharf. Like the *Mont Blanc*, it was a munitions ship, and its holds were filled with 30 cases of filled shells, 10,474 cases of shelled cartridges, 3,506 boxes of S.A. ("small arms") ammunitions and 1,981 drums of toluene, an organic compound used in the synthesis of TNT. It was also on fire. Broad sheets of flame shot up from its superstructure, just behind the funnel. One spark, one smouldering ash falling into the wrong hold, and downtown Halifax would be flattened.

Jefferson—more oblivious than ignorant of the danger to himself—had been following the unfolding drama from his office window for more than five hours. Just before 10 p.m. he'd heard a loud voice near King's Wharf yelling "Fire! Fire!" followed by the sound of the international fire alarm from the steam whistle of a nearby vessel. Luckily, the babble of harbour whistles and sirens was now so common and continuous—a backdrop to everyday life in the city—that few seemed to notice this sound or, if they did, to understand its import. So no one panicked. Or perhaps Haligonians were simply suffering from sensory overload: what was one more threat among so many?

Jefferson looked at his watch. It was nearly 3 a.m. It seemed like forever now but it had only been yesterday morning when the harbour patrol gate boats reported that a German U-boat might have slipped through the submarine net at the entrance to the harbour. At the time, more than two hundred ocean-going vessels filled the docks, the Basin and all available harbour anchorages. Just before the submarine alarm, the United States cruiser *Philadelphia* and nine destroyers had sailed into the harbour, shepherding four more large, overcrowded American army transports, which had had to wait at anchor in midstream because there was no space for them at the docks. As they waited, a flotilla of corvettes, minesweepers and harbour patrol boats darted this way and that, searching for signs of a submarine. Thankfully, the gate boats were wrong this time; no enemy sub had breached the harbour security.

But no one had to look very far to see what damage the U-boats could do. On the shores of McNab's Island, near the harbour mouth, sat the still-smoking hull of the Turkish tanker *Kars*, which had been torpedoed not long ago beyond the submarine net but within sight of the Citadel. Forty-six of its forty-seven crewmen burned to death. At Mars Rock, a submerged outcropping just a mile from the mouth of Halifax harbour, the remains of the Spanish tanker *Nueva Andalucia*'s cargo of aviation fuel also continued to burn fitfully, occasionally sending up bursts of flaming gas that lit up the countryside for miles around. Gasoline was now in such short supply that some local entrepreneurs had ventured out to the vessel in small skiffs to try to salvage its cargo to sell on the black market. Two had been burned so badly in a minor explosion, they were still in hospital.

That was nothing, Jefferson realized, compared with what would happen if the *Trongate* went up tonight.

As soon as the *Trongate* flashed the shocking signal from her Aldis lamp—"Require immediate assistance. Fire below decks. I have TNT aboard"—the blacked-out harbour came alive with flashes of light as wireless operators on other vessels began sending out their urgent dots and dashes, and port officials desperately tried to figure out what to do.

At first there had been no sign of the fire. Through his night glasses Jefferson could see the *Rouille*, a fire boat, and the *W.J. Hanrahan*, a tug with firefighting equipment—the two brightly lit vessels looked like floating Christmas trees, Jefferson thought—take up positions alongside the *Trongate* and begin pouring streams of water into the ship. Even with his glasses Jefferson couldn't see any flames, just thin clouds of smoke rising from inside the hull.

Just before midnight the *Trongate* had flashed another, even more ominous message: "Fire out of control. Sending crew ashore."

The crew were well known ashore, but not well loved. The *Trongate* was a hard-luck vessel. It had been stuck in port for nearly five months dealing with one problem or another—she'd most recently been at the South Terminal for repairs—and "her people," Jefferson would note later in his journal, "had gained the reputation of being the toughest, 'fightingest' crew that ever entered Halifax Harbour. A typical sample is one of her men who, in being ejected from a seamen's hostel, had bitten a policeman's finger, causing blood poisoning. Then he had gone to a local dance and got into a fight in which he had both jaws broken. He was taken to hospital and patched up, and the next night was back at the dance hall ready to fight his opponent of the previous evening—broken jaws and all."

Just before the *Trongate* announced that its crew was giving up trying to control the fire, the newspapers finally got wind of the affair from city firemen and began calling Jefferson to find out what was going on. The answer: plenty.

Jefferson had just picked up a signal from the dockyard: "Have decided to scuttle. Explosives party on way from dockyard. *Chedabucto* will stand by to sink by gunfire if necessary." The *Trongate*'s captain, perhaps mindful of the reaction of his ship's owners, immediately came ashore to plead with authorities to beach the ship rather than scuttle it, so it could be salvaged at minimal cost. At 2:45 the *Chedabucto*, normally a minesweeper, used its PA system to order the fire boats to "chop your lines and go." As the little vessels cast off and pulled away, Jefferson watched the *Chedabucto* train its searchlight along the *Trongate*'s waterline. Suddenly there was "a vivid flash of white fire from the minesweeper's four-inch gun, followed in two or three seconds by a hollow 'Boom!'"

It was dangerous, risky. Each shot had to penetrate the hull exactly along the waterline. If it landed too high, no water would enter the hole to begin filling the ship; if the shell hit the water instead of the vessel, it would likely ricochet and endanger other ships or even buildings on shore. Although the *Chedabucto* was using practice shells—standard four-inch shells filled with sand instead of live ammunition—there was no question that a solid shot to the wrong location could detonate the whole cargo, creating a larger and more catastrophic blast than the Halifax Explosion of 1917. But, as Jefferson noted in his journal, "this had to be chanced as the lesser of two evils."

The shelling also increased the potential for panic ashore. Authorities had already handed telephone operators a statement to read to frightened callers. "A burning ship is being sunk by gunfire and there is no danger," it declared optimistically.

"The scene at this time was extremely spectacular," Jefferson would later write. "The bright searchlight, the dim shapes of the surrounding ships, the flashing of the signal lamps, the movements of a myriad tugs and harbour craft, the booming of the four-inch gun, the leaping flames, the repeated explosions and flights of rockets and burning material from the *Trongate* presented what corvette men on leave said was a rather close replica of a night engagement at sea.

"Every few seconds, red and gold signal rockets, which seemed to form part of the cargo, roared aloft singly and in groups; while at this stage of the fire an incessant rattling like the crackling of firecrackers told of the explosion of thousands of rounds of small arms ammunition.

"Throughout all this hubbub, the crews of the adjacent American and Allied warships and transports showed no signs of panic or alarm, and not even the nearest of these vessels lifted anchor and tried to move to safer anchorage.

"The civil population also showed no signs of panic, although it is reported that a few nervous people living on or near Water Street did lock up homes and go to Citadel Hill to await the outcome. In one office close to the ship, night workers sat calmly down to tea and cakes while the fire and shooting were at their liveliest.

"Calmest of the lot," Jefferson added, "were the merchant seamen, just in from the North Atlantic blitz, whose hostel near the waterfront could hardly escape obliteration in event of such a blast. It happened that an airplane passed overhead just as the *Chedabucto* fired her first shot. These hearty Mariners listened a minute to make sure it was not a bomb, then turned over and went to sleep, entirely indifferent to danger from shells."

For forty-five more minutes the *Chedabucto* patiently fired shell after shell—twenty-five rounds in all—into the hull of the *Trongate*, which gradually settled lower and lower into the water. Finally, at 3:25 a.m., "she turned slightly on her side and disappeared, her high funnel being the last to vanish."

ARNOLD EDGAR'S PLEA was heartfelt. The petty officer from Fort William, Ontario, was appearing before Magistrate R.J. Flinn on a charge of assaulting Halifax Police Constable R. Watts. Edgar wasn't disputing the allegation, but he did think the sentence—a month's imprisonment in Rockhead, the city lock-up—was excessive. Besides, he told the judge in what turned into a five-minute speech, there were extenuating circumstances.

"Here we are," he began, "far from home and among strangers. I left my job to go in the navy at twenty-five dollars a month. We come in from a long cruise and we have nowhere to go for entertainment and relaxation and a glass of beer. So we are forced to buy liquor from the government stores, and to drink it we have to go to cheap restaurants. There we meet the wrong kinds of people, and sometimes we get into trouble. We used to have a good place to go, a place where we could meet and talk and have our beer in pleasant surroundings. That was the Ajax Club. But now we find that our government has closed it up. So what are we to do?"

Judge Flinn, the stipendiary magistrate for the City of Halifax, listened quietly, and when Edgar was finished, he reduced his sentence of a month in jail to a twenty-dollar fine.

THE LETTER FROM HIS UNCLE arrived unexpectedly in early May. Eric Dennis hadn't even been aware that Uncle William knew about his many abortive attempts to sign up for military service. But he clearly did. As William Dennis explained in his letter, he had been diagnosed with a heart condition that prevented him from serving in the Great War. Like Eric, he had been disappointed when he was turned down, but he'd eventually accepted he had an equally important role to play at home, by publishing a newspaper to drum up support among Nova Scotians for the campaign to defeat the Hun. "[I] held the view in the last war and it hasn't changed in this war that our newspapers are playing a most vital role in the United Nations efforts," he wrote to his nephew. "I would naturally think if you are not accepted for overseas service or a vital fighting position on the home front that every moment of your thought and effort should be devoted to the important work you are now engaged in."

In truth, Eric had finally given up dreaming that he could somehow slip in under the radar of the military doctors. Besides, he was married now, and his earlier romantic notions of glorious heroism or equally glorious death now seemed mindlessly naive and self-indulgent.

There were compensations, of course, for being among the dwindling number of journalists in the newsroom of the province's biggest and most powerful newspaper. His pay kept increasing, in part to compensate for the extra work he'd been forced to take on because so many of his colleagues had left to join the services. That meant he and Maxine, who was now pregnant, could afford to move into a converted attic in a bungalow in the city's west end. Unlike their single room with no cooking privileges, this apartment boasted two rooms and its own kitchen. As soon as Eric heard it was available, he literally ran a mile from the newspaper office to stand in line for the chance to see it. Though he was, the landlord told him, the one hundredth person to want to rent the place, Eric somehow managed to talk him into renting it to him. Halifax was probably one of the few places in the country where *not* being a man in uniform offered a social—and sometimes economic—advantage. Being a newspaperman probably hadn't hurt either. It gave him, he had come to understand, a certain cachet with a lot of people.

Thanks to his job, his circle of friends and contacts just kept growing. For example, he'd become friends with the captain of a British navy rescue ship, who would tip him off whenever his vessel brought in survivors from a convoy attack. In return, Dennis would occasionally take the man out for dinner at the Nova Scotian Hotel and then find a lady friend for him. Dennis knew all kinds of ladies in Halifax—another benefit of the reporting trade.

He also had what he called "friendlies" in the upper echelons of the local police forces. The Halifax police department's chief of detectives would phone him with tips and occasionally let him trail along on one of his investigations. Once, he'd been present when the police arrested a prisoner of war who'd escaped while being transferred to a train that was to transport him to an Ontario POW camp. That had been a big scoop. Not that he could always publish the information he got this way. Sometimes the navy would object; at other times, Jefferson himself. And sometimes Dennis knew better than even to ask permission to publish.

One of Dennis's other good contacts was the city's mayor, William Donovan, who'd recently approached him to enlist the newspaper's backing in rallying community support for HMCS *Halifax*. The navy's new corvettes had been named after Canadian cities, towns, rivers, bays and other geographic locations, and many communities had "adopted" their namesake vessel. People in the community might get together and raise money to buy the men a radio, or church groups would knit them socks or caps. In some places, Donovan told Eric, people had even taken to knitting specially designed "mittens" the men could use to keep their privates warm. "And the sailors accepted them gratefully," he added. "It can be damn cold all over out there in the middle of winter when your ship is coated in ice." Though he knew he wouldn't be able to mention such things in the paper, Dennis was more than happy to write a story encouraging the readers of the *Herald* and *Mail* to do their patriotic part for the crew of the city's own naval vessel. It seemed the least he could do for those who were overseas.

BERT BATSON PUT HIS CIGAR back between his teeth and picked up the small piece of sheet metal flashing, turning it over in his hand thoughtfully, as if admiring its heft. Batson knew better than to ask where it had come from, and Billy Mont certainly knew better than to volunteer that he'd ripped it off a chimney on the roof of a Water Street warehouse. Still, Billy was proud of himself. There were fewer and fewer roofs along the waterfront that he and his fellow scavengers hadn't already picked clean of lead, metal, brass, copper—anything, in fact, that junk dealers like Mr. Batson were prepared to exchange for cash.

Mr. Batson carefully placed the piece of flashing on his scale and added weights to the balance tray to determine just how much he would offer Billy for this treasure. Some of the other scavengers claimed Mr. Batson fiddled with his scales so he wouldn't have to pay full value for what they brought in. Billy watched carefully, but he'd never noticed anything suspicious. Some of the kids, of course, also claimed the other scrap metal dealers—Whitzman & Son and Leventhal's, both of which were further north, on Upper Water Street—cheated too. As for Billy, he simply patronized whichever shop happened to be nearest to his latest find. Today, that was Bert Batson's From a Needle to an Anchor Scrap Metals on Lower Water Street, next door to the Nova Scotia Light & Power generating station.

Billy had become an excellent scrounger. After school, on weekends, even on his way to and from his summer job chipping out boilers at the Shipyards, Billy kept watch for items of value. His grandfather had made a carrier for the bicycle he used to ride back and forth between Greenbank and the Shipyards, and Billy kept it full of all sorts of treasures. He collected everything from scrap metal to beer bottles. The latter were worth a penny apiece at the Provincial Bottle Exchange just down the street from Batson's.

Billy's backyard was, quite literally, the CN rail yard, his playground the maze of piers, warehouses and storage sheds that snaked north along the harbour's edge. He knew his turf and, like a good farmer, he understood how to turn a profit from it.

In the CN rail yards he staked out the refrigerator cars, climbing aboard when no one was looking and then rummaging in the ice packing for loose carrots, cabbages, lettuce, apples—anything he could sell door to door.

The Ocean Terminals offered an even richer cornucopia of foodstuffs for the taking. Billy knew that the refrigeration system in Pier 36 tended to break down a few times a week, so he would hang around waiting for it to happen, then join the stevedores helping themselves to the hams and meats. If he didn't take them, he would point out, they'd spoil. Pier 27, the next wharf north, boasted a heated shed often filled with ripening bananas. Billy would wander among the crates as if he were shopping in a store, gathering bunches to put in his bike cart. Even the pigeons that lived in the sheds were fair game; he would catch them and sell them to the Chinese restaurants downtown. General Seafoods, a fish processing plant located on the Ocean Terminals docks, offered the enterprising scavenger a variety of potentially lucrative treats from the sea. For starters there were big barrels of mackerel and herring left untended on the dock. Billy would fill up his bike carrier with them and then ride through south-end neighbourhoods selling them to housewives and their domestics for ten cents a dozen. Because the company pumped its fish waste—heads, tails and guts—directly from its processing line back into the harbour, other fish came to dine at the outfall. Billy was able to hook scores of fat fish there—halibut, haddock and cod. "You couldn't help but catch them," he would later recall, "and they were big, too. As big as Dido." Dido, a dwarf who also hung around the fish plant, was Billy's main competitor for fish.

If the fish at the outfall weren't biting, or if he was looking for a more entertaining catch, Billy would sometimes scoop up fish guts in a bag and head south a few blocks along the water's edge to the breakwater beside the Royal Nova Scotia Yacht Squadron. There, he'd dip the bag filled with bait into the water and use a scoop net to gather the lobsters attracted to it. Sometimes the old admirals from the yacht club would yell at him to go away, but more often than not they'd offer to buy his catch.

And there were still more ways to make money on the waterfront. Sometimes he'd hang around the docks when the troopships were loading. Bored soldiers would often entertain themselves by tossing coins into the harbour and watching the local boys dive for them. You had to be very fast to catch the coins before they sank.

His various enterprises earned him more than enough to treat himself well. Once a week he'd stop by the Riviera Restaurant on Spring Garden Road, spend seventy-five cents for a hot hamburger sandwich and a Coke, and have enough left over for the Saturday movie matinee—ten cents—at the Family Theatre on Barrington, which usually boasted a double bill of a mystery and a western along with a cartoon. If it had been a good week, he'd buy a five-cent chocolate bar to eat while he watched.

Much of his other entertainment was free. Sometimes he'd hang around outside the Woolworth's store on Barrington Street and listen to the blind man play his accordion. At nights he'd amuse himself by climbing to the top of the huge sand pile at Hubley's Sand & Gravel near the Ocean Terminals and watch young sailors and their girls having sex. "They went there because you could hear the cops coming when they climbed up to take a look around." The sand pile wasn't the only place where a curious thirteen-year-old boy could indulge his pubescent fantasies. There was a popular outdoor dance hall in Franklyn Park on the Northwest Arm where Billy and his friends would crawl in under the raised dance floor and look up the girls' skirts.

Perhaps it wasn't surprising, then, that the idea of going back to Tower Road School in a few weeks for grade six had less and less appeal. It wasn't that he was having any problems there; he'd been near the top of his class last year. But he didn't feel comfortable hanging out with the rich kids. When June Parker, a beautiful blonde girl from South Park Street, invited him to her birthday party, he didn't go. What would he have to say to her or any of them? He couldn't tell them about the stamp collection he'd fished out of the trash on Young Avenue. Besides, he'd rather fish—or scavenge—than play Red Line with a bunch of kids he was sure would look down their proper south-end noses at a boy from Greenbank.

Tonight's party—ostensibly to celebrate the return of Nova Scotia's "respectable communist" from a government internment camp, but really just an excuse for everyone in their circle to get together again—was taking place at Cai Sather's small apartment at the corner of Hollis and Morris streets.

Marjory Whitelaw first met Cai—and most of the dozen or so others at the party—through her roommate Barbara Eaton. They were part of an informal, eclectic group of left-leaning, mostly young people who liked to argue about issues like the inequities of modern capitalism and the relevance of Karl Marx to the modern world, but whose real ties to each other were more often of friendship—and occasionally romance. Barbara, the linchpin of the group, was among the most political of the lot, but also the most outgoing. Just about everyone attending tonight's party, including Marjory, could trace their connection with the others back to Barbara, the radical daughter of a Wolfville dentist.

Cai, for example, had first met Barbara while he was visiting the Norwegian shipping company offices where she worked. He'd been a shipboard biologist in the Norwegian whaling fleet when his vessel was among those diverted to Halifax after the Germans overran his homeland. These days Cai worked on the Halifax waterfront, chopping up fish at a local market.

Inviting Marjory and Barb to his party tonight was, in part, Cai's payback for their inviting him and his friend Olaf Bratteli, another Norwegian refugee, to a recent dinner party at their apartment. Bratteli, the president of the Norwegian Seamen's Association, was a legend among local Norwegian expatriates. When the Nazis' puppet government ordered the whaling fleet to make for German ports after Norway fell, Bratteli led a mutiny, locking his ship's pro-Nazi captain in a cupboard while he and the crew made for Halifax instead. Bratteli had his own connection to Barbara: he was in love with Marjorie Mitten, one of Barbara's friends from Acadia University.

Barbara and Marjory had had no ulterior motive for inviting the two handsome young Norwegians to dinner. Barbara already had a boyfriend, and Marjory was still pining for Thane, about whom there had been no news. The real point of the dinner party, Marjory would allow, was that she and Barbara wanted to prove "you could make a very good meal for four dollars a head." They did. They'd served a delicious roast pork with apples and potatoes, and homemade pie for dessert. There was also plenty of wine to wash it all down, which they'd cadged from friends who hadn't used up their ration cards. By the time the dinner was over, Cai was drunk and talking happily—and loudly—about his days at Oxford University, where he told them he'd had to explain to British acquaintances that he was "not Christian," by which he meant only that he wasn't conventional.

The telephone rang. It was Mrs. Gough, their landlady, who lived in the apartment next to them. "Get that Jew out of here," she hissed.

As liberal as Marjory and her friends imagined themselves to be, most still knew better than to flout convention too much by dating Jews. "Jews were untouchables as boyfriends," Marjory admits in retrospect, even though some of her best male friends—including Len Kitz and Simon Webber, two up-and-coming young lawyers—were Jewish. Marjory had met Kitz through his mother, Yetta, who ran the Allied Servicemen's Canteen where Marjory volunteered. If Gentiles weren't keen on their daughters dating Jews,

Marjory knew that Mrs. Kitz was equally unhappy at the idea that her son might end up with a shiksa. Whenever Len went out with a Gentile girl, "she always used to say to him, 'What's wrong with the Glube girl?'" Simon Webber did fall head over heels in love with a non-Jew at a dance at the Nova Scotian one Saturday night, Marjory recalls. "By Monday they were making plans to go to the dance at the Nova Scotian the next weekend. But by the next Saturday she had all sorts of excuses why she couldn't go out with him."

Though they weren't romantically interested in each other—convention or no convention—Marjory and Simon had become close friends. In fact, it was Simon who was using his legal and military contacts to help Marjory find out what had happened to Thane. She still hadn't had a reply to any of her letters, and had just about given up ever finding out his fate. But that didn't mean she was ready for a new romance.

There were only two people at the party tonight whom Marjory didn't already know, and one didn't interest her at all. That was Charlie Murray, the guest of honour. He'd only just returned to Halifax after two years in an internment camp in Petawawa, Ontario, to which the government had banished him as a threat to security. The Mounties had picked him up in Halifax on September 29, 1940, the day before his wife was due to deliver their child, and immediately shipped him off to Petawawa, where Ottawa was warehousing a motley crew of communists, fascists, Germans, Italians and others the government considered potential troublemakers.

Murray, the business agent for the Canadian Seamen's Union, was less of a danger to the country than he was to the unfettered powers of Nova Scotia's business elite and their friends in the provincial government. The youngest son of a revered Presbyterian minister, Murray, whose sister was a missionary in Korea, was a fisheries scientist when he became radicalized by the appalling conditions he discovered in Newfoundland fishing villages during the Depression. He signed on as director of organization for the Canadian

Seamen's Union, which was trying to organize east coast fishermen into a union. He also joined the Communist Party, becoming secretary of its Halifax branch as well as the man in charge of the Halifax news bureau for the *Clarion*, the party's national newspaper.

As the CSU attracted more and more grassroots support—fishermen in Lockeport, Nova Scotia, defied not only the fish companies but also the government and its armed police in the late 1930s during what became known as the Lockeport lockout—Murray's communist leanings began to appear more sinister. When it became clear that the government's willingness to call in the Mounties was not going to deter Murray from continuing his organizing efforts, the province's minister of labour, Leslie Currie, wrote to Murray directly: "I must tell you that my patience in this is exhausted. You will not be permitted any longer to disturb industrial relations in the province of Nova Scotia . . . You are a Communist and as such you deserve to be treated in the same manner as I would be treated if I endeavoured to carry on in Russia as you are doing in Nova Scotia."

It probably shouldn't have been surprising that the authorities would invoke Section 21 of the Defence of Canada regulations—which allowed the detention without trial of those the government believed posed a threat to the war effort—to round up communist union organizers like Murray. That their concern had more to do with the union leaders' organizing successes than with their Communist Party credentials became clearer when Ottawa kept many of them in detention even after the collapse of the German-Soviet non-aggression pact in mid-1941 transformed the communists from foes into friends.

His incarceration had made Murray even more of a celebrity among left-leaning Nova Scotians like Barbara Eaton and her friends. Though she didn't think of herself as a left-winger "by instinct," Marjory was among those who shared the belief that Murray had been badly treated, and she was happy he had finally been freed.

But did that mean, she asked herself, that she had to like him too? She'd only met him tonight, but she already knew they wouldn't get along. A slight, wiry man with rimless glasses and a high forehead who seemed perfectly cast in his role as the radical intellectual, Murray's confidence leaped over the border into arrogance. He was happy to tell Marjory why the CBC had made some decision on policy—something he couldn't possibly know, she was certain—with a brook-no-dissent cockiness that annoyed her. She moved on as soon as she could extricate herself from the conversation.

Jim Clarkson, the only other person she'd hadn't met before tonight, was another matter. He was a Cape Bretoner, a miner's son who'd graduated from Dalhousie University and now found himself at loose ends, trying to figure out what he should do next. He was hoping to get into the military, he told her. Wasn't everyone, she thought? In the meantime his sister Philamena had helped him land a good government job as the chief clerk in the Regional Oil Control Office of the Department of Munitions and Supply.

Marjory thought him shy, almost vulnerable. He seemed to have no confidence in himself, or perhaps that was just in contrast to Charlie Murray's smug self-satisfaction. Jim, she also couldn't help but notice, was handsome too. There was something melancholy about him, something romantic.

Could she be falling in love again?

MAGISTRATE R.J. FLINN had long since lost patience with—and belief in—the fervent pleadings of those like the sailor who'd appeared in his court last spring and talked his way out of jail time by blaming the closure of the Ajax Club for leading him astray. This morning Flinn looked down at the two sorry specimens before him in the courtroom. "This kind of thing must stop," he thundered.

"This kind of thing" was a wave of petty—and not so petty— crime. The *Mail* reported last week that theft charges in the city had increased 1,000 percent in the most recent quarter. The perpetrators had become so brazen, the paper claimed, that most of the thefts were happening in broad daylight. Police Chief Judson Conrod blamed the "foreign element," "children growing up on the streets" and what he called "beachcombers" who'd been attracted to the city by the magnet of its wartime prosperity. But he was also quick to point out that he didn't have the budget to hire the number of policemen needed to cope with the dramatic increase in the city's wartime population. Instead of 120 to 130 policemen, which would have represented a reasonable ratio of one officer for every thousand citizens, Conrod's entire force totalled 78 men and one woman, and many of them were new, inexperienced replacements for veteran officers who'd left for active service. Far from being able to police the streets effectively, Conrod was now reduced to responding to newspaper complaints about public safety by attacking the victims. "Women who walk across the dark Common at midnight," he told the reporter from the *Mail*, "are only inviting trouble."

For his part, Magistrate Flinn had seen too many merchant sailors, like the two before him today, accused of one crime or another. These men, merchant seamen from Southampton, England, had barely been in town a day before they were caught committing a break and enter. Flinn sentenced them to six months each in Rockhead prison. Perhaps, he suggested, that would send a message to those who would despoil his city.

IN THE SPRING of 1942, Halifax's Civilian Emergency Committee announced that it had divided the city into fourteen districts, each with its own platoon of volunteers commanded by an air-raid warden. In August the committee staged its first "imaginary attack" on Halifax, to teach more than two thousand volunteers how to deal with fire and gas attacks or find people trapped in fallen buildings.

Those weren't the only ominous signs that authorities believed the war could spread to North America, and specifically to Halifax, at any moment. Military personnel were now required to carry gas masks with them at all times. The Boy Scouts had set up a depot on a west-end street corner where they sold sand for five cents a bag as protection against incendiary devices. A 1942 public opinion poll showed that one in three Maritimers did not believe a German attack "unlikely."

And yet . . .

Perhaps it was war weariness, or the fatalism that came with being on the domestic front lines. Or perhaps it was as simple as the fact that, in the first three years of the war, no German plane had bombed Halifax and no Nazi destroyer had shelled its coast. Whatever the reason, much of the patriotic fervour and sense of obligation to the community that had been the hallmark of the war's early days had dissipated by 1942, replaced by a feeling, even among some prominent citizens, that it was now a matter of every-one for himself. On November 2, the *Mail* reported that William Shaw, the president of Shaw Steamship Co. Ltd., had become the first person convicted under the Prices and Trade regulations for hoarding excessive foodstuffs. Though Shaw, who lived in the city's affluent south end, claimed it was for personal use and represented amounts he would normally buy, the judge convicted him anyway.

That same night, Lieutenant Colonel Sidney Oland, the beer baron, was charged with violating blackout regulations. In an attempt to remind Haligonians of the importance of continuing to observe the nightly blackouts, the authorities had staged a mock air raid on the city. But as the airplanes flew overhead dropping their payload of leaflets, Haligonians—far from staying inside with their blinds drawn as they were supposed to—gathered on the sidewalks to watch the spectacle in an almost festive atmosphere.

Ironically, Sidney and Linda Oland were hosting a society din-ner party that night for British Admiral Stuart Bonham-Carter and his wife. Bonham-Carter, an affable, gregarious man, had managed to fit in very well during his brief tenure in Halifax. He'd become friends with a number of prominent locals, including Oland and James McGregor Stewart, the legendary head of the city's most prominent law firm. He and McGregor Stewart, Bonham-Carter told the other guests, had even made a friendly wager on when the first German submarine would appear off Halifax harbour. Bonham-Carter had already lost five pounds to the lawyer because none had shown up yet, and he faced the prospect of losing another five if one didn't appear soon. He couldn't understand why the German navy hadn't already made Halifax one of its primary targets. "Why, damnit," he declared, "Halifax is the most important port in the world today."

The war seemed so close, yet so far away.

FROM THE BRIDGE of the *Restigouche*, Debby Piers surveyed the carnage in the waters around him. There were frightened, frightful-looking men everywhere—burned, battered, battling to stay afloat, to stay alive. He could see men in lifeboats, huddled together against the winter chill, and men in the water, bobbing up and down in the swells in their life jackets or clinging numbly to pieces of what had not so long ago been the *Parthenon*, or the *Empire Sunrise*, or the *Empire Leopard*. So many ships gone, so many men in the water, yelling, screaming. *Help! Over here! Help!* Debby tried not to hear their voices, tried not to think about what he had no choice but to do. He reached for his loudspeaker.

The Lucky Who's luck had finally run out. For 35 months, then 36 months and 37 months, and finally for 38 glorious, heroic months—Piers had kept expanding his boast as one month spilled into the next—the *Restigouche* had lived up to the nickname the merchantmen had given it. The H00, as its call number designated it, hadn't lost a single ship among the hundreds it had escorted back and forth across the North Atlantic.

Hitler's initial hope of quickly bombing Britain into submission had long since evaporated. The war against Britain had become a war of attrition. Hitler's best hope now was to cut off its sea lifeline. So, in the fall of 1942, the Germans redoubled their efforts in the North Atlantic where they had belatedly recognized the Allies' Achilles heel: the Black Pit.

The Black Pit was a vast chunk of North Atlantic real estate that was beyond the protective cover of Canadian, British and Icelandic mid-range aircraft patrols. Despite the strategic importance of the convoys' cargoes, American and British authorities had decided not to use their long-range aircraft, which could have provided much-needed cover for the convoys in the Black Pit, in the Battle of the Atlantic. The Americans deployed theirs to the war in the Pacific while the British committed theirs to the bombing campaign against German cities. What that meant was that the unprotected convoys were easy pickings for submarines. Worse, the Germans—perhaps because they'd broken the Allies' encryption codes or perhaps because, more ominously, they had spies in place in Halifax—seemed to know when the convoys were coming.

In mid-October 1942, Dönitz, the German Admiral now in charge of the entire German navy, launched *Veilchen*—Group Violet—an operation that involved dispatching thirteen subs to positions inside the Pit. He stationed three others south of Newfoundland to pick up and shadow the next eastbound convoy.

That convoy happened to be SC107, a slow-moving forty-two-ship fleet sailing from Halifax to Liverpool. The Canadian Escort Group C4, headed by Lieutenant Commander Debby Piers, steamed out of St. John's shortly before noon on October 30 to meet up with the ships and take over escort duties. By that point the three German U-boats had already got a fix on the convoy's position. At first, Hudson bomber patrol planes from St. John's buzzed over the convoy, keeping the Germans at bay. By the next night, however, SC107 and its five-ship escort were on their own in the Pit—and at the mercy of what quickly became a swarm of enemy submarines. The wolf pack, which had managed stealthily to sneak in ahead of the convoy on both sides, suddenly swung into its path and launched its attack at two o'clock on the morning of November 2, 1942.

Piers's escorts were ill-equipped to stop them. Like most experienced Canadian naval officers, Debby had been complaining almost since the war began that British vessels were invariably better equipped than their Canadian counterparts. When it came to installing improved sub-detecting radar, or weapons for actually attacking the enemy, Canada's escorts seemed to lag about eighteen months behind the British navy.

It was no contest. For five days the German wolf pack attacked relentlessly, firing almost at will at the ships under Piers's protection. He did what he could. He would declare an Operation Raspberry, a signal to all the ships in the convoy to fire off snowflake flares to light up the night sky and, hopefully, catch a submarine on the surface, where the escorts could fire back at them. But the Germans evaded the flares. Piers also tried evasive manoeuvres, changing the convoy's course several times in quick succession to try to lose their pursuers. Instead, the thick fog confused many of the merchant captains, and the convoy itself became scattered and harder to protect.

One by one the U-boats would zero in on a merchant ship, sink it and move on to the next. One night the *Jeypore*, a British merchant ship, staggered among the convoy, a mass of flames. Another night the *Hobbema*, a munitions ship, blew up with such a powerful explosion that many sailors on other ships, including the *Restigouche*, were convinced their own vessel had been hit. As the explosion shook the fleet, the *Restigouche*'s record keeper wrote simply, "Ship hit," put down his pen and inflated his lifebelt.

At another point, Debby Piers had watched through his binoculars as the stern of one of the torpedoed vessels rose sixty degrees into the air and then eased almost gently into the ocean. He put down his glasses and turned to Reverend Waldo Smith, a navy chaplain from St. John's who'd come along on this trip to get a better understanding of what life on convoy duty was really like. "Say a prayer for them, Padre."

And now here he was staring into the roiling waters yet again at still more men from still more ships who would need all the prayers the padre could muster. Piers's own orders were clear: he was to press on, get whatever part of the convoy he could to its destination. He put the megaphone to his lips and spoke to those in the water. "Stay alive, fellows. The rescue boat will be by soon."

But Piers knew that the rescue boat, the SS *Stockport*, was already overfilled with more than 250 survivors from earlier sinkings. It was running dangerously short of food and water and would soon have to break off from the rest of the convoy and try to make it to port in Iceland. He knew some of those struggling in the water might be saved, but not all of them. The truth was, probably very few.

Shortly before noon on the fifth day, an RAF Liberator aircraft from Iceland finally reached the battered convoy. By then the Germans had sent fifteen ships, more than a third of the convoy, to the bottom.

CHAPTER 5

1943
– Murder Mystery –

N ext!" Dorothy Hendsbee shuffled forward a few more inches. How long had she been standing in this recruiting office line, anyway? Oh well, only two more ahead of her now. Soon it would be her turn. Soon . . . She felt a sudden clammy rush of panic. Would they be able to tell just by looking at her? What would happen if they caught her? Would they put her in jail? Oh God, whatever had made her think she could get away with this?

Desperation, that's what. If she thought about it for even a moment, she knew that would have to be her answer. She was desperate to find a job, desperate to make it on her own, desperate, most of all, not to have to go back to Half Island Cove.

Half Island Cove was an isolated fishing and farming community at the northeastern tip of Nova Scotia's eastern shore, roughly halfway along the fifty-mile stretch of coastal highway between the county seat of Guysborough and the fishing village of Canso. Half Island Cove was where Dorothy Hendsbee had come from most recently. She didn't consider it home, simply the place where her mother and stepfather happened to live. And that made going back even less appealing.

If you'd asked her where her real home was, Dorothy would have been hard pressed to answer. For the first ten of her sixteen years she'd been raised in North Ogden, about thirty miles inland from Half Island Cove. North Ogden, a still smaller community, was where her grandparents had had their farm. Esther and Thomas Cahill's three-hundred-acre mixed farming operation had provided a relatively comfortable life for them and their grand-daughter even in the worst years of the Depression.

When Dorothy conjured up memories of those days on the farm, she could still feel warm, enveloped, loved. When the other kids in school had laughed and taunted her—"Bas-tard! Bas-tard! Bas-tard!"—her grandmother provided comfort. "You do have a real father and mother, Dorothy," Gran'ma would say, sweeping her up in her arms. "We're your real father and mother."

Dorothy knew, even then, that that wasn't quite so. She knew her biological mother was Tom and Esther's daughter Lillian. But Lillian had left the farm—and gone out of Dorothy's life—shortly after giving birth to her. Eventually, she married a local ne'er-do-well named Roy Hendsbee, who didn't much like Dorothy. That was OK, because Dorothy didn't like Roy much either. Dorothy used to tell herself that her mother, who suffered from poor vision all her life, must have been practically blind when she picked *that* man for a husband. "My stepfather," she would later confide, cryptically and without elaborating, "was very, very mean." Roy and Lillian settled in Half Island Cove and eventually had a daughter of their own.

Until Dorothy was ten, her mother was little more than a casual, very occasional visitor in her life. But then, in the fall of 1936, her grandfather died suddenly and her grandmother became too ill to look after her any longer. So she was bundled off to Half Island Cove to live with her mother and stepfather, who didn't seem thrilled to have another mouth to feed. The family—mother, step-father, stepsister and Dorothy—subsisted on a five-dollar-a-month government relief cheque. Food, Dorothy would recall with delib-erate understatement, was "scanty."

Three years later, on September 10, 1939—the day Canada officially joined the war—her stepfather shipped twelve-year-old Dorothy off to live with her mother's half-brother, his wife and their two children, at Whitehead, an island five miles off the Atlantic coast, where her uncle had a job taking care of the lighthouse. No one asked Dorothy if she wanted to go, of course, just as, a year later, no one bothered to explain to her why her uncle decided to ship her back to Half Island Cove. The adults made the decisions; she just went where she was sent.

Having managed to complete grade eight by correspondence on the island, Dorothy was eager to return to what now seemed the bustling Half Island school—seventy-two kids, nine grades, one teacher, one room—to begin grade nine. But her family couldn't afford to buy the school books she needed, so she ended up doing grade eight all over again.

The best thing about school that year was Robert Cluney. He was a handsome young man, nearly three years older than Dorothy, who had also been raised by his grandmother. Though Dorothy thought of him as a platonic school pal—"I'd go with him to his grand-mother's house at lunch and she'd feed us cookies"—Robert clearly had more romantic visions. After he quit school and joined the army, he came home for a few days' leave before he shipped out. He asked Dorothy to go for a walk with him.

He was awkward, shy. "I have something for you," he told her, "something to remember me by."

It was a small gold, heart-shaped locket on a delicate chain, Dorothy's first-ever piece of jewellery. When she opened it up, there were spaces for two small photos. Robert promised to send her one of himself—he'd get his picture taken once he got over-seas—so she could put it together with her own in the locket. She said she would. He said he'd write her with an address as soon as he got to Europe. She said she'd write him back.

They never got the chance. Three weeks later she heard from a neighbour that Robert Cluney had been killed in action. He was the first person she knew who'd been killed in the war.

And now here she was, nearly three years later, standing in line at the Army Recruiting Office on Cogswell Street in Halifax, waiting to join up herself.

Just one person ahead of her now.

She'd read the ads in the newspaper. "Fifty-one jobs for you!" shouted the headline above a come-on for the Canadian Women's Army Corps. "It is your duty, girls . . . to take one of these essential jobs . . . so that men might fight Hitler." The problem was that Dorothy wasn't qualified to fill any of them. Worse, at sixteen, she was still two years too young to be signing up in the first place. Would they take one look at her and know the truth?

The larger truth—as Dorothy had already discovered during her first month in Halifax—was that she wasn't really qualified to do much of anything. She didn't have grade nine.

On November 13, 1940, her fourteenth birthday, she'd quit school for good. Her first job was as a live-in helper for a family of four in Boyleston, where she did the cooking and looked after the kids and the house for five dollars a month. Her most recent job was as a cookie packer in nearby Pictou. She'd fudged her unemployment record book to make it appear she was already sixteen, and got work on the conveyor belt at the Hamilton's Biscuit Factory. The work turned out to be mindlessly monotonous.

"Next!"

She was now first in line at the recruiting office. Dorothy wanted to turn and run, but her feet refused to move.

Three months ago, just before Christmas, she and six other women had been laid off. She'd had to go back to Half Island Cove to regroup, but she didn't want to stay there. That's when she decided to try Halifax. She'd never been to the province's capital city, but three unmarried cousins lived there. Lila, Viola and Kathleen Hendsbee used to come home to Half Island Cove every summer to visit their parents, and Dorothy would listen carefully to their descriptions of the city.

Armed only with those fuzzy images, a battered suitcase and a letter from her mother to her cousins, asking them to take Dorothy in while she established herself, Dorothy set off on the six-hour train trip to Halifax in early March 1943.

Halifax turned out to be exactly as she had envisioned it—teeming with people and uniforms and noise and busyness—but finding a job, even in the midst of a booming wartime economy, was far more difficult than she'd ever imagined. The problem was that as the war-goosed economy shifted into overdrive in the early forties, thousands of young people just like herself had abandoned their Depression-ravaged rural communities and streamed into cities like Halifax in search of a job and a future. There were jobs, but not for someone with outsized ambition and little experience or education. Dorothy was qualified to be a waitress or a maid, but those jobs didn't appeal to her. Working as a stenographer or as a sales clerk in a shop did, but they required skills she simply didn't have.

That was how she'd ended up at the army recruiting office this afternoon, through sheer desperation. The recruiting office was located at the corner of Cogswell and Gottingen streets, just down the block from her cousins' house. She'd passed it often during her daily walks around the city. Some days she'd head west along Cogswell, cross the dust bowl of the Halifax Commons and explore the leafy residential streets of the city's west end, off Quinpool Road. On other days she'd head east along Cogswell past the Army Provost barracks where her cousins' brother Floyd lived, and then, at the corner of Gottingen and Cogswell by the red brick recruiting office, choose her day's direction. She could walk north along Gottingen, admiring the fancy dresses she couldn't afford in shops like Kline's Ltd., "ladies' and men's ready-to-wear," or south along Brunswick to Buckingham and down to the Barrington Street business district. The purpose of these walks, of course, was not just for Dorothy to window shop at stores she couldn't afford to enter, but also to scope out job prospects. "It got to be very discouraging. When I passed the recruiting office this one day, I suddenly had this brainwave," she would recall. "I'd join up!"

It was now her turn.

The man behind the counter looked at her expectantly. She looked back at him for a moment, then quickly turned on her heel and walked away.

DEBBY PIERS HAD KNOWN, from that moment in early November when the first Allied aircraft from Iceland swooped low over the tattered remains of his decimated convoy and drove the German wolf pack away from its feeding frenzy, that there would be consequences for what had happened. Someone would have to pay for the loss of fifteen merchant ships and their vitally important cargos. And that someone, he knew instinctively, would be him.

"There went the ball game for D.W. Piers," he confided to colleagues as the *Restigouche* and what remained of Convoy SC107 finally limped into Liverpool harbour a few days later. Piers was immediately summoned to Derby House to account to the British Admiralty for himself and his convoy. He did try to explain. And there were plenty of sound explanations for the debacle, not the least of which was the Allies' failure to provide much-needed air cover through the Black Pit, or to provide additional escort vessels whose job would be not simply to protect the convoy but to hunt down and destroy German subs before they could attack. To complicate matters, Canada's navy, while it had grown dramatically from its standing start of just six old destroyers in 1939, was still woefully under-equipped for the job it was supposed to do. Piers and the other Canadian escort commanders could only envy their British counterparts their new and sophisticated gear for detecting submarines.

When British admiral Max Horton prepared his report on what had happened to Convoy SC107, he ignored most of those realities. Instead, he pointed out that 80 percent of convoy ship losses had occurred under Canadian command, and singled out Piers's youth and inexperience, as well as the lack of training of Canadian sailors, as the major contributing factors to the latest disaster. Although Piers's immediate superiors supported him—after reading the report, Canadian captain Roger Bidwell called it "ruddy nonsense" and even wrote Horton a note: "How about giving us a few decent destroyers, Maxie?"—the Canadian government accepted the essence of Horton's conclusions. In December 1942, British prime minister Winston Churchill cabled Canadian prime minister Mackenzie King to say, in effect, thanks for all your help, but how about letting us run the show from now on? Soon after, Angus L. Macdonald issued the orders transferring command of the main convoys back to the British navy. So now, in the spring of 1943, Piers himself was on his way back to Canada, this time as a passenger rather than the commander of a convoy. Officially, he was going back to Halifax to serve a stint as a training commander while Canada awaited delivery of his next command, HMCS *Algonquin*, a destroyer Canada was negotiating to obtain from the British and which was intended to operate under the command of the British home fleet at Scapa Flow. Unofficially, it was clear that Piers was being punished for what had happened with SC107.

Piers took advantage of his quiet time at sea to prepare a memo on the Canadian navy's conduct of the war. In it, he criticized headquarters' failings. Officers in the field, he complained, "had no idea who was running the navy in Ottawa." Anti-submarine warfare, which was the most important thing the navy did, "was number seven on the list of jobs to do in Ottawa."

When he reached Halifax, Piers shipped off his report to his superiors in Ottawa. Although it would be twenty years before he received any feedback about it, it became clear soon enough that someone in Ottawa was paying attention.

DOROTHY HENDSBEE LOOKED again at the words in the letter she clutched nervously in her hand. "In connection with your application for mechanical training for war industries," the mimeographed form letter began, "would you please report for an interview at—"

Someone had filled in the blank at the end of the sentence in ink: "7:30 p.m. o'clock on Tues. Apr. 6 at Geological Lab, N.S. Technical College."

Dorothy was in the right place, all right. But so too were about three dozen other women—all shapes and sizes of them. She found a seat at one of the schoolroom desks and looked around. Who were all these other women? Had they all answered the same small display ad on the back page of last Saturday's *Chronicle*?

WOMEN WANTED
TO LEARN ELECTRIC WELDING

Under the Dominion-Provincial War Emergency Training Program a limited number of Halifax women with suitable qualifications will be selected for training as electric welders. Applicants should not be under 20 years of age, weigh at least 130 pounds and have Grade IX education. Living allowances will be granted during the three months training period and employment will be arranged with local Shipyard upon the completion of the course. Write for application to the War Emergency Training Office, Nova Scotia Technical College, Halifax.

It was perhaps a measure of just how desperate Dorothy Hendsbee's job search had become since the day fear drove her out of the army recruiting office that she'd skipped like a flat rock on a smooth bay over the daunting reality that she didn't meet a single one of the ad's prerequisites. She was four years younger than the minimum age, she weighed—soaking wet with a full meal in her tummy—maybe 120 pounds and, of course, she was still a full year of study away from being able to claim a grade nine education.

She'd even had to borrow her cousins' dictionary to find out what a "welder" was. And afterwards, as she'd sat down that afternoon to write her letter of application—in her careful schoolgirl script with its fancy curls and swoops—she still wasn't exactly sure what she was applying for. All she knew for certain was that the ad promised not only training but also a living allowance while she trained. She could finally find a place of her own instead of mooching off her cousins. And the ad claimed there would be a real job for her at the conclusion of her training. That meant she wouldn't have to go to back to Half Island Cove. Ever.

Dorothy wasn't the only one who was desperate. The federal government had begun to apply itself to recruiting women workers only a few months before, long after the last of the million unemployed males left over from the Depression had been scooped up for war work of one sort or another. Ottawa was now projecting the country would need to employ close to a million and a half women—many in non-traditional jobs like welding—to sustain the national war effort. So there were now new rules: all women between twenty and twenty-four had to register for possible war duties. Women had become Canada's "most important available reserve of manpower," Prime Minister King declared, apparently without irony. This scheme to select and train five women in a crash course in welding was part of that new, desperate effort to keep the war machine functioning.

Electric welding? Whatever it was, Dorothy thought as she waited for her promised interview to begin, it was almost certain to be more interesting than the other positions she'd read about in the classifieds today: nurse, general maid, part-time maid . . . It also didn't appear to require the kind of credentials—"*Competent* stenographer," "*Experienced* operator for modern beauty parlour," "*Capable* girl for general office work, typing"—that were more difficult to fake.

Electric welding—how hard could it be?

"Ladies." A man had suddenly appeared at the front of the classroom. They were all going to take a test, he explained. So much for the interview Dorothy had been dreading. He handed each of them a blank sheet of paper and a pencil. They were to draw a series of straight lines—left to right, right to left, top to bottom, bottom to top—on the paper in front of them, he said. No rulers allowed. After that, they should sign their name, age, address and phone number, and hand in the paper. And then they could go. That was all there was to it.

Dorothy was now even more frightened than she had been at the idea of an interview. "He was talking about how important it was to have a steady hand and I never thought I could draw much of anything," she would say later.

She completed the test, handed it in and left. She wasn't hopeful. She might have to admit defeat and begin looking for a job as a maid. Or, worse, give up and go back to Half Island Cove.

"What do you mean he's ok?"

"He's alive is what I mean."

"And . . . ?"

"And that's all I know."

Marjory Whitelaw couldn't decide whether she was relieved or frustrated or angry. Thane Parker had survived the torpedoing of the *Lady Somers* two years before. He was alive. But where was he now? Had he been injured? Was he in a hospital somewhere? Could she go and see him? And if he had survived, why hadn't he written her? Or answered any of her letters?

Captain Joe Connolly couldn't—or wouldn't—answer any of her questions. He had already said far more than he was supposed to. Marjory, after all, wasn't a relative, so she wasn't entitled to information about military personnel, and Thane wasn't in the Canadian navy, so Captain Connolly had had no official reason to ask after him in the first place. But Connolly, who'd grown up on Young Avenue just a few houses from where Marjory had stayed with Alex and Tina, and who was friends with Marjory's friend Simon Webber, had agreed to make discreet inquiries.

So now she knew. But what did it mean? For Thane? For her? And perhaps most importantly, for her blossoming relationship with Jim Clarkson? She and Jim were now a couple. It had happened unexpectedly, almost by accident more than any design on her part.

After the night of the party at which she'd met him, Jim's weekend trips to Molly Hunt's father's tree farm had become fewer, though he couldn't seem to tell Molly their relationship was over.

Marjory would have preferred a more definitive declaration of love, but what she saw as Jim's shy ineptness was part of what charmed her. Jim was bright and smart and funny, but he lacked self-confidence. Nothing he did worked out. Take his military commission, for example. He'd got into the army, gone away for three months' training and then returned to Halifax with a bunch of his new army mates to await deployment. One by one, the army informed them that they'd been awarded army commissions. Everyone got their notice except Jim. It turned out to have been nothing more than a bureaucratic mix-up, but Jim considered it further evidence he was still the miner's son from Cape Breton, the first in his family to go to university, the poseur who didn't quite belong.

Alex and Tina certainly thought so. When Marjory introduced Jim to them, Tina made it clear she didn't consider Jim suitable. It was ironic really: Tina's father had spent time as a copper miner in Colorado. But that had been forgotten. I think you could do better, Tina said. Of course, she had also thought Thane too old.

Thane . . . Why hadn't he written?

LEONARD MURRAY OPENED the desk drawer, took out the official-looking notice of appointment, held it in his hands, admired the words one more time. And why not? As of April 1, 1943, he had become Rear Admiral Leonard Warren Murray, Commander in Chief, Northwest Atlantic. What that impressive-sounding title signified wasn't just that he was in charge of the Canadian naval forces in the Northwest Atlantic; he was in charge of *all* of them—Canadians, Brits, Yanks, every one of the Allied naval forces operating in the waters off Canada's east coast. He was the first—the only—Canadian military man ever to be placed in charge of an entire theatre of war. And he was damn proud of it.

Not that his success had come easily. Thanks to the Yanks he'd had to wait a full month longer than he should have to take command. But that seemed to be par for his career course these days. Ever since 1938 he'd had to fight for everything he got. In 1939, when Jones became the Vice Chief of Naval Staff, Murray had had to make do with a consolation prize as Director of Operations and Training. But Murray, as he always did, had made the best of it. As Ops Director he presented the navy's case for war funding to the cabinet finance committee. Defence Minister J.L. Ralston had been so impressed, he told Murray his group was the first "to justify everything you asked for—and the first . . . to have gone away with what they asked for." The job also brought him into close contact with British navy commanders, including Admiral Sir Dudley Pound, Britain's First Sea Lord. In 1919, Murray had served as a midshipman under then Captain Pound. He had been so impressed with Pound that he even imitated his peccadillo of using only green ink to write his official notes and memos. Twenty-two years later Admiral Pound personally urged Admiral Nelles to appoint Murray head of the new convoy operations headquarters in Newfoundland, because it "would give us great confidence" if he were in charge. Murray did such a good job in St. John's that he had been promoted again last year, this time to be the RCN's Commanding Officer, Atlantic Coast, in charge of all Canadian naval forces on the east coast.

From his new office in the naval dockyard Murray could see "the magnificent harbour, the warships tied up side by side, the merchantmen coming down from that inner sanctuary, Bedford Basin, warships pulling out to join them in convoy . . . ships under repair . . . sailors swarming about in their bell-bottom trousers . . ."

Halifax—and the city's naval establishment—had changed dramatically in the few short years Murray had been away. The total population had doubled to 120,000, of which fully 20,000 were sailors under Murray's direct command. That represented half the Canadian navy's total complement. Halifax was the navy's most important base: besides overseeing the convoys and coastal patrols, it had become the navy's "principal manning and supply depot, operational training centre and base for the working-up of new construction ships." Forty-seven Canadian and fourteen British warships were based here permanently, and they were responsible not only for protecting ships on the convoy routes between Nova Scotia and Newfoundland but also for providing escorts between Halifax and Boston or New York, which were now also threatened by German U-boats.

The problem was that there were far too many brass hats from too many countries trying to run all those convoy operations. The U.S. and Canada each had three naval bases along the northeastern seaboard, and each naturally wanted to put its own oar in the water when it came to operations. To make matters worse, there were two separate, independent operational air headquarters providing overhead security for the convoys. Convoy escorts at sea often got conflicting instructions from the Americans and the Canadians—and sometimes from the British as well. While Murray had sole charge of Canadian coastal convoys, he reported to American Vice Admiral Roland Brainard at Argentia, Newfoundland, if the convoys were heading east to the U.K.

In spite of the fallout from the *Restigouche* disaster, Murray's appointment as the Halifax-based officer in charge of all the Royal Canadian Navy's east coast operations was in fact part of a larger scheme by some senior Canadian officers to eventually make Canada the "responsible authority" for Allied operations in the Northwest Atlantic. During a two-week Atlantic Convoy Conference in Washington in March 1943, Canada made a successful pitch for operational control of all the waters north from New York and westward as far as the forty-seventh meridian. That meridian, east of the eastern tip of Newfoundland, was known as the CHOP, or Changeover Place, where the convoys swapped escorts. The total area under Canadian control would not be geographically large, but it was significant symbolically because it was the first area in which Canada would have command responsibilities that reflected the contribution it had long been making.

And who better to exercise that command than Murray, who was already based in Halifax, the heart of the convoy operations, and was well known and respected by his British and American peers?

The British Admiralty had dutifully signed off on the arrangement, but the Americans had seemed to be looking for ways to delay the handover. After the Washington conference, Admiral Ernest J. King, the American Chief of Naval Operations, proposed putting off the Canadian takeover for at least a month so his officers could be "reasonably confident that we shall have overcome the difficulties inherent in a somewhat abrupt transition and that the best available talent has been used to full advantage in the common cause." He had even suggested Murray might benefit from spending some time in Argentia, training as Vice Admiral Brainard's deputy, and that Brainard could then continue to act as his adviser for some unspecified time.

Murray had been livid. Convinced the Americans were playing for time so they could eventually "seize control again," he fired off a number of cables to Nelles in Ottawa, urging him to give the American offer the back of his hand. Admiral King, he had noted, "is very blunt in his statement that they do not think we are capable of handling the job, and it may be necessary to be blunt in return. It may be necessary to point out that 'the experienced services' of Admiral Brainard extend over about a year whilst the RCN has been concentrating on the escort of convoy, not unsuccessfully, for three-and-a-half years, and that the duties now carried out by Admiral Brainard were carried out by me until American control was established."

In the end, Nelles agreed to King's requested one-month delay to ease American concerns, but he declined—more decorously than Murray might have—King's offer to have Brainard act as Murray's mentor or adviser.

So, on April 30, 1943, Murray finally took charge. He was now the commander of eleven naval bases from Montreal to St. John's. He oversaw all the convoy escort services from Quebec to Newfoundland, including the Gulf Escort Force at Gaspé, the Halifax Force for Coastal Convoys, the Western Local Escort Force for ocean convoys between the North American east coast and St. John's, and the Mid-Ocean Escort Force from St. John's to Londonderry. He also supervised the operational side of the RCAF's east coast anti-submarine forces.

To get to all the bases under his command, Murray had his own amphibian airplane on permanent standby. The plane was one of the few perks of his new job. He and Jean would sometimes use it to slip away for a few quiet hours on a remote lake, where they could indulge their shared passion for trout and bass fishing. But these days, those opportunities were few.

His new job would not have been easy at the best of times, and these times were anything but that. Murray was taking command in the middle of the worst year of the Battle of the Atlantic. The German admiral Karl Dönitz, focusing all of Germany's sea strength on attacking the convoys, had sunk close to a thousand Allied ships during the fall and winter of 1942–43. Murray urged Ottawa and the other Allies to provide more ships, more trained senior officers and better air support to launch a counter-offensive against the subs, but so far to no avail.

Without such support, Murray realized, he was sending many of his own men, as well as thousands of merchant sailors who depended on them, to their doom. That's why he made it a point to attend, and speak at, every convoy briefing. After his officers had informed the masters and their chief engineers of their sailing orders, Murray would address them, quietly reassuring them that the navy was doing everything it could to make sure their journeys would be smooth and sub-free. But he knew—and he knew *they* knew—that fully one-quarter of them might not make it to the United Kingdom in their own vessels, and that half of that number might not make it all.

Obsessed with improving those daunting odds, Murray clocked countless hours inside his cavernous war room in a nondescript red brick building on Barrington Street, across Cornwallis Park from the Nova Scotian Hotel. Once the home of the Navy League, it had been converted to Murray's combined air-sea headquarters. Murray referred to it as "the holy of holies." A huge map of the North Atlantic dominated one wall. On it, sailors moved markers showing the positions of the convoys, the locations where intelligence had placed the German wolf packs, and the areas where air power had been deployed to keep the U-boats from the convoys.

Each morning at 10:30, Murray would meet with his operations staff in a small theatre off the main war room. After listening to their reports on what had happened during the previous twenty-four hours, getting a detailed briefing on anticipated weather for the next day's daylight hours, and hearing shorter reports on the disposition of forces, the state of ships in the fleets and so on, Murray would quietly, efficiently ask questions and then—just as straightforwardly—announce his decisions: which convoy should alter course to avoid straying too close to another convoy that was already under fire, which convoy should get priority for air coverage and which convoys, thanks to fog cover or the presence in the convoy of a mercantile aircraft carrier, could be left to their own devices.

It was never simple. Murray often had to try to link up, preferably in daylight hours, small, rump convoys sailing from Sydney or St. John's with the main body of a convoy already en route across the Atlantic, or deal with westbound ships that needed to split away from their convoy escorts to make for various east coast ports, from St. John's to Boston. And the German wolf packs weren't the only enemy. Even as Murray kept the convoys to the tightest possible schedule, he had to worry about the dangers of vicious storms, thick fog and drifting icebergs. "The situation," he lamented in a letter to a friend, "changed from hour to hour and each situation demanded individual treatment. Nothing could be left to routine."

Or to others. Murray kept a telephone by his bedside, and there would be hell to pay if he wasn't called in the event of an emergency. Though he rarely raised his voice, no one ever doubted who was in charge. Even when things went wrong, Murray would remain stoic. "Outwardly," recalls W.F. Ganong, the meteorologist responsible for delivering the daily weather reports, "he showed no emotion, but I am sure Admiral Murray felt those losses keenly."

Given the weight of all his various responsibilities related to the conduct of the Battle of the Atlantic, Murray had little time for—and less interest in—the deteriorating relationship between the navy and civilian authorities in Halifax. The situation was worsening by the week. While Ottawa had been busily throwing up prefabs to try to meet the city's housing shortage, those new homes were designated for civilian war workers, not for sailors or their families. Overcrowding had become so severe that Premier MacMillan had recently demanded publicly that Ottawa forbid the wives and families of those serving overseas from so much as setting foot inside Halifax. As if to underscore his concerns, the newspapers were now reporting water shortages too. The city's new mayor, Jack Lloyd, was organizing a civic delegation to travel to Ottawa to beg for "special consideration" of Halifax's needs as Canada's prime wartime city. Those needs, of course, included more money to hire more policemen to control the thousands of unruly servicemen under Murray's command.

Murray knew that. His own sub-commander at Stadacona was pressing him to take action where the city had failed so abysmally: at providing recreation facilities to keep his sailors from getting into the kind of trouble that called for added policemen. But how could anyone compare the city's piddling problem of coping with a few unruly naval ratings with his never-ending battle to save his sailors and merchant seamen from almost certain death at the hands of the German wolf packs? Murray knew what his priorities had to be. He only wished local officials would get their priorities straight too.

JEFF JEFFERSON WAS EXHAUSTED. He'd hardly slept at all last night. How could he with all that noise? It didn't help that he and Lennie were still living in the Nova Scotian Hotel, which was not only downtown in a city that never slept but also too close for comfort to the incessant racket of the harbour.

Although he had been noticing the increasing cacophony for months, "last night was probably the worst since the war began," he wrote in his journal this morning. He had decided to try capturing the audio panorama on paper. "A convoy of fifty ships was crawling in all night, and in addition to the usual loud blowing for the medical boat, pilot launches, coal barges, navigational signals, etc., each vessel blew a fog warning every few yards . . . The whole thing was bedlam, which made sleep almost impossible."

If anything, the din onshore was even more bothersome. "Motorcycles, army and commercial trucks roar through the streets, dozens of locomotives shunt day and night with the usual bell-ringing and whistling, and last but not least, the streetcars, now about eighty or ninety in number, pound over the dilapidated rails with a clatter that makes conversation almost impossible . . . On the streets crowds throng the sidewalks until late in the night and every evening sees swarms of drunks reeling, singing or fighting on all the principal thoroughfares."

The aural assault came from the skies too. "Overhead, there is the continuous monotonous droning of all kinds of planes. In fine weather they never let up even for one hour out of twenty-four."

Was this war—and this noise—a permanent state?

BOB SUTHERLAND had been to Nova Scotia before. His father's family came from Pictou County and he'd spent part of one summer there as a child. What he remembered most was that everyone he met was Presbyterian and no one seemed happy. Now he was here again, this time as the program officer for a new Knights of Columbus club on Hollis Street, just across from the Nova Scotian Hotel.

The Knights of Columbus Services Club, which had been built by the federal government specifically for the Roman Catholic group, was designed in the shape of an *H*, with a central lobby and wings on either side. In one wing there was a cafeteria and overnight hostel for up to two hundred; on the other, a ten-lane bowling alley, a library, a chapel and a large, high-ceilinged entertainment room with its own stage, where Sutherland planned to show popular movies after the theatres had finished with them, and produce live stage shows and dances. His job was to make sure there was something interesting going on every single night of the week. To help him in that task he had hired Mrs. Yell, a widow from Vancouver who'd come to Halifax to be close to her daughter, the principal of the Convent of the Sacred Heart School. Mrs. Yell's role was to recruit good young local Catholic girls to attend all the dances, which was not a difficult task, and then to chaperone them, which required considerably more skill and finesse.

Though he was only twenty-two himself, Sutherland wasn't new to this line of work; he had done a similar job at an air force base in Arnprior, Ontario. There, however, the war had seemed far off, and the base had resembled a country club. One of Sutherland's duties had been to build a ski lodge in the beautiful Ottawa Valley for the men at the base. He was also in charge of planning entertainment for the base officers. If a film didn't arrive in time for a showing, he would recall, "someone would fly me down to Toronto to pick it up. War might have been hell for a lot of people, but not for me."

He knew Halifax would be different—and it was. The war was everywhere. The job of catering to the needs and wants of thousands of sailors, soldiers and airmen ate up twenty-four hours of every day. He was told he'd get two weeks off at Christmas. He considered himself lucky he wasn't married. Hughie Creagen, his boss, who'd run a similar club in Newfoundland before being dispatched to Halifax, had a wife he saw once a year. Sutherland and Creagen lived in the hostel. So did Father Wingle, an air force chaplain who conducted services in the non-denominational chapel upstairs.

Most of the local men they hired tended to be either too old or not quite up to the task of fighting a war. The guy who ran the bowling alley, for example, was the ne'er-do-well scion of an old Antigonish Catholic family, the man in charge of the tuck shop was an out-of-work meteorologist and the stationary engineer was a wino who liked to spend his evenings in the basement shooting rats.

Bob Sutherland knew he wasn't in Arnprior any more.

DOROTHY HENDSBEE SMILED as she reread the article from this morning's newspaper one more time. FIVE PIONEER WOMEN WELDERS IN TRAINING, the headline read. "Five women—two of them former school teachers, one office clerk, a laundry worker and a clothing factory employee—are in training to become Halifax's pioneer female welders and break into a heretofore strictly man's domain . . ."

Lying on her bed in the small room she shared with fellow "pioneer" Bertha Roche, Dorothy knew she should stop reading. She was exhausted. But she couldn't help herself. She'd read the article just one more time and then go to sleep.

She took out a pen and carefully printed in block letters the names next to the figures in the photo below the headline: BERT, ME, MR. BOWMAN, PAULINE MACKAY. Across another photo showing her friend Helen, goggles pushed back into her hair, staring intently at a sheet of metal she was cutting, she wrote HELEN RICE. Dorothy didn't want to forget any of them, ever. Then she underlined each reference to herself—"the youngest of the group . . . Dorothy Hendsbee of Half Island Cove, Guysborough County"—in both the story and the photo caption, almost as a way of reassuring herself that all of this was indeed happening to her.

Because she planned to cut out the story and save it for her scrapbook, she also took the time to correct some of the errors she'd noticed. A subhead in the story's first column, for example, claimed, "Youngest is 17." Dorothy carefully turned the seven into a six. Near the end of the story, where it described her as an "acetylene welder," Dorothy blacked out the word *acetylene*. For someone who, three months ago, didn't know what a welder was, she'd come a long way. And her expectations had changed, too. Where the paper noted that she "makes 59 cents an hour," Dorothy added pointedly in pen: "to start."

But there were some corrections she didn't make. The article misidentified her hated stepfather Roy as her father, and noted that she was "deeply attached to her parents." She'd told the reporter the truth about that but asked him not to write it down. He'd done her one better and made up a daughterly quote for her: "The only reason that would make me quit would be if my mother told me," Dorothy had supposedly said, adding for good measure: "But mother says it's great for me to be working here. I get a great thrill knowing that I am helping to build Canada's new destroyers and I'm glad mother and dad are thrilled too."

Dorothy had to laugh at that.

Just as she had to blush at the reporter's fulsome description of her as a "dark-eyed, dimple-cheeked . . . comely maid." She looked appraisingly at the picture of herself staring back from the newspaper page. In the photo she was dressed in coveralls, the flipped-up faceplate of her welder's helmet perched atop her head, the long brown hair Mr. Bowman had urged her to cut off—"a fire hazard," he'd called it—spilling out from beneath her leather skullcap. In the photo she had been smiling for the photographer as she readied her welder's rod, and the smile did indeed highlight her dimples.

She'd been smiling a lot lately, ever since the moment she got that form letter—addressed to "Dear Sir"—instructing her to report to the Nova Scotia Technical College for a course in electric welding beginning April 12, 1943. Despite her fears, the letter made no reference to her being too young or too thin or too uneducated for the program. "You are accepted on probation for a period of three weeks to see whether or not you have the natural abilities for this particular type of work," the letter explained. "Your employment has been arranged with Halifax Shipyards and you will be expected to work for that firm when you complete your three months training period . . . Your living allowance will be $9.00 per week."

Nine dollars a week! Dorothy had earned five dollars *a month* in her first job, less than three years ago. And the news had got even better on the first day of classes. Harold Bowman, a senior welder at the Halifax Shipyards who'd been lent to Tech to teach the women, had transformed one of the college's basement labs into a combination classroom and welding shop, with makeshift cubicles divided by heavy canvas curtains. After he handed out coveralls and welding helmets, copies of their textbook, *Lessons in Arc Welding*—"a handy guide for the man behind the mask"—and a green Duo-Tang folder full of mimeographed lesson notes, Bowman had announced that the living allowance would be eleven dollars a week. After their formal training and some on-the-job experience, he added, they could expect to earn up to ninety cents an hour plus time and a half for overtime—and there'd be plenty of overtime, he said.

Dorothy couldn't wait.

When classes began on April 12, the three dozen women who'd taken the straight-line test the week before had been winnowed down to five. Inez Charron, the oldest, had been a schoolteacher in New Brunswick before moving to Halifax with her carpenter-husband, who'd taken a job with a local construction firm. She'd applied to train as a welder, she said, because she "didn't have enough to do and I wanted to do what I could to help out the war effort." Pauline MacKay had also been a schoolteacher on the province's south shore for three years before the war, but there was no work for schoolteachers there once the conflict began, so she'd moved to Halifax and taken a job in an office. "It wasn't very exciting," she said simply. Boredom was Helen Rice's explanation too. She was twenty-one, living at home with her parents in the city's north end and working as a bookkeeper at Clayton & Sons, a local men's clothing manufacturer. "Office work was awful boring," she said. "I spent most of my time looking at the clock and waiting for the day to end. Welding seemed exciting." Bertha Roche had applied because she needed a job. She was in her late twenties, divorced, with two kids. Her parents were taking care of her children at their farm in Shubenacadie, about forty miles from Halifax, while Bertha completed her welder's training in the city.

Perhaps because she missed her own children, or because Dorothy, at sixteen, seemed so young and vulnerable, Bertha quickly became a kind of surrogate mother for her. "She took me under her wing," Dorothy would later recall. By the end of their first day of training, in fact, Dorothy and Bertha had agreed to share a room in a house in Dartmouth. Edith, the landlady, whose husband was a naval officer serving overseas, charged them five dollars each a week but offered to reduce the rent by half if they'd look after her two pre-school-aged children on the weekends. When Edith said "weekends," she meant *all* weekend, *every* weekend. "She really partied," marvelled Dorothy. "Most of the time she'd take off Friday afternoon and we'd be lucky if she'd get home again by the time we had to go to work on Monday morning. She said we could help ourselves to her food from the fridge on the weekends. For some reason the fridge always seemed to be full—chicken, hamburgers, vegetables—so we ate well on the weekends."

During the week, she and Bertha bought bread and sandwich spread (mayonnaise and chopped-up pickles) and made their lunches in their room. After breakfast they'd catch a ferry across the harbour, then walk close to a mile south to the Technical College. They attended classes each weekday from eight in the morning to five in the afternoon.

Although their training—420 intense hours of shop practice and 60 hours of theory—paled in comparison with the four-year apprenticeship process their male counterparts had had to survive in the pre-war era, it was twice as long as the training that women welders in the U.S. were being given.

Although the Halifax women began with little in common beyond the fact that none of them had ever done anything like this before, they bonded instantly. They began calling themselves the Electric Five. Over lunch they'd talk about Mr. Bowman's frequent invocations of a higher power ("He's a Jehovah's Witness," Helen said), and about how he would insist that welding was not a craft but an art. They shared rites of passage, too. Although Bowman emphasized they should never, ever, look directly at the brilliant but hazardous light of the welding arc with their naked eyes, they did. "We were all blind for a few days after." And they learned to accept the occasional flash burn on their neck or chest. It was simply the price they paid for bodies that didn't fit comfortably into the work coveralls they'd been issued. To compensate, Bowman taught them how to use their blowtorches to warm their coffee.

They were such quick studies that, near the end of their training period, he told the newspaper reporter: "They are all as good as men in every respect. There is no doubt about that."

From the beginning Bowman made only one allowance for their gender: the women were forbidden to attempt overhead welding because of fears that falling sparks could ignite their hair. These days, it seemed, every young woman was trying to look like Veronica Lake, the Hollywood actress whose trademark was her long blonde hair cascading down over one eye. The U.S. State Department was so concerned about the number of young women war workers whose hair ended up tangled in machinery, they convinced Paramount to make Lake wear her hair pulled back for the duration of the conflict. Bowman tried to convince his female students to do the same, but without success. If only they'd cut their hair, he lamented to the reporter, they could turn out to be better than the men they were replacing. "They have a very steady hand. That is quite necessary in this work and something that many men can't overcome."

Perhaps it was Bowman's confidence in them that had made Dorothy and Bertha imagine this might turn into something more than a temporary, wartime job. "I'm going to make it my life profession," Dorothy had told the newspaper reporter enthusiastically.

"This is too good to give up for a kitchen." Added Bertha: "I'm going to keep right on this job after the war is over. I might get married but I'll make my husband keep the home."

Now, as she reread the article, Dorothy couldn't imagine what had possessed them to say such things to the reporter. They'd been told from the beginning that their jobs would last only as long as the war. They'd have to give them up whenever the veterans—*male* veterans—returned to claim them.

Dorothy tried to put that out of her mind. She would soon have a job, a place of her own, money in her pocket, and the prospect of more, and better, to come. She turned out the light and tried to sleep. Morning would come soon enough.

BILLY MONT WAS FOURTEEN years old. He had his grade six. It was time to get on with his life.

His mother didn't object when he quit school; she was already gone from Billy's life. During her stay in the City Home she'd met a man, got married and disappeared. His step-grandmother was only too happy when Billy landed a year-round job that meant he could contribute more to the family's precarious finances.

If he'd had a choice, Billy would have signed up to fight overseas. But he was too young, and too small to convince the recruiters he was really eighteen. So, in the summer of 1943, he went to work for the Canadian National Railways. It wasn't much of a job. He and an old guy spent their days picking up papers and trash alongside the tracks outside the station, or emptying and cleaning boxcars. Though his supervisor told him that, if he worked hard, he might someday get to move inside the station to clean the floors and brass fittings, or maybe, if he was lucky, even become a redcap and get to carry luggage, Billy wasn't sure he wanted to do anything but what he was doing. He hadn't given up his lucrative scavenging sideline, and his new job offered him lots of opportunities to pick up new treasures he could sell or trade. Why would he want to be promoted?

BYRON HIMMELMAN WAS READY to go back to sea.

"That's nice, son," Tom Skinner, the foreman, replied, "but we think we'll keep you here for a while yet."

"Here" was the Halifax Shipyards. It was ironic, really. Byron had begun applying at the Shipyards shortly after he left his victualling assistant's job aboard the *Montrolite* more than three years earlier. His plan then had been to train as an electrician so he'd be able to go back to sea with a better job. While he waited to get hired as an electrician's helper at the Shipyards, he'd taken night classes at the Nova Scotia Technical College. But he knew he needed hands-on experience too. That's why he was so pleased when he finally landed a job last fall apprenticing with Bill Jennings, a fabulous shipyard electrician who could take motors apart and put them back together better and faster than anyone else. Byron had already been promoted twice: to temporary light man, setting up lights for workmen at night or inside ships, and more recently to "improver," which meant, as he explained to friends, he was "not quite an electrician but no longer a helper."

Now he thought he was ready to move on. His supervisors didn't disagree, but they weren't prepared to let him go that easily. It was easy to understand why. There were so few trained tradesmen who weren't in uniform that places like the Shipyards were now full of boys and old men, even women. And there was plenty of work for all of them—and more. There were, quite literally, thousands of ships to repair each year. Sometimes workers had to patch up a ship with a gaping torpedo hole in its side. As often as not, however, the problem was as simple and as troubling as sand in the engine bearings, put there by crew members who didn't want to go back to sea. More and more of them didn't. Some were simply afraid for their lives, and with good reason. Others were motivated by anger over low pay or frustration at living conditions aboard the vessels. Whatever their reasons, Byron sometimes thought, sabotage had become the great untold story of this war. In fact, right now down at Pier 28 there was a French merchant ship whose crew had scuttled it to prevent it from sailing.

And then, of course, there was the federal government's massive wartime shipbuilding program. The Shipyards' major responsibility these days was building new Tribal class destroyers like the *Micmac*, which was scheduled to be launched soon. Byron had been kept busy lighting that site so the men—women too, he supposed—could work after dark.

His job had its perks, of course. He'd recently been able to buy a car, a 1937 Hudson Terraplane, for $100 from a girl who'd joined the army. While gasoline had been rationed for a year and a half and rubber for tires was still rationed (one infamous Halifax taxi had had to replace a worn rubber tire with a wooden one), defence workers, which is what the government considered shipyard employees, were entitled to a larger allotment.

Because Byron lived at home and didn't have to pay rent, he could also afford some of the pleasures the city had to offer. On Saturday nights he would go to the dances at the Nova Scotian, sometimes with a friend's sister, sometimes with his cousin, a beautician who was boarding at his house. He'd taken her to the New Year's Eve dance there last year. One of his school chums, Don Warner, was the band leader. And of course there were movies to go to, even live shows, so long as you were prepared to stand in line. Recently, Byron had seen *The Navy Show* at the Capitol Theatre. It was a revue designed to boost morale among servicemen and civilians, and it had certainly done that for Byron. The best part was when a fellow by the name of John Pratt sang "You'll Get Used to It." Byron couldn't get the song out of his head. "The first year is the worst year . . ."

He didn't know about that, but he did know that, unlike those who sabotaged their ships, he didn't want to get used to being a landlubber. He was ready to go back to sea.

AGNES MACDONALD STOOD at the edge of the flag-bedecked launch platform surrounded by what the newspaper reporters would describe as five "full-blooded, feather-festive" Native chiefs, all of them dwarfed beneath the "sharp-nosed glistening grey prow" of the massive destroyer towering over them on the slipway. Agnes—better known as Mrs. Angus L. Macdonald, the wife of Nova Scotia's former premier, now federal naval minister—raised the bottle of champagne above her shoulder and spoke into the microphone. "I christen thee *Micmac*," she declared solemnly, "and God bless this ship and all who sail in her."

Dorothy Hendsbee stood a few hundred feet away, watching from the deck railing of Hull #13, *Micmac*'s soon-to-be sister ship. The usual clang of hammer on steel, the staccato rat-tat-tat of rivets penetrating plates and the hollow whoosh of welding torches had stilled. Dorothy and her fellow construction workers had downed tools and were taking a few minutes from building this new ship to celebrate the completion of their last project. It was a big event—and not just in Halifax.

Ottawa had proclaimed September 18, 1943, Ships for Victory Day, and was marking the occasion by launching a dozen ships—two destroyers, two frigates, two 10,000-ton merchantmen, a minesweeper, a corvette, a Fairmile patrol vessel, a tanker and two tugs—at shipyards across the Dominion. They were, as Angus L. had been proud to point out to the local press, among the 620 ships—not to mention hundreds of smaller vessels—launched so far under the Department of Munitions and Supplies' shipbuilding program.

HMCS *Micmac* was not only the biggest ship launched today—377 feet with a beam of 37.5 feet and a displacement of more than 2,000 tons, which made it 50 feet longer and 300 tons heavier than the next largest—but the biggest ever built in Canada.

Smash. Macdonald brought the bottle down hard on the hull, breaking the glass and sending a spray of champagne over the reporters assembled below the platform, much to the delight of the hundreds of guests, workers and spectators who'd gathered for the occasion. She was then handed a pair of scissors and snipped the ceremonial ribbon. While the crowds cheered and the harbour filled with the sounds of boat horns and whistles, the *Micmac* glided gracefully down the slipway and into the harbour. As it did so, the crib work on the other side of the vessel became visible to the spectators. Effigies of Hitler and Japanese emperor Hirohito hung by their necks from the crib work. The crowd applauded even more loudly.

The cheering finally stopped only when the Micmac elders—three chiefs and two band councillors in full regalia—stepped up to the microphone and began to chant a blessing on the ship that invoked the tribe's patron saint, Saint Anne. Two naval chaplains, one Protestant and one Roman Catholic, had offered their blessings earlier in the ceremony. Earlier too, John Ferguson, a rivet passer who, at sixteen, was the youngest member of the construction crew, had presented flowers to Mrs. Macdonald on behalf of the crew.

Dorothy could no longer claim to be the youngest, but that didn't mean she'd been forgotten. The *Mail* had printed her picture again, the one of her in her welder's gear, as part of a montage of photos of "Workers Who Helped Build 'Micmac.'" The caption described her, as usual, as a "pretty 17-year-old." Being described that way still embarrassed Dorothy, but she was getting used to it. Defence officials had liked that photo so much that they used it in official publications to promote the war effort and boost morale among the troops. That must have been how Warren Zagata had seen it, Dorothy guessed. Zagata, a young American GI training in Texas, had sent Dorothy a picture of himself in uniform, along with a letter promising to send her an airline ticket if she would only visit him in Texas. Dorothy knew it was foolish to think of such a thing. She'd written back, thanking him but declining his offer as gently as she could.

As Dorothy and the rest of the crew returned to their work on Hull #13, the next, still-unnamed destroyer, the dignitaries and their guests retreated to the loft in the shipyard's main administrative building for the formal reception. Vice Admiral Percy Nelles, the Chief of Naval Staff, was there, along with Arthur Cross, the president of Dominion Steel and Coal Co., which owned the yard, and various military and civic dignitaries, suppliers and, of course, the press. H.B. Jefferson, the official press censor, stopped by as well, mingling and sampling the cold cuts.

Angus L. Macdonald spoke briefly. He recalled the time he and Percy Nelles flew to England to persuade the Admiralty to let Canada build the Tribal class destroyers. One of the factors that had helped persuade the British, he claimed, was that four of the ships would be built in Halifax, "in a province where people have followed the sea and have known its crafts for hundreds of years." There were now 73,000 Canadians serving in the navy, he pointed out, of whom between 6,000 and 7,000 were Nova Scotians. "No province," he argued, "has given more generously of its men to build and man these ships than Nova Scotia."

And women too, he might have added.

CHURCHILL IS CHEERED BY CROWDS IN HALIFAX boasted the headline over Eric Dennis's fulsome report in the Tuesday, September 21 edition of the Halifax *Herald*. But the phrase in smaller type above the headline—"Now It Can Be Told"—was more revealing.

Churchill had indeed been applauded by enthusiastic Haligonians during two separate visits to the city, and his very public appearances had been the talk of the town. It was now a full week since he flashed his final V-for-Victory salutes to the cheering throngs from the topmost bridge of HMS *Renown*, as the warship eased out of the harbour to the strains of a marine band playing "Rule, Britannia!" Until today, however, the press had not been permitted to publish a word about it. It was only now that Churchill was safely back in England that Jeff Jefferson, an unabashed admirer of the great man, was opening the floodgates to stories of Churchill's two triumphant visits to the city.

Churchill and his party, which included his wife and daughter, had slipped quietly into Halifax harbour aboard the *Queen Mary* on

August 9. But his arrival didn't stay quiet for long. Sailors from his ship crowded the deck, cheering so loudly as Churchill walked down the gangplank that they attracted the notice of sailors aboard other ships, and even of locals walking along Barrington.

"One of the first to see the prime minister," Eric would write in his belated news report, "was a six-year-old dirty-faced boy at the dockside. 'I'm gonna run home and tell Mom Churchill's in town,' he shouted to a companion." By the time Churchill's motorcade reached the train station, hundreds had gathered to catch a glimpse of the legendary British war hero. Churchill didn't disappoint. As he walked along the train platform to his waiting car, his ever-present cigar in his mouth, he tipped his cap to the crowd and gave them a V-for-Victory salute.

This Halifax stopover was understandably brief. Churchill, along with key advisers Lord Louis Mountbatten, Sir John Dill and Sir Dudley Pound, was on his way to Quebec City and Washington for critical meetings with Canadian prime minister Mackenzie King and U.S. president Franklin Roosevelt.

His return visit was supposed to be equally quick. "I hope you'll like the city," Mayor Jack Lloyd declared as he officially welcomed Churchill back at a train-side ceremony on September 15. "I hope you'll enjoy your stay."

"Stay?" Churchill shot back, bemused. "I'll only be here twenty minutes." In truth, he spent more than an hour and a half touring the city with Rear Admiral Murray, visiting historic landmarks— Point Pleasant Park, the Public Gardens, Citadel Hill and the Northwest Arm—and surprising many along the way.

During his walk through the Gardens, Churchill encountered two airmen with ice cream cones relaxing on a bench. Seeing Churchill, the men immediately sprang to attention and saluted stiffly, but they couldn't quite figure out what to do with their cones. They "clung to the cones in their left hands," Eric wrote, "like swords held at attention." Churchill, smiling, simply tipped his cap in response.

Of course, not everyone was quite so impressed by the British visitor. Walking over a stone bridge leading to the Gardens' exit at the corner of Spring Garden Road and South Park Street, Churchill noticed a "little boy with torn trousers bent over its wall. Chuckling to himself, the prime minister walked up to the lad, pinched him in the thigh, but the boy took no notice. Something in the stream below held his fixed attention."

Later, when Churchill's motorcade got stuck behind a streetcar in a traffic jam while leaving the Public Gardens, one of the RCMP officers accompanying him got out to see if he could move the traffic along. But the tramcar driver, catching a glimpse of Churchill staring out of the car window, didn't move along as the Mountie obviously hoped he would. Instead, he jumped out of the vehicle, pointed to Churchill, tossed his hat in the air and led his passengers in a lusty cheer for the British prime minister.

On the dock later, waiting to board the *Renown*, Churchill turned to one of his colleagues. "Now we know Halifax is not just a shed on the wharf as we had known it to be before . . ."

It wasn't quite as ringing an endorsement as British Rear Admiral Stuart Bonham-Carter's earlier declaration that Halifax might just be "the most important port in the world today," but Eric knew that his local readers—and his editors—would still lap it up. In fact, when the story was eventually cleared for publication, the *Herald* accompanied Eric's news story with a front-page editorial entitled "Halifax Honoured." "It was altogether appropriate that Mr. Churchill should choose Halifax as his gateway to Canada," the editorial declared. "Halifax is essentially Empire history . . . Churchill, the historian, who knows his British history as well as any man, realizes it; and as he trod historic ground in Halifax a few days ago, he must have felt that here, more than in any other part of the Overseas Empire, he could find the authentic foundations of the British Story beyond the seas."

As Eric watched Churchill shaking hands with Premier MacMillan's wife—"I would like to have the chance to visit the different hostels and see more of Halifax but I'm afraid it cannot be this time," he told her—he noticed Jeff Jefferson and his wife on the periphery of the official delegation. Jefferson was practically beaming.

To coincide with release of the news of Churchill's visit, Eric had heard the navy was planning a special press junket for national journalists to unveil the still-secret story (though it was well known locally) of its success this spring in thwarting the Nazis when they attempted to mine the entrance to Halifax harbour. Eric realized he would have to look up his notes on that story soon.

"Got something very interesting for you, Eric." For some reason George Fox, the deputy chief of police, liked the *Herald* better than its rival and would often call Eric to tip him to breaking news stories before the *Chronicle* could catch wind of them. "There's been what looks like a murder-suicide down in Marlborough Woods," Fox said, adding mysteriously, "and the circumstances . . . well, let's just say they seem a little strange."

Even though he'd been in the newsroom since before seven this morning, and had been planning to make an early day of it—Maxine was in the hospital waiting to deliver their second child, and Eric was anxious to visit her—murder-suicides weren't an everyday occurrence in Halifax, and certainly not in Marlborough Woods, one of the city's swankiest addresses.

The circumstances were indeed strange—and horrific. Sometime last night, according to the police, Commander Frank Johnson, the Royal Navy's paymaster in Halifax, had murdered his eleven-year-old daughter, Nadia, with an axe and then killed himself. Near a boathouse fifty yards from the Johnson home, police had discovered spattered, frozen pools of blood staining the whiteness of the season's first snowfall, along with clumps of what looked like human flesh and blonde hair. Although an axe and a red canoe were missing from the boathouse, leading police to believe he might have dumped her body in the Northwest Arm before killing himself, they had not yet recovered either body.

The investigation had begun around 2 p.m., Jim Baker, the Inspector of Detectives, told Eric. Commander Johnson had arrived home from New York last night but hadn't shown up for work as expected this morning, so Lieutenant W.A. Kibble, his chief of staff, had called his home around noon. The Johnsons' maid searched the house but found no trace of him. She did, however, discover a letter addressed to Lieutenant Kibble. As soon as he read the letter—and saw the blood on the snow—Kibble called the police.

"What was in the letter?" Eric wanted to know.

"I can't tell you that," Baker answered, "but I will tell you that Commander Johnson did say in his letter he'd put his affairs in order." The contents of the letter, he added, convinced him he was investigating a murder-suicide.

According to the police, the actual story had begun a little over a week earlier, on American Thanksgiving Day, when Johnson's wife, Vava, was hit by a car while crossing a New York City street. The family had lived in Manhattan during the early days of the war, and their daughter was keen to return there to the private school she'd attended previously. Vava wanted to move back to New York too. Halifax, she'd told friends, was boring and bland. She'd gone to New York on November 15, Baker said, to look for an apartment for herself and her daughter.

As soon as he heard about the accident, Johnson flew to her bedside. Vava, who had fractured her skull, was still in a coma in New York's Welfare Island Hospital. According to police, Commander Johnson had spent three days with his wife before returning to Halifax last night. A navy chauffeur picked him up at the train station, drove him to his office so he could pick up some papers, then dropped him off at his home sometime between midnight and 12:30 a.m. The Johnsons' live-in maid said she'd seen him later that night in the drawing room. Another family staying in the house at the time—an American navy lieutenant and his wife—told police they'd heard Commander Johnson moving around downstairs most of the night.

"It seems our friend Commander Johnson was a busy fellow last night," Baker said to Eric. "The maid says he was burning papers in the fireplace. Now why do you suppose he'd be doing that?"

"It's all very funny," agreed Bill Cleary, one of Baker's deputies. He smiled at Eric. "You could say this is one of those cases with many of the mysterious elements of fiction."

"It looks like a murder and a suicide," Baker added, "but anything but a simple murder-suicide." Though he wouldn't say so for publication, Baker confided to Eric that it appeared Johnson might have been embezzling funds from the Royal Navy's accounts and was burning the incriminating evidence.

While that could explain why Johnson killed himself, Eric thought, it didn't account for him murdering his own daughter—and so brutally. There must be more to all this than anyone yet knew.

Back in the newsroom, Eric put fresh paper in his typewriter and began to compose his story. "The mysterious disappearance of a Halifax naval officer and his nine-year-old daughter from their Northwest Arm home yesterday while his wife lay near death in a New York hospital was under investigation by police last night with its circumstances leading to fears in some quarters that one of the most pathetic tragedies in the city in years had taken place . . ."

Maxine! He hadn't gone to the hospital to visit her. Was he a father again? He picked up the telephone.

"YOU TWO GIRLS are just the greatest," the young lieutenant declared happily as he watched Dorothy Hendsbee and Bertha Roche work their green-wrapping-paper-and-red-ribbon magic on the boxes of housecoats, sweaters, scarves and slippers in front of them. The lieutenant and his roommates—navy officers all—had bought the gifts to send home to their girlfriends, wives and parents for Christmas but then discovered they were all thumbs when it came to wrapping them. "Could you . . . ?" one of them had asked tentatively tonight after supper. "Of course," they'd said, and within a few minutes there were a dozen or more boxes from Eaton's,

Simpson's, Kline's, even one from Mills Brothers, the high society lady's shop on Spring Garden Road, piled on the kitchen table.

Dorothy didn't mind. She liked the young men she and Bertha were now rooming with. They were the only females among the dozen boarders. The men seemed to be an ever-changing cast of navy officers "from the higher ranks, nice, decent people," who would arrive in Halifax, spend a few weeks at the house and then ship out for Europe, never to be heard from again. Dorothy didn't think of any of them as romantic prospects—they all seemed to have sweethearts somewhere else, and besides, she was far too busy at the Shipyards to worry overmuch about finding a man right now—but she did enjoy just being around so many older "brothers."

The atmosphere at this boarding house was a far cry from their first place, in Dartmouth, where Dorothy and Bertha were left to look after the landlady's kids. The next place they'd rented—on Barrington Street near the Shipyards—was noisy and rowdy and not a place they wanted to stay. It was a good thing, Dorothy would tell her friends, that everything they owned fit neatly into one suitcase. They moved into a room in another house on Windsor Street, but that lasted only a few weeks before the landlady's cooking convinced Bertha they should look for something better. They'd found this rooming house on Lady Hammond Road, just a few blocks from the Shipyards, a few months ago. For nine dollars each a week, they got to share a room in a nice house owned by a widow who not only made them all breakfast and a hot meal at night but also packed them a lunch to take to work each day. "She was nice, just like what I figured a real mother would be like," Dorothy says. "We thought we were the luckiest people alive."

If only she could shake this awful cold, Dorothy thought, as she took a final appraising look at the red bow on the package she'd just finished wrapping and handed it back to the young lieutenant. She was glad the foreman at the Shipyards hadn't asked her to work tonight. The *Iroquois*, whose hull had been damaged by a torpedo, was in the yard for emergency repairs. For the past few weeks

Dorothy, perhaps because she was among the smallest of the welders, had been assigned to work in tight quarters deep in the bowels of the vessel. The smoky, dirty work seemed to be making her cold even worse.

"Any news on that Limey bastard who killed his little girl?" one of the officers asked as he watched Dorothy pick up another box and place it on a sheet of green wrapping paper.

"They're burying the little girl tomorrow afternoon," one of the others answered. "But I don't think they've found him yet. If he's alive, hanging's too good for him, I say."

There were murmurs of agreement around the table.

What were they talking about? Dorothy wondered. Between work and this cold, she hadn't had much time for—or interest in—the news. She was just too tired for any of it. As soon as she finished wrapping these last few presents, she thought, she'd go to bed.

ERIC DENNIS STOOD near the back of the overcrowded little chapel in Cruikshank's Funeral Home taking notes as the navy chaplain finally raised his bowed head and broke the awful silence. "Would you all please stand now," he asked the dozens of mourners, many with tears in their eyes, "and sing with me, 'There's a Friend for Little Children in the Bright Blue Sky.'"

Police divers had recovered Nadia Johnson's body from the bottom of the Northwest Arm shortly before noon on Friday, December 3, two days after she and her father disappeared. Her small body had been weighted down with eight large stones. Although there was a gaping wound in the back of her head where she'd been bludgeoned with the axe, it turned out that that was not the actual cause of death. It was much worse. "Her lungs were filled with an exceptional quantity of water," the medical examiner noted, "indicating she was still alive when she hit the water and also that she put up a struggle in the water." Eric Dennis thought of his new son, William Richard Eric Dennis, who'd been born the day after the murder. That anyone could do such a thing to his own child was beyond his imagining.

The murder-suicide, if that's what it was, was the talk of Halifax. The fact that the police hadn't found any sign of Commander Johnson's body, despite dragging the seabed near the house for nearly a week, only added to the public fascination, and deepened the mystery.

Though the Johnsons had been in Halifax for only a year, they were already famous, or perhaps infamous, for their lavish entertaining. Last July, for example, they'd thrown a large dinner party featuring special Russian dishes, "red, white and blue candelabra, summer flowers and . . . place mats [with] flags of all the United Nations" to honour Lieutenant-Governor Henry E. Kendall and his wife. The event became notorious, not so much because the guest list included the cream of the city's social, military, diplomatic and political elite, but because of the description of Vava's dress in the write-up in the *Mail*'s "Women's Activities" pages. "Mrs. Johnson was attired in fuchsia-coloured cocktail pyjamas with Royal blue feathers in her hair," gushed the paper's Social Notes editor, who also happened to be a dinner guest. "Her 10-year-old daughter Nadia, dressed in blue taffeta, acted as portress . . ."

When he read that description of Vava's outfit, Don Fraser, a dour Pictou County curmudgeon who was the editor and publisher of the New Glasgow *Eastern Chronicle*, saw red. He not only reprinted the entire offending item in his newspaper but then also penned a scathing editorial denouncing the frivolous Johnsons and their prominent guests for taking part in what he called "ridiculous shenanigans" during a critical time in the war. "Canadian boys are fighting in the heat and choking dust of the barren hills of Sicily . . . Young men, the very lifeblood of this young nation, are offering their all in behalf of home and country," he thundered before concluding: "Fuchsia-coloured cocktail pyjamas may sound smart in high society, but it has a very depressing effect upon the people at large and the Canadians bearing arms."

In light of the rumours now circulating about what could have led Johnson to murder his own daughter, the family's extravagant lifestyle had taken on new meaning. How had they afforded it all? Their forest green, two-storey, five-bedroom house nestled on spacious grounds in tony Marlborough Woods boasted prime water frontage, a boathouse and its own dock on the Northwest Arm. At first blush the rent—$125 a month—might not have seemed excessive for a Royal Navy paymaster who earned $350 monthly. But Frank Johnson was also footing the bills for all the other accoutrements: a live-in domestic, tuition for Nadia at the Halifax Ladies' College, a local private girls' school, membership in the Bengal Lancers, the elite horse-riding club to which all the children of everyone who was anyone in Halifax belonged, and, of course, all the dinner parties. Though some had already questioned, albeit in a gossipy, never-to-their-faces way, how the Johnsons could afford all this, most had assumed that one or both of them must have come from money. Vava certainly talked, and acted, to the manor born.

Though no longer beautiful, Vava, thirty-seven, who claimed to be a Polish countess, was nonetheless a striking woman: heavyset, bosomy and with a commanding presence that made her difficult to ignore. She had a button installed under her place at the dining-room table so that she could summon her maid, even if the maid was just ten feet away and dinner was no more formal than a borscht lunch with Nadia. She had flashing dark eyes, wore her long black hair pulled back in a bun and liked to drape dark, sweeping capes over her shoulders. Her thick Russian accent only added to her aura—and now to the rumours swirling around the family.

There were, in fact, two main theories about the mystery among Haligonians. The first was that Johnson was, as the police had suggested to Eric, misappropriating money from the Royal Navy to support his family's lifestyle. But that didn't explain why he would murder his daughter. Neither did the other popular scenario: that one or both of the Johnsons were spies who were about to be exposed.

To complicate matters, the police were no longer sure Johnson had committed suicide. "We are not completely satisfied that

Commander Johnson's body is at the bottom of the Northwest Arm," Police Chief Conrod had told Eric three days ago, adding that he was urging everyone in the area to "be on the lookout for any man acting strangely" and would soon be sending out circulars to alert other police forces in both Canada and the United States.

In response to their call for vigilance, the police had been inundated with Johnson sightings. He'd been spotted buying pop and cigarettes at a downtown store. Police had even swarmed into a local theatre one evening and arrested a man named Johnson who matched the missing man's description. It turned out he was a merchant seaman who just happened to look a lot like the man authorities were seeking.

The day before Nadia's funeral, Arthur Wills, a U.S. navy commander who'd been friends with the Johnsons for twenty-five years, arrived from New York to take charge of the burial arrangements—and to dispel what he called "a lot of nonsense" about his friend's disappearance. Johnson was not an embezzler; he and his wife weren't spies; they were not about to divorce. His friend, he said, was simply so distraught over his wife's accident and what seemed the likelihood that she would not survive that he became suicidal. He had killed his daughter so they'd all be together in heaven. "There is no doubt Johnson will be found at the bottom of the harbour," he insisted.

For now, however, there was only Nadia to bury. Hundreds of curious Haligonians had stood for hours in the rain and slush outside the funeral home this afternoon to pay their respects to the little girl who'd captured the city's collective imagination this past week—and, of course, to catch a glimpse of those local worthies who had come officially to mourn her.

Inside, the chapel was filled to overflowing. Eric saw plenty of familiar faces—Lieutenant-Governor Kendall and his wife, the Soviet consul and his family, Deputy Mayor "Gee" Ahern, Miss Dauphinee, the principal of Nadia's school, Lieutenant Commander Seeger, the commanding officer of the local Royal Navy base—and many others he didn't recognize, most in uniform. There was even an honour guard of naval ratings and Wrens.

Wreaths, sprays, baskets and cut flowers surrounded the small casket at the front of the chapel. Eric made notes of some of the more poignant messages. There was one, for example, from her "School Friends"; another, a flower-trimmed horseshoe that sat by itself near the foot of the casket, bore the inscription "Champ and the ponies." Champ had been Nadia's favourite horse at her riding club. But perhaps the most poignant of all was the bouquet of cut flowers with the note: "A Father and His Two Little Daughters."

THE FIRE THAT ripped through the ramshackle old building at the corner of Barrington and Sackville streets on December 11 perhaps provided local reporters with a few days of welcome respite from their seemingly continuous coverage of the Johnson mystery—about which there'd actually been no news for days—but it certainly didn't do much for Jeff Jefferson's mood. "This fire has cooked the goose so far as the local restaurant scene is concerned," he wrote despairingly a few days after the spectacular eight-hour Saturday night blaze.

The fire had caused $130,000 worth of damage and forced three downtown businesses to close. Among them was the Bon Ton Café, a second-floor walk-up "all-night dine and dance joint" popular among naval ratings and some of the reporters at the *Herald*. While Jefferson himself certainly wasn't a regular at the Bon Ton, its demise affected him too. "Norman's has been jammed to the gills every hour since, and the Green Lantern and others are in similar congestion," he noted in a report to his superiors in Ottawa. The government had recently put out to tender a new service canteen on Barrington Street beside St. Paul's cemetery and across from the lieutenant-governor's "palace," he added, "but this won't be worth a hoot unless it is thrown open to civilians as well as service people. Anything Ottawa HQ can do to bring this about by mentioning it to the great or near great encountered here and there, will be much appreciated."

Given Ottawa's record for providing facilities in Halifax, Jefferson wasn't holding out much hope.

SHE MUST REALLY look sick, Dorothy thought to herself. A soldier had taken one look at her and immediately offered her his seat on the standing-room-only train. Certainly, Dorothy had never felt worse. She was shivering one minute, sweating the next, with barely enough energy to drag herself and her suitcase onto the train.

The doctor had said it was pneumonia. Don't even think about going back to work for a while, he'd told her. Dorothy wanted to tell him about how busy they were at the Shipyards, about all the overtime she'd be missing, about how she had to keep working. She wanted to, but she didn't even have the energy to argue.

So now, two days before Christmas, she was on this train, heading back to Half Island to spend the holidays with her mother and stepfather. Perhaps, she thought, if she could just get a few days' bedrest there, she'd be well enough to return to her job by the beginning of the new year.

By the time the train pulled out of the station, she was already asleep.

THE SAILOR PULLED OVER to the side of the road and waited while the three hitchhiking sailors clambered into the back seat of his old DeSoto. It was Christmas Day, after all, and they looked cold standing by the side of the road, their thumbs in the air.

"Thanks, sailor," one of them said.

"No bother, fellas. Where ya headed?"

"Anywhere downtown is good."

"Say, who's that belong to?" one of them asked, pointing to the captain's uniform hanging by the car window.

"Captain Piers," the driver replied, straight-faced. "Just taking it to get it cleaned."

"Piers, eh?" the sailor said. "Not a bad old bastard."

Captain Debby Piers, sitting in the driver's seat in the uniform of the lowest naval rating, couldn't help but smile.

It was a naval tradition that, aboard ships in port on Christmas Day, the most junior sailor in the crew got to trade places with the captain. The sailor was allowed to dress up in the captain's uniform, inspect the rest of the crew and even issue orders to the officers and men. So Debby Piers had spent this Christmas morning aboard his new ship, the *Algonquin*, dressed as a sailor.

By the time the shipboard festivities were over, however, Debby was eager to get on with his own Christmas celebrations, so he'd asked the ship's coxswain to put his uniform in the car while he wore the sailor's uniform for the drive to Janet's parents'.

Now, as he drove down Barrington Street with his unsuspecting hitchhikers in the back seat, Debby decided to continue the game. "What you got in there?" he demanded, pointing to the bulge under one of the sailors' greatcoats.

The man opened his coat with a flourish to show off a large, fully cooked turkey. He ripped off one of the drumsticks and began to chew on it. Another sailor hauled a forty-ouncer of rum from inside his coat.

"I think it's time we all had a little drink," the sailor said, taking a swig and handing the bottle to Debby.

When he let them out at the corner of Barrington and Sackville, where the Bon Ton had burned down a couple of weeks before, they were all fast friends.

"Say, where'd you get the turkey and the rum?" Debby asked finally, as the three sailors stood together on the sidewalk.

"The captain's galley," one said proudly.

"Where else?" added another.

"Merry Christmas, fellas," Debby said.

"You too, sailor," they replied as he drove off. "And thanks for the ride."

While the sailors sought out a dark alley where they could celebrate Christmas Day devouring ripped-up pieces of purloined turkey and sharing swigs of rum straight from the bottle, Debby headed for his parents-in-law's warm and cozy Young Avenue home, where Janet was waiting and the smells of roast turkey and plum pudding filled the air.

NO ONE WOULD admit as much, of course, but the disaster that had beset Convoy SC107 nearly a year earlier might have been Debby Piers's most important contribution to the Battle of the Atlantic. It served as an icy North Atlantic wake-up call to those running the convoy operations: they were losing the battle if not the war.

Shortly after he agreed to hand operational command of the convoys back to the British, Canada's Navy Secretary, Angus L. Macdonald, ordered his chief aide, John Connolly, to figure out just how badly the Royal Canadian Navy was doing its job. While going through the files at naval headquarters, Connolly came across the report Debby Piers had written that spring, along with letters from other commanders begging for more up-to-date equipment or complaining about bureaucratic snafus that kept them from doing their jobs. Connolly's eventual report not only blamed Admiral Percy Nelles and his top staff but also claimed they'd been covering up their own ineptitude. By the end of the year Nelles had been shuffled out of his job as the country's top naval officer and exiled to London to be chief "liaison officer" to the British. There were rumours in naval circles that Nelles had recommended Leonard Murray as his successor but that Angus L. Macdonald had held out for George Jones, who became a vice admiral and Chief of Naval Staff. Jones had finally, as he'd claimed he would many years before, "beat them all" to become the navy's top commander.

By then, the Allies had recognized belatedly that they not only had to commit more and better aircraft to protecting the convoys but also needed to bolster the convoy escorts with vessels whose job was to aggressively seek out and sink submarines. While the regular escorts continued to focus on shepherding their convoys to their destinations, the new hunter-attack ships were free to break off and chase German subs. Thanks largely to these changes, the Allies sank close to two hundred German subs in 1943. In retrospect, it had not been a bad time for Leonard Murray to take charge of the Northwest Atlantic theatre of war.

Even as the Allies began to dominate the sea lanes, however, Nazi saboteurs became even bolder. In late May 1943, a German submarine had slipped, undetected, through Halifax's outer defences and laid fifty-six mines across the mouth of the harbour. Luckily, a convoy escort vessel spotted one of the devices floating on the water just before a large convoy was scheduled to depart. For the next twenty-four hours Halifax harbour was closed while a flotilla of Royal Navy and Royal Canadian Navy minesweepers—whaler-like vessels some called the "ugly ducklings" of the navy—cleared a 1,200-yard-wide channel to allow the convoy to go on its way. The only casualty was a two-thousand-ton merchant ship that strayed outside the cleared channel, struck a mine and sank.

Virtually everyone in the city knew about the attempted mining within days, but it remained officially hush-hush until September, when Ottawa belatedly decided to release the story to coincide with Churchill's safe return from Canada, even though the two stories were unrelated. In hopes of getting favourable publicity for its role in the war effort, Ottawa invited national and international news-paper, magazine, news service and radio reporters to spend a day on one of its minesweepers so they could see how the officers and crews went about their "monotonous but sometimes dangerous job" of keeping the port safe from the enemy.

Maclean's asked Thomas Raddall, a Nova Scotia writer whose first historical novel, *His Majesty's Yankees*, had just been published to favourable reviews in the *New York Times*, to cover the story for them. For Raddall the real story "was not the day's wallowing in the war channel, which made many of the passengers very sick, but the denouement after our return to the dockyard, which sickened us all. Navy PR refused to answer even routine questions; when he did make one or two quibbling replies, the [navy] intelligence offi-cer cut in and said we mustn't use this and we mustn't mention that." After one too many evasive answers, Raddall had finally had enough, and walked out.

"Are you doing this story for *Maclean's*?" someone asked.

"No, certainly not," he replied.

"Why don't you do an article on navy censorship?" one of the CBC reporters suggested.

Raddall was tempted, but why waste the effort? "I knew it would never get printed," he would later say. Instead, he wrote to the editors of *Maclean's*, explaining why he wouldn't be writing the article they'd asked for, and adding that "as long as this stupid policy continued to hide the tasks and doings of the Canadian navy, the rest of the world would go on thinking, as it did now, that the war in the Atlantic was being fought mainly by the U.S. navy and partly by the British navy, and with some fringe assistance by Canadian, Brazilian and other little tinpot outfits that didn't really matter much."

Raddall, who knew that letters addressed to newspapers and magazines were routinely opened by the mail censor to make sure they contained no official secrets, wasn't surprised to get a call from the navy's chief public relations officer a few days after he sent his letter to *Maclean's*.

"How's the *Maclean's* story coming together?" the PR man asked solicitously.

"I guessed that he had my letter in front of him," Raddall would later write. "In case he hadn't, I repeated my remarks and said I'd heard the words and music of 'Hush-hush-hush, Here Comes the Bogeyman' when I was a child and I didn't like it any more now than I did then."

The PR man said nothing. There was really nothing to say.

CHAPTER SIX

1944
– Vindication, VD and Planning for V-Day –

They didn't look much like Nazis in their nineteenth-century Scottish kilts and busbies, but that didn't matter to Harold Masterman or Lawrence Perry, his next-door neighbour and best friend. They could fill up hours around the train table in Harold's basement firing pencils from the gun tubes of their spring-loaded tanks at the soldiers they'd carefully lined up across the table.

The train table, a converted Ping-Pong table, had belonged to the O'Byrnes' son. Mr. O'Byrne had designed and built it, complete with three tracks looping in and out around the perimeter, electric trains, a papier mâché mountain, a small village complete with buildings and an impressive collection of toy soldiers to defend it. After Harold came to live with them, Mr. O'Byrne said they were his.

Harold had become so enamoured of Junior's toy soldiers that the O'Byrnes had begun buying him additional sets for birthdays and Christmases. Sometimes his stepsister Mary would take him on the tram to the five-and-dime on Gottingen Street to pick out the soldiers he wanted. They were all carefully hand-painted and came in boxes of a dozen soldiers each. Harold liked to save the elastics that were looped over the soldiers to keep them in their places and use them for slingshots.

Since Junior's soldiers had been hand-painted in Japan before the war, his Scottish soldiers looked vaguely Japanese. Or so Harold imagined. He and Lawrence made them the enemy—sometimes the Nazis, usually the Japanese—and fired at them with their tanks, or used Harold's soldiers to knock them down.

In the basement, the good guys always won.

IT WAS TIME to leave this city. There were many memories here, but too few worth remembering. First Thane, now Jim. Marjory Whitelaw knew how Molly Hunt must have felt. Jim Clarkson had not told Marjory he was breaking up with her; he had simply stopped coming round. And then, without warning, she'd learned he was marrying an old flame from a time before either her or Molly. Two weeks later he was married and gone, off to Europe to fight, without so much as a word of explanation or goodbye. Now, Marjory was left alone in her garret with only her memories. This wasn't nearly as romantic as she had imagined it would be. She was just lonely, sitting on the bed in her apartment tonight. And cold. Very cold.

She'd moved into this tiny attic apartment on South Street last fall. The building was owned by the sister of the city's most notorious landlady. Lottie Frame had been in and out of court—and in and out of the newspapers—many times to face charges for everything from overcharging tenants to failing to provide adequate heat. Marjory had heard that Mrs. Frame would sometimes sneak into her tenants' apartments while they were out and use their stoves for cooking so she wouldn't have to run up her own electricity bill. The last time Mrs. Frame had been in court—she'd faced eleven separate charges of gouging—Judge R.E. Inglis fined her twenty dollars on the first charge and forty dollars for each of the others. The Prices and Trade Board, which had asked for a fine of $1,000 on each charge because she was such a flagrant violator, appealed, but Marjory hadn't seen anything in the newspapers about the outcome. Not that it mattered; everyone knew the fines were simply a licensing fee. There were, according to one report she'd seen, thirteen thousand people looking for rooms in Halifax. Most would willingly and quietly have paid more than the officially posted rent just to have a roof over their heads.

Marjory was lucky. For some reason, her landlady charged only five dollars a week for this garret. Marjory had been living on her own ever since Barbara Eaton left town for a better job in Moncton, two years ago. That was around the time Marjory too changed jobs. The mother of one of her friends had told her the Children's Hospital was looking for a receptionist, so she applied and got the job. It paid $90 a month, $30 more than she'd got for counting fish for the government, but she had lots more responsibility, too. The Children's, on Morris Street near the Victoria General Hospital, was a small, eighty-bed infirmary for kids, so Marjory ended up doing everything from admitting patients to handling the accounts to preparing salary cheques. For the first few months, she lived in the hospital's nurses' residence but quickly found the matron's Victorian regulations too restrictive. Even though she wasn't a nurse, Marjory was expected to abide by their rules, which meant she couldn't get married without permission of the matron, and if she did receive permission to get engaged, she would have had to sign a paper agreeing not to sleep with her husband-to-be before the marriage. She didn't stay long.

Marjory's landlady turned out to be not quite so notorious as her sister, but she was not much more accommodating, either. Marjory's apartment had been advertised as furnished, but the furnishings consisted of one lumpy bed and a small table. There was a small pot-bellied stove in the kitchen—the only heat in the apartment—but it was hard to obtain wood to burn in it. Marjory had had to depend on friends with cars to bring her occasional bundles of wood from the country. When it was cold, she stayed away from the apartment as long as possible—went to a movie or had a snack at Norman's—then came home and crawled quickly into bed, burying herself under the covers and trying to sleep.

She should do that now. She looked across the room to the kitchen sink and couldn't help but recall pleasant evenings not that long ago, when Jim would be standing by that sink, holding a book in one hand while he helped her wash the dishes.

Marjory had come to Halifax just four years ago in search of adventure, romance and the chance to dance until dawn. Instead, she'd found monotony, heartache and disillusionment. Wartime romance, like the city itself, had turned out to be shabby around the edges. She blinked back the tears.

It really was time to leave this town, go home to Montreal.

IT WAS ALMOST as if none of it had ever happened. When Dorothy Hendsbee finally returned to Halifax in early April, her job was gone. "You signed an agreement," the man in the front office reminded her. "Remember?" She had, and she did. The agreement she and the rest of the Electric Five signed when they began work at the Halifax Shipyards last June was explicit. Their jobs as welders would last only until male veterans returned to reclaim them. Sometime during the three months she'd been recuperating from pneumonia at her mother's in Half Island Cove, a male veteran had come home and taken her job. And no, the man said, he didn't know where Bertha or the others were. There were lots of veterans back from the war now, he explained matter-of-factly, and they needed work.

Dorothy had had no choice but to return to live with her old-maid cousins while she looked for another job. That made her sense of déjà vu more acute—and her desire to find a job more urgent. Within two weeks she found one, but it was a comedown from welding. She would be a waitress, serving customers at the lunch counter in Simpson's, the big department store in the city's west end. The pay, eleven dollars a week, was the living allowance she'd earned a year ago during her welding training. Somehow, it didn't seem nearly as much any more.

JEFF JEFFERSON CHUCKLED. The *Chronicle* had telephoned to ask him to render his censor's judgment on a story it wanted to publish about a fifteen-minute brawl on Spring Garden Road the night before between some army and navy men. As far as Jefferson was concerned, this was the best news he'd heard in months. And not because the Shore Patrol and provost officers had arrived quickly to quell the "affray . . . The war has been entirely too ladylike around Halifax," he wrote in his diary. "Fighting between the services is a sure sign of victory, and when they get around to joining forces and trying to burn the city hall, as they did in 1918, we shall know for certain that we are in the VICTORY YEAR."

As a reporter, Jefferson had covered those riots at the end of the Great War. A lawless mob of servicemen, fed up with service life and eager to be discharged, had gone on a rampage through the downtown, wrecking nine shops and causing $20,000 worth of damage. It had been quite a party, Jefferson recalled. There were rumours—he had certainly heard them—that some sailors were planning a similar spree when this war finally ended.

Jefferson passed the "affray" story with the mildest of admonitions to the *Chronicle* editors that the "army versus navy feature shall not be too strongly played up."

NOT EVERYONE BELIEVED the increasing lawlessness on city streets was a matter to cheer about, or even to take lightly. Bob Rankin, the *Herald*'s managing editor, certainly didn't. Drunken sailors had taken over his downtown. They openly cursed at passersby, and made lewd comments to unescorted females doing nothing more provocative than walking along the street minding their own business. On payday nights some of these louts had even taken to randomly smashing out plate glass windows in Barrington Street shops, seemingly just for the sport of it. They'd made city streets so inhospitable, even dangerous, that decent folk were telling him they hesitated to venture out of their homes at night.

Rankin, who'd served in the army himself during World War I, believed the real problem was the increasingly lax discipline among the younger navy recruits. Instilling and enforcing discipline was the responsibility of their senior officers, up to and including—perhaps especially including—Rear Admiral Leonard Murray.

If George Jones were still running the show, Rankin would have had no hesitation in taking up these concerns with him. During Jones's tenure as the commander of naval forces in Halifax, he and the Commodore had become friends. Jones would often take Rankin into his confidence, and Rankin in turn kept Jones apprised of anything happening in the city that the head of the navy should know about.

But Jones's successor, Len Murray, was a different sort. At first Rankin had done his best to court Murray, but his efforts were invariably rebuffed. Their occasional encounters in public were now awkward, even embarrassing.

It might have been as simple as the fact that Murray didn't like, or trust, journalists. He once confessed to a friend that the "closest I ever came to panic" was in London early in the war, when a PR man at Canada House convinced him to take part in a daily briefing at Britain's Ministry of Information. As he described the situation to a friend: "I had been stacked up against the international news gatherers who might not be as kindly disposed to a trusting naval officer as would those who were naturally on our side." His belief that the press was "them" to the navy's "us" undoubtedly made Murray reluctant to exchange confidences with a newspaper editor. Rankin came to believe Murray actually hated the press, and he had to admit he eventually came to hate Murray back.

He wasn't the only one. "Murray was one of those kind of guys people either liked greatly to disliked greatly," Eric Dennis would say later. While Eric himself liked the Admiral and found him reasonable to deal with, Brian O'Connell, a reporter for the competing *Chronicle*, thought Murray was "aloof and uncomfortable with the press," and that the navy he ran, perhaps not surprisingly, "regarded all newsmen as a cut above Hitler but not one whit superior to Goebbels."

If Murray had few friends in the media, his relations with the local civilian establishment were just as frosty. While the Murrays entertained frequently, their guests were usually visiting naval officers rather than members of the local gentry. As was the case with the naval establishment, much of the local antagonism to the Admiral stemmed from a dislike of his wife, Jean. "The Murrays were unpopular," allowed one society hostess, "mainly because of her." Jean was dismissive of locals, whom she referred to as "parochial peasants." At a time when the government was rationing gasoline and calling for personal sacrifices from the civilian population, Mrs. Murray was frequently spotted driving around the city dressed in one of her two mink coats, using her husband's chauffeured car to shop for herself or do errands. The locals were not amused.

This was all part of the larger divide between the navy and the city. The antagonism between the two, conceded Mayor Jack Lloyd, "seemed to be strong and mutual." It only worsened as the war came closer to an end. The discipline that danger had brought to everyday life in Halifax began to diminish. Ordinary citizens became less tolerant of the military's dominance of their city, sailors less willing to put up with the privations they had been required to endure.

Little had improved during the five years of the war, and much had noticeably deteriorated. The lack of adequate housing had become so critical that E.L. Cousins, the Wartime Housing Act administrator for Halifax, had recently announced plans to put signs in every Canadian railway station warning people to stay away from Halifax except on official business. The National Film Board had released a new documentary featuring scenes of sailors and their wives sitting on their luggage in the streets of Halifax because they had no place to live. And although there was now a wet canteen at the Navy League Recreation Centre at the Wanderers Grounds, there were still far too few welcoming places for an ordinary sailor or soldier to go for a drink, or for relaxation and recreation.

So they made their own fun. And the situation was much worse now even than two years ago, when Judge Flinn had issued his "this must stop" proclamation from the bench. Street fights pitted soldiers against sailors. Gravestone toppling had become a popular pastime. And window smashing was now so common that insurance companies refused to provide coverage to businesses in some parts of the city. As a result, some storefronts had been permanently boarded over with sheets of plywood.

Petty vandalism escalated into petty theft—and worse. The week after Jefferson wrote approvingly of the "affray" between soldiers and sailors, Rankin's newspaper carried reports of a "crime wave" sweeping the city, and complained that the city police force—now a collection mostly of raw recruits and superannuated veterans because so many former members were overseas—simply couldn't cope with the criminal element. A few weeks later, on April 29, the paper editorialized: "Day after day, and night after night, the safety of citizens in the streets of the city becomes less certain . . . People are robbed and beaten; houses entered and robbed; business premises are looted—but there is a marked shortage of arrests and there are still fewer convictions."

Publicly, Rankin's newspaper defended the navy. In an April 27 editorial the *Herald* claimed citizens should be proud of the "magnificent manner" in which the navy had been doing its job. "Mistakes and shortcomings have been few," it noted, adding pointedly: "No one familiar with the facts has anything but impatience at the small minds that snipe at the navy."

Privately, however, Rankin was far less sanguine. In early May he invited two young navy officers—the local public relations officer and the head of the Shore Patrol—to his office for an "informal conference" to discuss the problems as he saw them. He was being inundated with complaints from readers about the "shore activities" of naval personnel, he pointed out, and they were demanding "that the newspapers should have something to say about the matter on behalf of the people of this community." Just that morning, he told them, he'd had a call from Bill Schwartz, the owner of a coffee and spice import firm in the city's north end, who'd reported naval personnel had broken a number of windows in his Barrington Street plant the night before. What did the navy plan to do to deal with this sort of objectionable behaviour?

The officers' answers were far from satisfactory. The Shore Patrol officer even allowed he wouldn't want his wife to walk alone on Barrington Street after 10 p.m., which Rankin took as "pretty good evidence he did not consider the streets safe." But while they'd received plenty of complaints themselves, the officers said, there was little they could do about them. Though they didn't explain, Rankin took that to mean that the navy's higher-ups—and Murray in particular—didn't see the issue as a priority concern.

As the meeting broke up, Rankin warned them that if the navy couldn't control its own men, "it might be necessary for us to take a hand in calling [publicly] for protection [from Ottawa]."

A few days later Rankin got a phone call, not from Admiral Murray, as he might have expected, but from the mayor. And not to say that the problems would be dealt with, but to let him know that the navy was warning the mayor that if the *Herald* went ahead with a story on the sailors' lack of discipline, the navy "did not propose to accept responsibility for what might transpire following publication."

Rankin was livid. He called the navy officer who'd called Mayor Lloyd, a Captain Armstrong, berating him for going over his head "and advising him that anytime he had anything to discuss with the Halifax *Herald*, it would be a matter of courtesy to communicate direct with the Halifax *Herald*." When Armstrong replied that he'd been "instructed" to call the mayor, Rankin knew better than to ask who'd done the instructing. Murray. He simply reiterated his point that the newspaper was the place to call to talk about material that might be planned for publication, adding sarcastically that Armstrong should "convey my compliments to whoever had instructed him."

Since he had Armstrong on the line—and he was sure Armstrong would pass on the gist of their conversation to his superior—Rankin took the opportunity to pursue his case.

"Are the men of the RCN not taught discipline?" he demanded.

Armstrong's casual, almost offhand reply shocked him. "They don't know the meaning of the word, sir."

"What about respect for the uniform they wear? Surely they are at least taught that."

"There's no time for that either, sir," Armstrong explained as patiently as he could. "All the recruits are desperately needed for service, and there isn't time between the time they sign up and the time they go to sea to teach them everything they need to know."

Rankin couldn't believe what he was hearing. "That's a pretty sad picture," he said. "If the navy can't even control its own men while they're in service, imagine how terrible it will be when this war is over."

Armstrong, it was clear, had thought about that. "I hate to think, sir," he replied.

Shortly after this unsatisfactory exchange with Captain Armstrong, Rankin sat down to write a "personal and confidential" letter to his old friend Vice Admiral George Jones, now the Chief of Naval Staff in Ottawa. After laying out the problems and his unsuccessful efforts to get the navy to deal with them, Rankin concluded, "I thought it might be of interest to you to have the background which this letter contains."

It was. Three days later Jones wrote back a "personal and confidential" reply, thanking Rankin for "bringing the matter of the conduct of the naval ratings in Halifax to my attention. Unfortunately, I am out of direct touch with the situation now. However, I am giving the matter my personal attention and will have somebody there before the end of the week to look things over quietly to see what can be done."

Jones didn't ask Admiral Murray to respond to Rankin's complaints. In fact, Murray wouldn't even know Rankin had written such a letter—or that his nemesis had dispatched a junior officer to investigate the conduct of his command—until a year later.

Ironically, just three days before Rankin's letter to Jones,

Murray himself had issued a memo complaining that the discipline "situation has steadily been deteriorating" and ordering his officers to smarten up the sailors. In a follow-up memo a month later, Murray praised the fact that "considerable smartening up has taken place," but added there was still room "for much improvement in the general smartness and appearance of naval officers and men."

While the Allies' recent successes—in both the Battle of the Atlantic and the land war in Europe—had finally given Murray the opportunity to focus more on "parade ground and polish" instead of simply trying to instill some battle discipline as quickly as possible in the masses of raw recruits who passed through his hands, shore discipline was still far from the top of his priority list.

JANET PIERS AND HER DAUGHTER had spent the day visiting with her parents on Young Avenue. A few after minutes after Janet's father disappeared upstairs to his study to listen to the news, they heard him calling urgently to them. "Jannie! Anne!" Murray Macneill shouted. "Come up here and listen to this."

The news broadcast was almost over when they got to his study. It seemed, as far as Janet could understand it, that British and Canadian forces had landed on the beaches of Normandy, in France, and were attacking German forces there.

"This is it," Murray Macneill announced grandly. "This is the one." He'd wanted them to hear history in the making.

Janet couldn't concern herself with history. She could think only of Debby. Was he there? Was he all right?

CASE CLOSED.

The Johnson murder-suicide mystery that had gripped all of Halifax last December sputtered to a sudden, unexpected and most unsatisfactory end on July 12, 1944, when police finally found a man's body at the bottom of the Northwest Arm, just two hundred feet from the spot where Nadia Johnson's body had been recovered seven months earlier. Police weren't sure at first that this body was Frank Johnson's. The face and lower jawbone were gone, along with both hands and feet, and the body was badly decomposed. But what remained of the remains, which had been weighted down with fourteen pounds of shale rock stuffed into the pockets of a blue gabardine overcoat, was still clothed in grey flannel trousers. The coat and pants matched the description neighbours had given of the clothes worn by a man they'd seen paddling a red canoe near the Johnson boathouse that day. There were no identification papers on the body, but the other items recovered from the coat pockets—"six undischarged large calibre pistol shells [and] 35 British, Canadian and U.S.A coins of small value"—also pointed to Johnson. More telling, police found laundry tags on some of the clothing. Chief of Detectives Baker quickly traced them to a local laundry. Its records indicated the clothing belonged to a Commander Johnson.

Case closed.

Under the headline JOHNSON CASE CONSIDERED SOLVED BY CITY POLICE, Eric Dennis's story the next morning began: "Halifax City Police were ready last night to close their books on the 'Johnson case.'" But there remained some unanswered questions. What was Johnson burning that night in his fireplace? Had Johnson, as Baker originally hinted to Dennis, been fiddling the books? Had Vava, or Frank, or both, been spies? And even if Johnson was a thief or a spy, why had he decided he had to murder his own daughter?

The police weren't saying. Case closed.

The Royal Navy wasn't much help either. Despite an announcement in December 1943 that it planned to conduct internal inquiries into Johnson's disappearance, naval authorities now seemed eager to put all the unpleasantness behind them. Two days after the body was recovered, it was buried—with full naval honours—in Halifax's historic Camp Hill cemetery, a few feet from where Nadia had been laid to rest seven months earlier. Hundreds of curious Haligonians once again lined the perimeter of the burial grounds to catch a glimpse of the flag-draped grey casket containing what remained of the mysterious British officer who—inexplicably still, and perhaps forever—had murdered his daughter and then taken his own life. High-ranking British officers, along with hundreds of dragooned naval ratings, attended the brief service: two verses of the hymn "Eternal Father, Strong to Save," a three-volley salute and a lone bugler's rendition of the "Last Post." There were a number of floral wreaths at the gravesite. The most interesting, to Eric Dennis at least, was marked, *From Vava.*

Vava Johnson was indeed still alive. She'd been transferred from the Welfare Island State Hospital to the Manhattan State Hospital for the Insane. Eric spoke to Arthur Wills, the family friend who'd taken responsibility for Vava's care after Johnson disappeared. Her recovery had been slow, he told Eric—"She lives entirely in the present"—but she was making progress. She'd finally been told that her husband and daughter were gone. When he told her, Wills said, she was "terribly shaken but not entirely surprised. Naturally," he added, "I did not tell her the details."

The details? What were the real details? No one could—or would—tell Eric that. Like plenty of others in Halifax at the time, Eric wondered if there was more to the story than he'd been told. For a while he even hoped to find time to get back to it. But he never did. In a city at war, there were always too many stories and too little time.

Case closed.

The details of the Johnson case, or at least the ones police and military investigators pieced together after the incident, were not what Chief of Detectives Baker had suggested to Eric Dennis. According to a report that remained locked away in city police files for decades, investigators concluded that Vava Johnson had been a spy and that her husband was either her willing accomplice or a dupe. According to their report, Vava had copied some of Commander Johnson's confidential documents and taken them with her to New York to turn over to her spymasters. During his visits with her at the hospital after the accident, police surmised, Johnson some-how discovered he'd been compromised. He returned to Halifax, burned the originals, murdered his daughter and then killed himself.

SITTING QUIETLY on the platform, listening to the other speakers and waiting, less and less patiently, for his own turn to address the crowd, Halifax mayor Jack Lloyd knew he had to say what had been on his mind for months now.

The Department of Health had organized this day-long conference of a hundred or so provincial police chiefs, heads of social service organizations, health officers, armed forces representatives and family doctors, ostensibly to talk about how to combat an epidemic of venereal disease in Nova Scotia. But it had degenerated into an orgy of self-congratulation and smug self-satisfaction.

Nova Scotia's "intensive" campaign against venereal disease had been fought with "vigour, imagination and drive"; the results had been "highly gratifying," not to mention "remarkable," and so on and so on. Even Eliot Ness, director of the U.S. government's Social Protective Division of the Federal Security Agency, who had been brought in from Washington as the keynote speaker, declared that Nova Scotia had "a fine record in meeting the menace," and that, if the police and provincial authorities continued to co-operate in such a fine manner, venereal disease would be practically "wiped out" in the province within two years.

Lloyd wondered how Ness knew that. And did he know about the military's quarantine station, which had been operating on Lawlor's Island in the middle of Halifax harbour since the spring of 1941? At any given moment there were as many as ninety soldiers and sailors being treated for venereal diseases there.

Ness was a famous lawman, of course, the G-man who'd created the Untouchables and put legendary gangster Al Capone away for tax evasion in the early thirties. But it had been more than a dozen years since Ness's glory days, and there were those who would tell you Ness had spent most of the intervening time—first as

Cleveland's Director of Public Safety, and now with the government's security agency in Washington—trading on his crime-fighting reputation. And partying. Ness had a reputation for living well. Lloyd had even heard rumours—nothing specific, of course—that Ness had spent the evening before today's conference "enjoying" the city's underground nightlife.

Not that Lloyd disagreed with much that Ness said, except for his presumptions about the state of Nova Scotia's fight against VD. In fact, there was much that Lloyd liked about what Ness had to say, especially when he talked about the "great political interference" and attacks from "financial interests" he'd faced in the U.S. as he tried to convince local officials to stamp out red-light districts in American cities.

Lloyd wasn't the only one who had taken special note of those remarks. In his own speech Premier MacMillan had felt compelled to argue that there had been no political interference in Nova Scotia, emphasizing that "any measures to erase law-breaking will not be interfered with."

Then it was Lloyd's turn. He began carefully enough, thanking the province and the minister of health, Dr. Davis, for organizing the gathering, and welcoming all the distinguished guests on the platform: Ness, the premier, Len Murray and the other heads of the local military establishment, RCMP Commissioner Eames, Michael Morrisey, the president of the International Association of Police Chiefs, and W.G. Dixon, a consultant to the federal health department's Division of Venereal Disease Control in Ottawa. He was careful not to downplay the success of local efforts to combat VD, and he praised the premier, his health minister and the RCMP for their co-operation with his officials. "No stone has been left unturned to wipe out venereal disease in Halifax." And yet . . . And yet he too was under enormous pressure, he told his audience bitterly, to go easy in the campaign against this scourge. "Such pressure comes to me from politicians right here in Halifax," he declared. "'You can't close this place [they say]. They spend four hundred dollars a month for groceries alone.' That's the kind of thing I heard when we tried to make a cleanup. You'd be surprised," he said at last, "at the various business angles that are tied up with it."

Afterwards, a few people came up to congratulate him on his forthrightness. Others studiously avoided him. He was—and wasn't—surprised to see that the next day's *Herald* quoted only his upbeat comments on co-operation. The sole newspaper to deal directly with his criticism of the local political and business establishment was a small labour weekly known as the *Citizen*. The editorial in that paper repeated the mayor's claim that local brothels managed to survive "because they're good for business and votes." In a stinging editorial the paper asked: "Why doesn't that same group of politicians and businessmen who drove the Ajax Club from Tobin Street—acknowledged as the best-conducted service club in all of Canada—get busy to close down the venereal-infected dives and whore houses protected by business and political pressure as so declared by the Mayor of Halifax?"

The Ajax Club might have been long gone, but it—as well as those who forced it to close—was still far from forgotten.

"NEVER BEFORE HAVE I been where the skies were more blue and brighter, or when the invincible march of our forces has been more swiftly and inevitably directed toward its goal," the familiar voice began. The exuberant crowd instantly hushed as one. It was pure Winnie, Eric Dennis thought, watching the great man speak from the train platform.

Even before the *Queen Mary*, carrying Winston Churchill, had tied up at Pier 20, men, women and children began gathering behind the fences along the prohibited areas near the Ocean Terminals to catch a glimpse of their hero.

The British prime minister, dressed in his familiar tugboat captain's semi-naval sea cap and blue jacket with the gold buttons, didn't disappoint them with his waves and his victory salutes as he and his party walked behind the protective fencing from the dock to the waiting train. When he reached his private car, Churchill turned to a local official and gestured back towards the cheering crowd, 1,500 or more strong now. "Bring 'em down," he shouted. "Let them come down." The multitude didn't need a second invitation. They surged past startled, scarlet-clad Mounties and military security officers, and flocked around Churchill, who stood on the rear platform of the train, smiling and rolling his cigar in the fingers of his right hand.

The crowd, led by a local businessman, serenaded Churchill and his wife with a chorus of "It's a Long Way to Tipperary." "Can you sing 'O Canada' for me?" Churchill asked. Of course they could. And "The Maple Leaf" too. And "Land of Hope and Glory." Churchill beat time with his hands, Eric wrote in his notebook, and joined in singing the choruses. When the crowd began to sing "When the Lights Go On Again," he could see tears in Churchill's eyes. Could the British prime minister be thinking, Eric wondered, of the news that in less than a week, on the night of September 17, the lights of London were scheduled to be turned on again for the first time in five years?

"Mr. Churchill," someone asked when the song ended, "if we are perfectly quiet, would you consent to say a few words?"

The British prime minister didn't need a second invitation. This was not his first visit to Halifax, he told the throng, "but it is the first time I have been accorded such a welcome." The future, he said, was as positive as the crowd. "We are sitting on top of the world and we shall go on to a victorious end," he told them. The crowd cheered some more. Churchill waved again.

The signs of that victorious end were everywhere now. A year ago Eric hadn't even been allowed to write about Churchill's stopovers until the prime minister and his party were safely back in England. And somewhere along the line "An East Coast Port" had morphed back into Halifax again.

During the past few months, the *Herald* had been full of now-it-can-be-told stories from the early, dark days of the war. There was the tale of the attempted scuttling of the French luxury liner *Pasteur* in Halifax harbour in 1940. After France fell to the Germans, the ship tied up in Halifax harbour to await orders. Pro-Nazi crew members, fearing the *Pasteur* would be turned over to the Allies, damaged the engines and destroyed all the ship's electrical and other charts to make it difficult to repair and maintain her. They had been about to open the seacocks to fill the ship with water and make their escape when an armed RCN boarding party took command of the ship and arrested the crew. Police discovered at least one benzine-filled bottle that would have been used to blow up the vessel. The *Pasteur*, "saved from destruction," as the *Herald* put it, "went back to sea for the United Nations in a new war role."

While most such disclosures were intended to honour, after the fact, the heroic deeds of members of the armed forces—like Lieutenant Commander D.G. Jeffrey, "DSO, former columnist of the Halifax *Mail*" and head of the *Pasteur* boarding party, who bravely took control of the ship "not knowing all the time whether or not bombs had been planted in the ship to prevent it from falling into Allied hands"—some of the revelations had a purpose with respect to the ongoing war effort.

In July, the federal Department of Munitions and Supply announced that, at some unspecified point in the war, stocks of petroleum products for civilian and military use in Halifax had fallen so low that there had been enough for only three days of critical operations. Despite the recent positive news on the war front, the department was quick to add, "the availability of gasoline and fuel oil for Canada [is] still in the critical stage," and it released a blizzard of statistics to make Nova Scotians think twice before turning up the heat or travelling that extra mile. While Canadians had saved 568 million gallons of petroleum products since conservation began in 1941, the country's European invasion forces were swallowing 25 million gallons *a week* as they pushed their way towards Germany and victory. During the year-long pre-invasion air bombing campaign in Europe, more than 200 million gallons—"enough to run every AA car in Canada for more than five years"—had disappeared into thin air. Refuelling a single Canadian destroyer took enough fuel to heat the average home for 350 years.

The message was simple: it was not yet the time to begin celebrating.

But that certainly wasn't the mood at the CNR station today. When a dining-car conductor came out to offer Churchill a copy of yesterday's *Mail*, the prime minister held up the headline to the cheering crowd. ALLIES HAMMERING WAY TOWARD SIEGFRIED LINE, it declared. Churchill beamed.

When someone in the crowd jokingly demanded, "How about the nickel, Mr. Churchill?" he pointed to the newspaper and retorted: "This is lend-lease." The crowd roared its approval.

"How many cigars do you smoke a day?" a man asked.

"That depends on how big they are."

And then finally it was time for the British leader and his party to leave. Churchill was on his way to Quebec City for yet another meeting with Roosevelt, this one to discuss what the newspapers called "the changed military situation" in Europe and review their previous formulas for "unconditional surrender . . . not with a view to make things easier for a beaten enemy but to define its meaning in more detail so hostilities can be ended with the least sacrifice of life."

As the train pulled out of the station with Churchill still waving and making his V for Victory signs, Eric imagined that Hollywood couldn't have devised a farewell more moving, more dramatic. He'd have to remember to include that sentiment in his story for tomorrow.

JUST OVER A WEEK after Churchill and his party departed Halifax in triumph, Mayor Jack Lloyd called a meeting of civic and military officials to begin planning local events to celebrate the now seemingly imminent victory of the Allied forces over Hitler's Nazis.

The week before, U.S. soldiers had plowed through the Siegfried Line, a chain of forts and tank defences built during the First World War along the border between France and Germany, and they were now advancing hard on Berlin. The war in Europe, British Field Marshal Sir Bernard Montgomery confidently predicted to reporters, would be "all over" before the end of 1944, a forecast that was set in headline type in the *Mail* on September 20, the day after the mayor's first meeting to plan what everyone was beginning to call V-Day or, more properly, VE-Day celebrations.

At the meeting, they discussed the possibility of thanksgiving church services, a civic parade through the streets and an evening "pyrotechnic display" in the harbour—and even appointed a committee headed by Civil Defence Director Osborne R. Crowell to oversee the planning. But the real focus of the meeting seemed to be less on how to celebrate than on how to keep the celebrations from getting out of hand. Local business leaders in particular wanted to know "what protection the armed services could give against damage." Their concern was understandable. Rumours had circulated almost from the beginning of the war that disgruntled sailors intended to "take Halifax apart" when the conflict finally ended. And memories of the 1918 disorders were still strong.

A few days later, Police Chief Conrod met for the first time with the heads of the RCMP and the military police, as well as the chair of the provincial liquor commission, to discuss the matter. At that meeting, officials agreed the local liquor commission outlets as well as the military service canteens should be shut tight for the duration of whatever events the city planned, and that special precautions should be taken to make sure service personnel couldn't break in and loot the liquor stores.

The local military commanders, including Murray, got together in mid-November to follow up on these discussions. They suggested a number of ways to keep the military merrymaking from getting out of hand, including having each unit stage its own thanksgiving worship service or compulsory parade the day hostilities ended. Officers would read an agreed-upon proclamation "worded in such a manner as to discourage boisterous celebrations," and then everyone would spend the rest of V-Day in "regular service routine."

It all seemed so simple. But, like ending the war, it didn't turn out to be as straightforward as it seemed.

As 1944 closed, the war in Europe was still raging—and not just in Europe. On December 24 the minesweeper HMCS *Clayoquot* was torpedoed and sunk just five miles off the Sambro Lightship at the entrance to Halifax harbour. Eight more men had lost their lives. And Haligonians had one more reminder that the war was not yet over.

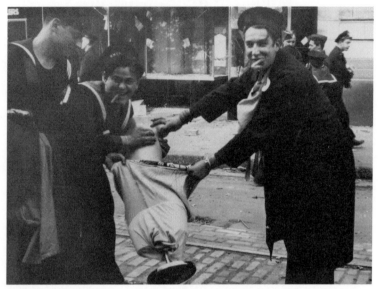

Three cigar-smoking sailors mug for the camera as they undress a stolen mannequin. (Courtesy Maritime Command Museum)

.

As the Barrington Street riot unfolds in the background, a man shows off his stolen Victory Bond poster while the sailors from the photo above show off their now naked mannequin. (Courtesy Maritime Command Museum)

Looking north along Barrington Street shortly after 4 p.m. on May 8, 1945.
(Courtesy Maritime Command Museum)

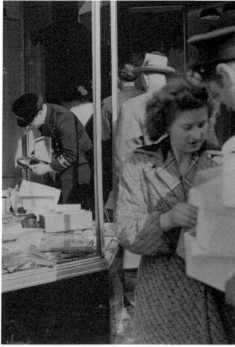

While the sailors led the riots, there were plenty of civilians, including school-children, eager to help in the looting. (Courtesy Maritime Command Museum)

Looters window-shopped their way through the devastated downtown. (Courtesy Maritime Command Museum)

Showing off their ill-gotten gain. (Courtesy Maritime Command Museum)

Making off with the spring suit collection. (Courtesy Maritime Command Museum)

Toasting the end of the war outside City Hall with cases of beer "liberated" from Keith's Brewery. (Collection of Bill Mont)

Admiral Murray's scheme to end the riots by parading his sailors through downtown streets goes horribly awry. (Collection of Bill Mont)

A sailor leads the window smashing on Hollis Street.
(Courtesy Maritime Command Museum)

The burned-out hulk of a city police patrol wagon ends up on a Halifax wharf. (Courtesy Maritime Command Museum)

.

Aftermath: Looters led into police court the next day. (Collection of Bill Mont)

CHAPTER 7

1945
– Riots and Recrimination –

For Admiral Murray's officers, the Christmas Eve sinking of the *Clayoquot* was yet another indicator of a pronounced shift in German submarine tactics. Since the Allies belatedly began providing air cover over the Black Pit and adding hunter-killer vessels to convoy escorts in 1943, the mid-Atlantic had become too dangerous for German U-boats. So, by mid-1944, the German high command was trying out an audacious new strategy: sending their submarines all the way across the Atlantic to hide out in shallow waters near the shipping lanes off the North American coast— where Allied detection systems tended to be less effective—and wait for ships to pass by. While not nearly as dramatic or devastating as attacking a convoy in mid-ocean, the new offensive, which the Allies dubbed "static tactics," showed that the Nazis weren't ready to give up on the Battle of the Atlantic. It also brought the war even closer to Halifax.

On January 4, 1945, a German U-boat sank two ships just east of Halifax, and then, ten days later, attacked a convoy on its way from Boston to Halifax. At the entrance to Halifax harbour a torpedo ripped through the hull of the merchant vessel *British Freedom*, sinking it. Fifteen minutes later the submarine struck again, this time blowing the rudder off an American cargo ship, the SS *Martin Van Buren*. The crew abandoned the vessel, which soon drifted ashore on Lobster Claw Ridge, near the Sambro Lightship.

As unfortunate as that loss might have been for the war effort, it was a bonus for those with access to boats big enough to get to the ledge. The *Van Buren* was filled with $3 million worth of cargo. While no one had any use for the locomotive the ship was ferrying to England, scavengers made short work of the rest: 350,000 cases of canned food, dehydrated potatoes, cigarettes and truck tires. For many Haligonians, the grounding of the *Van Buren* proved to be a late but welcome Christmas present.

BYRON HIMMELMAN WAS ASKING HIMSELF what the hell he was doing here, at the top of a ship's mast in the middle of a foggy night with the seas rolling, when heights scared the hell out of him. All to change a goddamn light bulb! Whatever made him think being a ship's electrician would be an easy job?

He'd been comfortably asleep when the watchman rapped on his cabin door. "Skipper wants you on the bridge," a voice announced. Byron got dressed, gathered his tools and headed up to see what was the matter.

"Mast headlight's out," the captain explained, his hand pointing skywards. "We'll need it for Boston."

Byron Himmelman had finally landed the job he wanted, as a ship's electrician. The *Trontolite* was heading to Venezuela to pick up a cargo of fuel oil for a convoy to Britain. The ship's regular electrician was on vacation, and Byron was available to fill in. He had gone down to Morris Goldberg's Men's Wear on Barrington Street and bought a uniform with his own money. The *Trontolite*'s captain, unlike many of his fellow merchant navy skippers, insisted his officers wear uniforms. Byron's uniform cost him $135, a not inconsiderable chunk out of his first month's lieutenant's pay of $235. But he wasn't complaining; he was finally doing what he wanted.

What he didn't want was to have to climb 50 feet up a ladder welded to the mast but so narrow he couldn't put both feet on a rung at the same time. He had tried to put off the inevitable, checked the juice at the bottom of the mast. There was electricity going up the mast. Damn. It had to be the bulb. Reluctantly he began to climb, the bayonet-mount light bulb in his hand. The ship, riding high with its tanks empty, rolled from side to side in the swells near Boston. He was at the top now, stomach churning, left leg planted firmly on one rung of the ladder, right leg and left arm wrapped around the mast to steady himself while he reached out with his right arm to remove the spent bulb from its mounting.

The ship's whistle, a loud air horn on the funnel directly in front of him, sounded sharply. Byron, his nerves already frayed, felt his body jerk involuntarily. *A-r-r-r* . . . The sharpest pain he'd ever experienced exploded in his left leg, midway between the ankle and the knee. He'd somehow managed to smack it against the rung above his foothold. It stung and burned and ached all at the same time. What the hell had he done to it? He couldn't stop now; he had to finish the job. And he did, gritting his teeth against the pain.

Finally, the new bulb in place, Byron was able to lower himself gingerly down the ladder to the deck. Back inside, he pulled up his pant leg. Much of his leg below the knee was already a purplish mess. He wondered if he'd broken it. He doubted that, but he had no way of finding out: there was no doctor aboard the ship. Finally, he limped back to his cabin and tried to sleep, but the pain wouldn't let him. What in God's name had he done?

KNOCK KNOCK. Two raps on the wall, that was the signal. But it was so early—too early—and much too cold. Dorothy desperately wanted to stay under the covers just a few more minutes, but if she did, she'd have to buy her own breakfast later, or do without again. She eventually forced herself to crawl out of the hard, uncomfortable army cot Mrs. MacDonald, her landlady, passed off as a bed. Dorothy shivered. She'd slept last night, like every night this winter, wearing a pair of thick socks she'd knit herself and a heavy woollen sweater over her pyjamas. But they weren't enough to keep her warm now. Mrs. MacDonald didn't believe in wasting heat—or in allowing her tenants to cook their own food.

She'd been living at Mrs. MacDonald's since last summer, when she saw an ad to share a room in this house-turned-rooming-house on Cunard Street. Her roommate Noreen, who came from Chester, worked as a waitress in the cafeteria at the Stadacona naval base. There were ten girls altogether, mostly young and working as waitresses, or packing chocolates at Moir's, the candy factory downtown. Dorothy Cook—the other Dorothy, the one who'd just rapped twice on her wall—was a clerk in a grocery store on Robie Street.

Dorothy Cook had a hot plate in her room. She wasn't supposed to. Mrs. MacDonald's rules: *No cooking in the rooms.* Mrs. MacDonald had all sorts of rules. The girls had to be in the house each night by eleven because that's when she locked the doors. If you weren't in by eleven, you spent the night on the street. And, needless to say, the girls weren't permitted to have men in their rooms.

Dorothy had a steady boyfriend now, an army provost officer named Reg Lutz whom she'd met through her cousin Lloyd. They'd been dating only a few months when he showed up unannounced at the lunch counter one day. "Come with me," he'd said. "I want to show you something." He led her over to Simpson's jewellery counter. He showed her a diamond ring. "Do you like this one?" he asked. "Yes," she answered. She didn't look at any others, not knowing what to look for. She did see the price tag, though. Fifty dollars. That was a lot of money, she thought. "OK," he told the clerk, "I'll take it."

It hadn't been like in any of the movies she'd seen. There was no music. No bended knee. No grand embrace. No tears of joy. But she and Reg were now engaged. They planned to marry this summer. However, that seemed a long way away this morning, when Dorothy could see her breath even in her cold bedroom.

For now, the Dorothys and the other girls each paid Mrs. MacDonald four dollars a week for little more than an army cot with rarely changed sheets in a shared bedroom. They all shared a single underwear-and-nylons-festooned bathroom. Dorothy couldn't really afford to be paying more than a third of her miserly weekly salary in rent, but what choice did she have? What choice did anyone have? Halifax was even more overcrowded now than when she'd left.

Opening her bedroom door, she felt a welcome blast of semi-warm air from the central register in the downstairs hall. If only Dorothy could leave her bedroom door open at night to allow that heat to fill her room. Another one of Mrs. MacDonald's rules: *Bedroom doors must be kept closed at all times.*

After toast and tea, Dorothy would return to her chilly room, dress as quickly as she could and begin the mile-long walk to Simpson's. Along the way, she'd remember the good times back at the Shipyards, the camaraderie of the Electric Five . . . She liked the other Dorothy. And Reg, of course, though she wasn't sure she was in love with him. How would she know? On Sundays when Reg had to work, she and the other Dorothy would sometimes treat themselves to a dinner they couldn't afford at Lohnes's, and share a few hours of gossipy girl talk about men and makeup and movie stars. But it wasn't the same as with Bertha and the rest of the welding crew. She missed them, missed being a pioneer, missed being a cog in the Allied war effort.

She tried to put it out of her mind, and most of the time she succeeded. But, sometimes, like today, on the walk to her not nearly as well paid, not nearly as satisfying job at the lunch counter, Dorothy remembered the times that were gone forever.

ON MARCH 19, Lieutenant Commander Reg Wood, the officer in charge of the navy's Shore Patrol in Halifax, flew to Ottawa for two days of meetings with his fellow naval police heads from across the country. The purpose: to figure out how to cope with the expected "boisterous" VE-Day celebrations and "make preparations against breakage of windows, overturning of vehicles and the customary forms of property damage occasioned by mass celebrations." Perhaps the group's most significant decision was that the naval police forces would not patrol the streets "but be held in reserve to answer calls of an emergency nature and then travel in strong units to the point of disturbance."

Back in Halifax, Woods—with Murray's approval—sent a memo to each member of the Shore Patrol, pointing out that the force's primary role on VE-Day would be to "try and control naval personnel rather than restrict them . . . No person is to be apprehended . . . unless absolutely necessary and it cannot be stressed too strongly that the success of the patrol on V-Day will rely solely on tact . . . Apprehending a rating on this day . . . may be the cause of a serious riot."

Three hundred copies of the memo were printed and distributed, even though there were only 233 Shore Patrol officers. There would later be suggestions that some copies fell into the hands of those who regarded the warning to the Shore Patrol as an invitation to them.

BYRON HIMMELMAN FINALLY ARRIVED back in Halifax on March 25, 1945, more than two months after he'd finally got his wish and been allowed to set sail as the electrician aboard the *Trontolite*. Now he'd had more than enough of life at sea. As soon as the ship docked, Byron headed straight to the office of Dr. Koch, the port doctor, in the immigration shed at Pier 21. He was scared.

The leg he'd injured while changing the light bulb early in the trip had not healed. In fact, it had become much worse. There were now three nasty nickel-sized sores just below his knee that wouldn't heal, each one oozing pus from under the scab. He'd already been to see one doctor in Caripito, the Venezuelan port where the *Trontolite* picked up its cargo of oil, and another in Boston on the trip north. Both had recommended amputation.

At first Dr. Koch seemed to agree with the previous diagnoses. Then he paused, looked again at the puzzling bruising and scabbing, and glanced up at Byron. "But why don't we try and save the leg first."

Byron Himmelman exhaled slowly. He had almost come to terms with the idea he would lose his leg. Almost.

"I'm not promising anything," Dr. Koch was quick to caution. "But it's worth a try. I've got some ointment I'll give you. Get the nurse to make you a couple of appointments for next week. We'll apply the ointment and see how you're doing then."

BOB SUTHERLAND WAS PLANNING to celebrate Victory Day by staging the biggest, most exciting party in town. Unlike the organizers of the city's official celebrations, whose main interest seemed to be figuring out how to keep the partying from getting out of hand, Sutherland wanted the Knights of Columbus to stage a dance that truly suited the joyousness of the moment. He'd been working with Mrs. Yell, the Club's hostess-chaperone, to make sure there would be hundreds of local girls on hand that night, supplemented by girls from the local ranks of the Women's Army Corps. He and his boss, Hughie Creagen, had been calling on local businesses to donate door prizes and souvenirs to give out to those in attendance. The Club's chef had promised the food would be plentiful. Sutherland was most proud, however, of the fact that he'd arranged for the Stadacona Dance Band, a group Sutherland believed were every bit as good as Glenn Miller's famous Air Force Band, to provide the dance music.

All he needed now was for the Germans to surrender.

IF SUTHERLAND'S GOAL was to organize the best party in town for servicemen on VE-Day, Osborne Crowell seemed intent on making sure party-goers would have no fun whatsoever.

Crowell's civic VE-Day Committee had been meeting since last September. While it had come up with a range of genteel events to mark the occasion, from parades and singsongs to thanksgiving services and fireworks, it seemed to want to discourage servicemen from joining the civic celebrations, by making it as inconvenient and unpleasant as possible for them to do so. There would be no tramcar service to ferry them between their bases and downtown, for example. If they did manage to get downtown, no restaurants would be open to serve them a meal. The local restaurant association had actually offered to keep its establishments open if the city would provide police protection, but the police chief said he couldn't spare any men. He told theatre owners he had no officers available for them either, so they too announced plans to shutter their box offices for VE-Day.

Arthur Mahon, the chief commissioner of the Nova Scotia Liquor Commission, didn't state his intentions publicly—and wouldn't until VE-Day dawned—but he did inform the police chief and members of Crowell's committee that all liquor stores would close on VE-Day. He'd also written to Admiral Murray and the heads of the other two services, urging them to shut down their canteens. After hasty consultations with his fellow commanders, Murray wrote back rejecting that request. He suggested that closing the liquor stores, coupled with "proper control" in the service canteens, "will go a long way towards keeping the crowds of service personnel off the streets where they might do harm to public and private property." Murray even hinted the navy might "set up singsongs and entertainment within the service establishments" to give sailors even less reason to leave their bases.

That fit nicely with Crowell's view that there should be separate celebrations for the citizens of the city and the members of the military. Police Chief Conrod had also become convinced, as a result of his meetings with military police officials, that he wouldn't have to deal with servicemen, who would be "quite happy in their respective headquarters."

The problem with all this was that no one bothered to ask the servicemen how happy they would feel to be left out of the celebration of a victory they felt was theirs.

LEONARD MURRAY KNEW he shouldn't be thinking that far ahead, yet he couldn't help considering his future.

He was exhausted. The war consumed him, fifteen hours a day, seven days a week. He'd finally had to give up playing hockey, his passion, though he was quick to point out that in his final game earlier this winter—playing defence against a Cornwallis team that boasted a former Toronto Maple Leaf named Andy Blair at centre ice—the opposition failed to score once while he was on the ice. And he was forty-nine years old.

These days, his only respite from the pressures of work was an occasional brief walk with Jean in Point Pleasant Park. His coxswain, William Cobham, would drive them there in their eight-passenger Dodge limousine, wait, and then drive them back again. By the time Murray returned to the office, visitors were usually lined up outside his door, anxious for a moment of his time. But he rarely had time any more to spend with his ratings, most of whom wouldn't have recognized him. He hardly saw his immediate subordinates either. He'd become so bogged down in the minutiae of command, they usually made their own decisions without consulting him. The result, one of his captains would recall, was that there was "no co-ordination in the management of the port."

Not that it seemed to matter any more. The Allies were pushing inexorably towards Berlin; Mussolini was on the run. It was only a matter of time. The headline in today's newspaper predicted, CAPTURE OF BERLIN ONLY A MATTER OF HOURS. That was probably optimistic, but not by much. Soon the long war in Europe would be over. And then what? What would Rear Admiral Leonard Murray—the only Canadian ever to command an entire theatre of war—do for an encore?

He tried to remind himself it wasn't over yet. Less than two weeks ago, in fact, just before dawn on April 16, the Germans had torpedoed yet another minesweeper, the *Esquimalt*, off Sambro Head. It had been an awful tragedy. The torpedo hit the ship's stern section, causing it to sink almost immediately. The crew had just three minutes to escape. Twenty-eight didn't make it. Worse, even though the sinking took place almost within sight of the harbour mouth, there wasn't time for the crew to send a signal, so it was six hours before anyone knew the vessel had been hit. Finally, the HMCS *Sarnia*, another minesweeper, chanced upon one of its carlyfloats. Of the forty-two sailors who'd managed to clamber off the sinking ship, only twenty-six survived.

No, the war wasn't over yet, which made it difficult for Murray to devote much attention to his subordinates' plans for on-base victory celebrations.

He looked again at the note he'd written, considered the green-inked message one more time. He would send it. Mackenzie King had announced that all Canadian troops assigned to finish the fight in the Pacific theatre would be volunteers. Murray's message to Ottawa was that he wanted to be one of them. What else was an old warrior to do now that this war was coming to an end?

On May 1, Eric Dennis attended a Government House ceremony where Allan MacDougall Butler took the oath of allegiance and office as the new mayor of the city of Halifax. Less than a month earlier, Mayor Jack Lloyd had quit unexpectedly to take a job in London, working on post-war reconstruction for the new United Nations Relief and Rehabilitation Agency.

Butler, the city's former finance commissioner, had been the only candidate for the job. Like Lloyd, he was a chartered accountant. But unlike the charismatic thirty-six-year-old Lloyd, who'd served as alderman for six years before being elected mayor, Butler was a colourless fifty-five-year-old with no practical political experience and—Eric believed—no real vision for a post-war Halifax.

After Butler had kissed the bible and signed all the official documents, Lieutenant-Governor Kendall congratulated him on his acclamation victory but warned him that, with the war ending, the next year in Halifax would require "a lot of service" from him. "You are expected to make the most of it," he said.

Butler didn't have much time to savour the moment or to follow through on his plan to move the mayor's highly polished $200 walnut desk to what he considered a more suitable corner of the office. Within forty-five minutes of being sworn in, he was whisked back to City Hall in a police department radio car so he could preside over a meeting of the VE-Day Committee. Butler hadn't realized that chairing the meeting was his job.

It was not an auspicious beginning.

ON MONDAY, MAY 7, 1945, Leonard Murray's steward woke him shortly after five a.m. The long-anticipated cable from the British Admiralty had finally arrived. Germany had surrendered! The war was over. Despite that news, the confidential message also "warned that the fleet in all waters is to remain on a war footing and in a state of constant vigilance" in case rogue German subs decided to fight on to the death. Murray didn't need reminding. On Saturday in Copenhagen, German warships, which had ostensibly surrendered, opened fire and shelled the city. The Admiralty's message also instructed Murray to keep the news secret until the heads of Allied governments had the opportunity to announce the good news to their own citizens. So Murray merely advised his commanders that VE-Day "would be tomorrow or possibly later."

Within hours, however, and well before Ottawa could issue any official pronouncement, radio stations were broadcasting excited reports of the German capitulation, and the Halifax *Mail* was on the streets with an extra edition featuring a three-inch-high banner headline: WAR END OFFICIAL.

At the YMCA, members of the Halifax-Dartmouth Ministerial Association interrupted their monthly meeting, joined in singing a couple of verses of "Praise God From Whom All Blessings Flow," then rushed back to their own churches to begin planned thanksgiving services. By the time they got there, the pews were already starting to fill.

Mayor Butler was in his new office in City Hall around 10:30 a.m.

when he saw the first newspaper headlines. He declared the rest of the day a holiday for civic workers, then drove his car to his house in the city's west end. He wanted, as he would explain later, to get it off the streets for "security reasons."

In the beginning there seemed little to worry about. Tramcar conductors who had hastily headed for the car barns as soon as the news came—just as they'd been instructed—were sent back into the streets after their bosses decided the celebrations had not turned out to be as raucous or destructive as they'd feared.

But there was certainly plenty of celebrating taking place. Despite heavy fog and a pelting rain, the streets flooded with Haligonians spontaneously "cheering, shouting, horn-blowing, whistle-tooting [and] bell-peeling." Flags and bunting sprouted from every downtown window, flag mast and even telephone pole. People on roofs and in the upper floors of office buildings tossed toilet-paper streamers into the air. A group of high school students marched through the streets cheering, singing and waving flags. The only damage came when some overenthusiastic young boys pulled four hundred pounds of carrots off the back of a vegetable truck and began hurling them around Barrington Street. A few windows were broken, but the rowdiness was quickly quieted.

Just before noon the rain stopped and, in the words of the *Mail*, "the sun broke through the clouds as if to herald the Allied victory." (Syd Thomas, a reporter at Canadian Press, had called Jeff Jefferson at 11:45 to ask if it would be OK to mention the weather in his report. The censor gave him the go-ahead but stressed he should not emphasize the fog in case German subs decided to take advantage of the "murky conditions" to sink a few more Allied vessels.)

Dorothy Hendsbee was serving a customer at the lunch counter in the west-end Simpson's department store when the lights suddenly blinked on and off three times. It was the signal. "When you see those lights flash," her boss had told Dorothy a few days before, "it means the war is over. As soon as that happens, you close up and go home. And don't bother coming back for at least two days—we'll be closed." She didn't even wait to count her cash, just took it up to the office in the elevator, turned it in and left. As she followed the stream of employees and customers out the door, Dorothy worried about Reg. He'd already warned her he'd be doing provost duty and not to expect to see him for a few days. They'd be busy keeping order. Dorothy hoped he would be OK.

Simpson's wasn't the only store locking its doors. Eaton's, Woolworth's, the Met and Zeller's all shut down by noon, as did most independent retailers. Eaton's closed so quickly, in fact, that many regular grocery orders weren't delivered. To assuage unhappy customers, Eaton's called the newspapers to announce it would replace any perishables packaged but not delivered when the store closed—but not, of course, until Wednesday, when the store would reopen.

The city's eleven movie theatres papered over posters advertising current attractions—Abbott and Costello's "newest and greatest fun" entitled *Here Come the Co-eds*, Edward G. Robinson's *Mr. Winkle Goes to War*, Dorothy Lamour's *Rainbow Island*, and *Youth On Trial*, featuring a no-name cast but a poster that promised "the screen blazes with the searing emotions of youth . . . wild . . . reckless . . . shocking!"—with hand-lettered signs announcing they were closing "so our staffs may celebrate with the rest of Halifax." There was some truth to that, of course, but not much. Most restaurants ushered out the last of the lunch crowds shortly after one and locked their doors too.

Chief Commissioner Art Mahon of the Nova Scotia Liquor Commission had already telephoned the managers of all the city's liquor outlets to tell them not to open for business at all. "We will be closed until further notice," he told the *Mail*.

At first, no one seemed to notice. For one thing, the bootleggers were doing a brisk business. One would later claim to have sold five hundred bottles of rum at $12.50 a bottle. And the wet canteen at Stadacona was well stocked too, with six thousand bottles of beer available for thirsty sailors.

The crowds were good-natured, the mood buoyant. At the police station, previously agreed policing plans went into effect. Liaison officers from the three military police forces took up residence at the police station so they could deploy their men to trouble spots if needed. This meant that in addition to his own 86 officers and men, Chief Conrod had 169 Shore Patrol officers, 169 army provost officers, 74 air force police and 43 Mounties at his disposal. Two of the police department's three platoons—forty men—reported for duty at 11 a.m., with the rest scheduled to arrive at 4 p.m. But it didn't appear they'd be needed. Chief Conrod, who was eating his lunch at his desk in case there was any trouble, was exultant. "Everybody is very, very good," he told reporters between bites. "Outside of a few traffic blockades, we have had no trouble. It is beautiful, just beautiful."

Dorothy Hendsbee wasn't so sure. She'd walked the mile from Simpson's along the surprisingly busy Herring Cove Road to Maplewood, where she was now renting a room in Edith Walker's house. When she got home, two navy officers who were also renting rooms there were already up on the roof celebrating the end of the war by firing their guns into the air. The noises scared the wits out of Dorothy. Was this really how people were going to celebrate?

Eric Dennis had been in the *Mail* newsroom since the news first came over the wire, ensuring he had reporters wherever the spontaneous celebrations were breaking out while fielding phone calls from scores of confused Haligonians. Some just wanted confirmation the war was really over, while others were phoning to find out when the official VE-Day celebrations would take place. Eric couldn't tell them because he didn't know the answer. It seemed no one did.

The original plan had been for Ottawa formally to declare victory in Europe and then designate a day for all Canadians to mark the occasion officially. But news of the German surrender had leaked out in press bulletins from Europe before the government was ready to make its own announcement. While officials in Ottawa scrambled to catch up with events, Haligonians spilled into the streets to start their own impromptu party, and those in charge of the city's official celebration watched helplessly.

Members of the VE-Day Committee had converged on City Hall as soon as news of the German surrender leaked out. They'd waited patiently in council chambers for the official announcement from Ottawa. When word didn't come by 12:15 p.m., they held a four-minute meeting, agreed to adjourn for an hour and went into the streets to canvass the crowds on whether they wanted the celebrations to be held today, tomorrow or perhaps even later in the week. By the time they reconvened at 1:30, there was no consensus—and still no word from Ottawa.

That announcement finally came through at 5:30 p.m., by which time Mayor Butler had convened a special meeting of city council, the VE-Day Committee, the heads of all the policing forces and military leaders, including Admiral Murray, to make sure they were all on the same wavelength. Ottawa declared Tuesday, May 8—tomorrow—Victory in Europe Day. That would be fine for most of the activities the VE-Day Committee had planned—but what about the fireworks? This afternoon had turned out to be warm and the skies were clear and bright, but everyone knew that in Halifax "you could never tell what [weather] tomorrow would bring." Besides, the crowds were already—and rightly—in a celebrating mood. Council decided the fireworks would go ahead tonight.

Eric Dennis, who was doing double duty as city editor and city hall reporter, had received a call about the meeting from the new mayor. He arrived in time to hear Admiral Murray address the gathering. Even though his officers had plans for their own on-base celebrations, and even though they'd made it clear to local officials that few sailors were likely to want to join in the civic celebrations, Murray didn't like what he felt was the anti-sailor tenor of the meeting—and of the mayor. His men, he insisted, had earned the right to participate in the city's festivities if they wanted to.

The others seemed more concerned about the potential for vandalism and violence. One of the aldermen asked if the police were anticipating any problems controlling the crowds tonight. Chief Conrod answered by getting up and walking over to the window overlooking Barrington Street. Through the window, everyone could see a clearly exuberant young man climbing a telephone poll to get at a flag flying from it. Conrod turned back to the others. "Nothing we can't handle," he said with a smile.

Leonard Murray felt the same way. Unlike the rest of the city, the armed forces had remained at their posts all day. At 3:15 p.m., Murray had issued a congratulatory but cautionary message to his subordinate officers, with orders that it be read to all ships' companies before the end of the workday at 5 p.m. "In wishing the personnel of this command a most joyful celebration of V-Day," the Admiral's message began, "I must draw attention to the fact that there are probably a number of submarines manned by fanatical Nazis still at sea and that responsibility for the safety of lives and property at sea remains upon our shoulders until all have been accounted for . . . I count on the common sense of all naval personnel and on their consideration for the feelings of those whose relatives will not return from this conflict to ensure that the celebration will be joyful without being destructive or distasteful."

With that, more than nine thousand naval personnel were freed to leave seven shore establishments and dozens of ships. They were not required to report back to work until seven o'clock the next morning. Thousands began to drift downtown. Most were not much interested in the street dancing, singsongs and other genteel events Crowell's committee had planned.

As for Murray, he returned home to have dinner with Jean. He planned to spend the evening catching up on his paperwork. The war might have ended, but the paperwork never did.

By the time Lieutenant Commander Reg Wood and his men arrived on the scene shortly after nine o'clock, the disturbance was already over. A few minutes earlier he'd watched from his office window in the Stadacona barracks as a crowd of a hundred or so sailors, who'd spilled out onto Barrington Street after the base's wet canteen closed, surrounded a southbound tram. They appeared to be menacing the driver. Wood gathered thirty Shore Patrolmen and hurried to the scene. By the time they got there, however, the tram-car had already escaped, leaving only shards of shattered glass on the street and a crowd of noisy ratings milling about. The men seemed to be in high spirits as well as high on spirits, and Wood didn't consider them dangerous. So, following the orders he himself had issued a little over a month before, he didn't try to arrest them or even order them back to barracks.

"OK, fellas," he told them, "you've had your fun. Time to push on." And they did. Wood watched them walking south along Barrington towards the downtown, laughing and joking among themselves. He and his men headed back to the office. He hoped the rest of the night would be this easy.

Eric and Maxine Dennis were among the fifteen thousand oohing and aahing Haligonians gathered on the eastern slopes of Citadel Hill to watch tonight's dazzling display of fireworks and pyrotechnics. It was everything the organizers had promised. For close to two hours, multicoloured flares, fired from George's Island and from navy boats in the harbour, painted the clear night sky with starbursts and streamers of light. Two fire boats steamed back and forth in the middle of the harbour, spraying water into the air over beams of coloured lights, adding to the spectacle for the crowds on the hill.

Amid the deafening kabooms of the fireworks, the cheerful cheers of the crowd and the joyous blasts from whistles and horns on the hundred or so ships in the harbour, Eric thought he could hear something else, faint but distinct. It sounded like smashing glass, and it appeared to be coming from downtown.

"WE COULD USE YOU DOWN HERE, SIR." Wood's liaison officer, Warrant Officer John Barbour, was calling from police headquarters at City Hall, and there was an obvious urgency in his tone. The downtown was now jammed with navy men, he said, and the crowd seemed to be getting out of hand. Sailors were blocking tramcars along Barrington Street and disconnecting the poles that linked them to the overhead electrical wires. Eight trams were now stranded, powerless, just north of Spring Garden Road.

"We'll be there as soon as we can," Wood said.

While Wood consulted with Barbour and Chief Conrod at City Hall, his men fanned out along Barrington Street in their patrol vehicles, attempting to clear a path so the conductors could get their trams safely away from downtown, where the mob was now close to seven thousand strong. The officers eventually managed to liberate all but one of the trams. Five hundred sailors had surrounded car 126 from the Windsor-to-Inglis Street run, which was stuck near the corner of Barrington and Blowers. After forcing the driver and passengers off the tram, a group of naval ratings smashed its windows, ripped out all its seats and began rocking the battered hulk from side to side, attempting to topple it. When they couldn't manage that, a sailor pried open one of the vehicle's journal boxes—metal boxes in which the tram's axles rested—to get at the highly flammable mixture of lubricating oil and waste material inside. He and his mates began setting wads of paper saturated with the gunky mixture on fire and tossing them inside the passenger compartment.

There were reasons why this torrent of pent-up rage had suddenly surged over Halifax's downtown streets with the irresistible force of a spring flood. To start with, there were these goddamn trams. Too few. Too old. Too uncomfortable. Too crowded. Not to mention too many drivers giving too much guff about how they'd had to put up with too many unruly come-from-aways like them. *They'd* had to put up with! Could the sailors help it if they weren't from Halifax? They certainly hadn't chosen to be here. Who would?

Nowhere to go. No restaurants worthy of the name. No place to get a drink. Who shut down the Ajax Club, anyway? Nothing to do. *Ever*. Nothing. Except stand in line and pay through the nose to merchants who didn't even smile when they took your hard-earned pittance. Oh, yes, and salute your superior officers. They'd had enough of "Yes, sir" and "No, sir" and military spit and polish to last them a couple of lifetimes.

The war was over. They'd done all anyone had asked of them, and more. They'd won the Battle of the Atlantic. They'd seen friends die. And now, on the very day when they should have been celebrating with their comrades and thanking whatever gods there are for the Allied victory and their own survival, the ungrateful, narrow-minded, mean-spirited burghers of this godforsaken city had shut down the liquor stores, shuttered the movie theatres, boarded up the shops, stopped serving dinner.

Reasons? Oh yes, they had their reasons, all right.

At the same time, of course, there was no reason at all. Just an hour earlier, a laughing, joking, rowdy crowd of a hundred sailors had attacked a tram outside Stadacona just for the fun of it. Now, something indefinable, perhaps impossible to explain to anyone who wasn't there, had transformed that small band into a menacing mob of thousands of sailors, soldiers and civilians bent on mayhem and destruction. This unruly lot were now flooding through downtown streets, trashing trams, setting fires and smashing windows, all for no discernible purpose. Perhaps it was anger-fired adrenalin, or random revenge, or just the giddy thrill of being caught up in a crowd that had developed a life of its own.

Whatever the reason, or lack of it, the cork was out of the bottle now, and there would be no putting it back in. Certainly not for a while.

ERIC DENNIS couldn't believe this was happening. Not in Halifax, not now that the war was finally over.

He'd convinced a slightly nervous Maxine to take a late night stroll downtown with him after the fireworks. Just to see what all that noise was about, he'd said. As they walked arm in arm south from Citadel Hill and then down Spring Garden Road towards Barrington, the cacophony—shouts, sirens, curses, laughter, breaking glass—grew louder and more intense, as did the acrid smell of smoke. Still, nothing prepared Eric for the sight that greeted them as he and Maxine rounded the corner at Barrington Street.

A block to the north he could see the burning wreckage of what had once been a tramcar surrounded by rowdy, roistering sailors. One of them, seemingly oblivious to the heat and smoke, had grabbed an iron bar and was using it to rip out the tram's brass fittings and railings. Clutching the treasures he'd collected, the sailor ran down the street towards Eric and Maxine. Then he stopped suddenly in front of the offices of Nova Scotia Light & Power, which were on the main floor of the Capitol Theatre Building, turned, and began heaving the fittings, one by one, through its plate glass windows. What had the electric company ever done to him? Eric wondered.

An older sailor, not one of the rioters, stood beside Eric, calmly smoking his pipe and taking in the action across the street. "It was a grim war, and now it's a grim celebration," he said to no one in particular. "I'm tired of everything . . . I want to go home."

Just then, a soldier, one of the few in the crowd, his uniform torn and his hair tousled, climbed up on the roof of the burning tram and began smashing at it with a metal bar. "They never should have made these things anyway," he shouted, to loud cheers from the crowd. "Fucking Toonerville Trolleys," someone else shouted derisively.

AT 11:30 P.M., Constable Fred Nagle got orders to ferry a squad of police officers to the scene of the tramcar fire in his patrol wagon. Carefully manoeuvring the vehicle along streets littered with broken glass and filled with menacing crowds was frightening enough, but what happened when he arrived at Barrington and Blowers would be worse.

By this point there were thousands of people—some would later estimate as many as twelve thousand, including many curious spectators who'd wandered downtown after the fireworks display—jamming the streets. Nagle had been on the force only two years. He'd never seen anything like this. But of course, neither had anyone else. The military riots of 1918 already paled by comparison.

The mob around the tram, which continued trying to overturn the now blazing hulk, spotted Nagle's police wagon and descended on it like a Nazi wolf pack on a lone merchant ship. They surrounded the wagon and began rocking it back and forth on its springs, until finally it tipped over on its side with a resounding crash. Nagle felt a sharp pain in his back as his body was sent flying across the seat and slammed hard into the passenger door. The officers in back scrambled out of the back doors, which had popped open on impact. Through the windscreen, Nagle, still in shock, saw a sailor carrying a flag dip it in the flames of the burning tram and then throw the fiery flag towards the wagon. There was a flash of light and a loud blast. The man had tossed the flag on gasoline that was leaking from the wagon's ruptured tank. The whole vehicle was now ablaze.

Nagle tried desperately to climb out of the inferno, but as soon as he pushed the door open, someone in the crowd would shove him back in—one even prodded him in the ribs with another flagpole—and then slam the door shut again. Finally, a burly young sailor, realizing the policeman might die if something wasn't done quickly, came to his rescue, forcing open the door and dragging a coughing, sputtering, terrified Nagle to safety.

SOON AFTER, SHORE PATROL trucks jammed with men arrived in force, but they were completely unarmed and no match for the rioters. They could do little but stand by and watch the vehicles burn.

By then the crowd had discovered a new target for its rage: the city firefighters who'd arrived to try to put out the fires. As soon as the firemen connected their hose to the fire hydrant, someone disconnected it. A fireman tried again; a rioter unscrewed it again. Before long, a couple of ratings put an end to that game by hacking the hose to pieces with axes they'd taken from the fire truck.

It didn't matter much by this point, anyway. There was little left of either the tram or the police wagon to burn. "To the Sackville Street liquor store," someone shouted, and most of the crowd moved north, leaving behind the smouldering wrecks.

They were not the first, as it turned out, to get the idea that it might be good sport to loot the liquor stores. A few minutes earlier, three merchant seamen had tried to storm the building, one tossing a flagpole through the front window. But as soon as a watchman confronted them, they fled. The watchman then called police headquarters, which dispatched six officers as backup. However, the policemen were powerless now, as the mob from the tram fire massed on the street in front of the store. Some began throwing rocks through the windows. One of the police officers stationed himself in front of the building as if to bar access.

"We've no problem with you and we don't want to hurt you," a soldier told him, "but they won't let us buy liquor to celebrate, so we're going to take it anyway."

The policeman stood his ground. "It's not mine to give," he said.

The soldier had heard enough. "C'mon boys," he called to his mates, brushing past the policeman, through a smashed window and into the store. Two dozen others followed.

CHIEF CONROD HAD INTENDED to call Admiral Murray, but somehow he dialed a wrong number and ended up with Lieutenant Tunney, the officer of the watch, instead.

"I need you to contact someone in authority up there right now," Conrod told him urgently, assuming Tunney's office was at naval headquarters, which it wasn't. "We're having real problems downtown. Some naval ratings are trying to break into the Sackville Street liquor store. I don't have enough men to handle them and the Shore

Patrol seems powerless to do anything. I need you to get through to Murray and get him to send us help as quickly as possible."

"Very well, sir," Tunney replied. "I'll see what I can do." Tunney didn't call Admiral Murray. Instead, he telephoned the Shore Patrol office at Stadacona to relay Conrod's message.

"We're on it already, Lieutenant," the duty officer there explained. "We'll take care of it."

At his home, Len Murray continued to plow his way through his night's worth of paperwork, oblivious to the hell breaking loose downtown.

AROUND MIDNIGHT, some energetic sailors decided to dump the cooling, burned-out police patrol into the harbour. They managed to push the zigzagging, driverless vehicle down the Sackville Street hill, careening into storefronts along the way, until they reached the Maritime National Fish Plant wharf, where they accidentally smashed it so hard into one of the wharf stanchions that they couldn't budge it further. Frustrated, they abandoned the effort and returned up the hill to look for other diversions.

By then the streets were awash in champagne, gin, rum and beer. Though the police had managed to drive off most of the would-be looters at the Sackville Street store, the mob had simply moved on to the Hollis Street liquor outlet, where they were rewarded with a veritable treasure trove of booze: 1,600 cases of spirits, 500 cases of wine and a staggering 2,500 cases of beer. Before police arrived to drive them out, the looters had made off with about half of that booty.

Now the partying could really begin.

INSIDE THE Knights of Columbus Services Centre at the south end of Hollis Street, more than a thousand sailors, airmen and soldiers were peacefully and joyfully celebrating the end of the hostilities. The place had been jammed with revellers since five o'clock this afternoon. The Stadacona Dance Band had begun playing shortly after six, around the same time the first of the hundreds of local girls arrived to act as hostesses for the jubilant servicemen.

Then, a few hours later, some Shore Patrol officers stopped by to warn Bob Sutherland there was a rumble on Lower Water Street near the government liquor store. The SPs there were calling for reinforcements, they said.

Some of the men who'd been dancing inside decided to go out and see what all the fuss was about. A short time later they returned wearing watches up their arms from wrist to shoulder, or loaded down with ladies' fur coats, even lingerie.

Father Wingle took up residence by the door, barring entrance to anyone carrying stolen booty. Some protested, but not too loudly. After all, Wingle, who stood six foot three and weighed 240 pounds, had been a collegiate wrestling champion. But a few of those who'd been kicked out sought revenge. A beer bottle came flying in through an open window.

Around midnight Sutherland happened to look out the window. Hollis Street was crowded with sailors, most of them carrying cases of beer or liquor. Some appeared to be headed for the gardens behind the Nova Scotian Hotel to drink their illegal booty; others simply plunked themselves down on a curb, cracked open a bottle and began to drink. The mood, so far as Sutherland could tell, was still mostly good-natured around the K of C building—but for how long?

A military policeman stopped for a coffee and imparted more chilling news. There was an angry mob roaming Barrington Street, he said, rolling over cars and setting fire to anything that would burn. The authorities, the MP said, were being overpowered; law and order had completely broken down.

Not inside the K of C Centre, Sutherland thought with relief. Not yet, anyway.

At this critical moment, the kitchen workers reported they'd run out of food supplies.

"What do we do now?" Hughie Creagen asked of no one in particular.

Sutherland shook his head. "There's nothing to do," he replied.

Perhaps not surprisingly, the Centre's switchboard was flooded with calls from anxious parents. Were their daughters safe? When would they be home? How would they get there?

Those were exactly the questions Sutherland, Creagen, Mary Yell and the pastor tried to answer as they huddled near the entrance. It was now after midnight and much of south-end Water Street behind the hostel was ablaze. As soon as firefighters snuffed out one small fire, the mob started another.

Their best hope, Sutherland and the others agreed, was to take advantage of the fact the crowd seemed so gleefully occupied with wreaking its own havoc on the streets at either end of the building that it wouldn't notice them spiriting the girls away by another route. They would put as many as would fit into the Centre's old Ford station wagon, head down Terminal Road between the hotel and the Centre to the now deserted waterfront docks, drive south until they were past the trouble and then head west towards the residential areas, where they could arrange rendezvous points with the girls' parents. To avoid attracting undue attention from those still inside the Centre, they decided to phase out the dancing gradually, substituting movies to keep the men occupied and inside the building.

In the end, the project took nearly six hours, and it wasn't easy. Even though the route they'd chosen avoided the worst of the disturbances, Sutherland could hear the sounds of shouting and shattering glass and smell the smoke from the fires. And he still had to drive by knots of drinking, often menacing-looking sailors. As he passed by them, he tightened his grip on the steering wheel, wondering anxiously what would happen if the sailors decided to stop the station wagon. Sutherland did all the driving, but the girls had to give him directions. He'd spent so much time inside the Centre over the past two years, he realized belatedly, he didn't know most of the street names, let alone how to get from place to place.

Finally, just before dawn, he dropped off the last of the girls and headed back downtown.

LIEUTENANT COMMANDER Wood was worried. Far too much liquor was in far too many of the wrong hands. Some of it had probably already made its way back aboard ships and into naval barracks, where it might fuel even more outbreaks in the morning. Wood had just been talking to Chief Conrod, who was beside himself with anger and frustration. Conrod wanted assurances the navy would shut down its wet canteens to keep tonight's awful situation from becoming worse tomorrow.

Even though it was now two in the morning, Wood decided he had no choice but to call his boss. But which one? His immediate superior was Commander Rendell James Johnson, the executive officer at Stadacona. But Wood, as the Shore Patrol officer of the Commander-in-Chief, was also on the staff of Admiral Murray.

Perhaps out of misplaced deference to Murray, Wood decided Johnson would be the one to be roused from his sleep. Wood reported on the looting of the liquor stores and passed on Conrod's strong recommendation that the wet canteens not open as scheduled later in the morning.

Commander Johnson thanked Wood and hung up. Although Wood hadn't said so, Johnson had the impression that Chief Conrod would be contacting Admiral Murray directly. He was wrong. Conrod had already spoken with the officer of the watch, whom he assumed—wrongly too, as it turned out—would have contacted Murray. Johnson, for his part, concluding that Conrod and Murray would sort things out themselves, went back to sleep without contacting Murray, his chief of staff, George Miles, or anyone else.

It was a fateful decision.

BUSINESS HAD DRIED up for Hollis Street's bootleg booze sellers. There was so much alcohol on the streets, people were giving it away to strangers, while bottles of bootleg liquor that had sold for as much as fifteen dollars earlier in the day were going begging at five dollars a quart.

Booze wasn't the only thing free that night in Halifax.

"Step right up now, sir, don't be shy." The drunken sailor had stationed himself in the middle of the display window at Wallace Brothers' shoe store near the corner of Barrington and Sackville streets. Men's and women's shoes were scattered in piles around him. "What can I do for you tonight?"

A passerby, in civilian clothes, seemed oblivious to the incongruity of it all. "I'll take a size eight. Men's. Black," he said, as calmly as if ordering a coffee at Norman's.

The sailor reached around, rummaged through his stock, found what he was looking for, handed it to the man. "Here you are, then. Next!"

It was 4:30 a.m.

BOB SUTHERLAND WAS DISGUSTED. This wasn't Rome or Berlin; this was Halifax. And it wasn't Canadians fighting the enemy; it was Canadians fighting Canadians.

He and some of the K of C Centre staff had decided to take an early morning walk through the downtown to see for themselves what the riots had done. It was quiet now, almost eerie. There were disheveled bodies everywhere, not dead but dead drunk, sleeping off the excesses of the night before. On lawns. On sidewalks. In the gutters. Even in the middle of the street.

They'd walked up and down the streets—north on Lower Water to Duke Street and then up to Barrington, south along Barrington through the worst of the broken glass and ravaged storefronts to Spring Garden Road, up and down Spring Garden back to Barrington, and then finally cutting past the Lieutenant-Governor's to Hollis Street for the last few blocks back to the Centre.

Sutherland thought it couldn't get any worse. Then it did. They were just a block from the Services Centre, hurrying now to escape the foul smells of stale beer, vomit and charred wood, when they saw a couple huddled together on the steps of what had once been a small variety store. When he first saw them, hugging each other, Sutherland couldn't help thinking they looked like young lovers. But they weren't young—and they were both sobbing. Then he recognized them. They were the husband and wife who owned the shop. Sutherland used to stop there occasionally for a candy bar or some shaving cream. He'd talked to them, heard their stories of a son who was a career navy man and their two grandsons and granddaughter who had served overseas. One of their grandsons, they'd told Sutherland with grief and pride, had been killed on the beaches of Normandy. The mob didn't know any of that. They'd simply run riot through this tiny store because it was there. They'd stolen what they wanted and smashed the rest. Now the business, this elderly couple's livelihood, was destroyed.

Sutherland felt revulsion, but confusion too. Didn't these hooligans know that hundreds, perhaps thousands of their fellow servicemen had walked out of this little store over the past six years with free cigarettes, or candy, or pop, because the couple knew that many of them didn't have much spending money left after sending most of their allowances home? Didn't they know that these grandparents were always trying to do a little something nice for "the boys"? Didn't they know any of this? Or didn't they care?

As Sutherland walked up to the man and woman, they at first looked frightened. Then they recognized Sutherland and threw open their arms. He hugged them. So did the others.

"Come back with us," Sutherland said finally. "There's nothing you can do here."

He took them into the Centre's cafeteria, where dozens of young men, most of whom had spent the night in the residence, were still eating their breakfast along with a few exhausted Shore Patrol officers on their way back to barracks for a few hours' rest.

One of the SP officers, after hearing what had happened to the old couple, began to cry. He grabbed Father Wingle's priest's cap off his head, took his wallet out of his pocket and dumped all his bills into the cap. Turning to the diners, tears streaming down his cheeks, he barked like a drill sergeant. "Come on," he said, pointing to the cap.

Within a few minutes he'd collected close to a thousand dollars, which he handed over to the shopkeepers. By then, everyone had tears in their eyes.

DEBBY PIERS'S VE-DAY celebration was very different. After commanding *Algonquin* through the successful D-Day invasion, Debby had finally been sent home to Nova Scotia's idyllic Annapolis Valley to serve as training commander at HMCS *Cornwallis*, now the largest naval training base in North America. Janet and Anne had joined him there; it was the first time they'd been together as a family in two years. On VE-Day they attended a thanksgiving ceremony where the base commander, Captain J.C.I. Edwards, thanked his officers and men and read a message of gratitude and congratulations from Piers's original mentor, Admiral Murray. After everyone listened to Prime Minister Churchill's radio address, which was broadcast over loudspeakers to the entire base, Captain Edwards declared a "make and mend," navy talk for a holiday, and the partying began. Anne, who was now eleven, led a conga line around the hall and everyone chanted, "Coo-ey, Coo-ey Conga! Coo-ey, Coo-ey Conga!"

The next morning Janet telephoned her mother to tell her about the "terrific party" the base had staged. That's how they learned what had happened in Halifax. Debby was saddened, but angry too. Though he was still a member in good standing of the city's social elite, he was a sailor as well. The same civic narrow-mindedness that had led to the closure of the Ajax Club three years before was alive and well and, he was convinced, had sparked the riots. When Janet's mother told them authorities had closed the liquor stores on VE-Day, this only reinforced Debby's anger. Janet's reaction was instant. "Idiots," she said. Debby couldn't have agreed more.

ERIC DENNIS BEGAN TYPING. "I have just walked, crawled and climbed through the ruins of Halifax business districts," he wrote, barely having to consider the words that flowed through his fingers almost as quickly as this morning's images tumbled across his brain. "There is devastation everywhere. The business areas look like London after a blitz. The streets are littered with broken plate glass, with paper, shoes, whiskey bottles and beer bottles. The jails are jammed with civilians and service personnel, men and women alike. The hospitals are overflowing with injured, some of them dying—" Dennis still had some facts to sort out. Had the police confirmed the story of the eighteen-year-old Vancouver sailor who was supposed to have drunk himself to death in the dockyard last night? And what about that civilian whose body had been found aboard a navy ship? Had he been killed in the riots?

There was so much more to write, but Eric knew that further work on this freelance piece for tomorrow's Toronto *Star* would have to wait until this afternoon, after today's *Mail* hit the streets. Eric forced himself to focus again on the job at hand. He banged out a few paragraphs of the *other* story Jefferson had just OK'd:

> Now it can be told—just how close the war came to Halifax. More than a dozen ships—warships and merchantmen—went down with torpedo holes in their sides inside or within sight of the entrance to Halifax harbour, seven of them in the last six months.

Strange, he thought to himself. In any other circumstances that would have been banner-headline front-page news. Today it would be lucky to get a couple of columns on page three. There were so many incredible photos from last night he still needed to find space for. Which one should they play on the front page? Eric favoured one taken early this morning, showing the charred police patrol wagon sitting abandoned at the edge of the pier. One of the other editors was pushing for a shot of the blazing tram taken in the mid-dle of the night. He had plenty of photos to choose from, but he wasn't sure he had enough reporters to cover whatever might happen next. Was there more to come? Would the official VE-Day program go ahead as planned? Or would the Mayor cancel it?

Eric's friend George Fox, the assistant deputy chief of police and his best contact on the force, had called him at home just before dawn. He was sending a squad of city detectives into the devastated downtown to begin their investigation and he wanted to know if Eric was interested in going with them. Of course he was. It would be a great story for Eric, but Fox had his own self-interested motives. There'd been so much looting overnight, he wanted an independent witness to accompany his policemen in case anyone later alleged they'd been pilfering too.

As awful as last night's riots had been—Eric and Maxine had walked the downtown streets for nearly two hours, stunned into silence by what they witnessed—this morning's aftermath seemed even worse. Eric wasn't exaggerating when he wrote about having to crawl and climb over debris. The rain- and liquor-slicked sidewalks and streets were literally covered with smashed display cases, abandoned merchandise, mannequins and store furnishings, as well as acres of broken glass and bottles.

"How much damage, you think?" Eric had asked one policeman.

"All told? At least a million, I'd say."

Eric knew it was just a guess, but he needed a number for his story, and a million certainly seemed within the realm of possibility. It might even be too low.

The policeman also told him that, from what he'd heard, almost none of the shopkeepers carried riot insurance. Whoever expected such a thing could happen?

ADMIRAL MURRAY DIDN'T KNOW anything about the dramatic events of the night before until a steward brought him the morning newspapers shortly after 9 a.m. Murray had finished his paperwork around 1 a.m. and gone directly to bed. The phone he kept beside his bed for emergency calls had not rung.

The *Herald*'s report called it "the maddest night perhaps old Halifax had ever seen" and said "soldiers, sailors and some civilians" were involved in looting the liquor stores. Those newspapers were at it again, Murray thought angrily, always trying to blame his men whenever anything untoward happened in the city. Murray knew better. Still, since the newspapers were reporting that sailors had been involved, he called his chief of staff, Captain Gus Miles, to ask for a report, and then left his office for an official "Service of Praise and Thanksgiving to Almighty God" at St. Paul's Anglican Church at 11 a.m. There he listened, along with 1,500 other worshippers, to the prophetic words of Archdeacon T.W. Savary: "The days ahead will not be easy." Murray could not have guessed just how difficult they would turn out to be.

It was nearly noon before Captain Miles managed to report back to Murray. The Chief of Police, Miles said, was calling for the closure of the wet canteens and the suspension of today's leaves for sailors, but it was too late. Murray had already ordered that the signal to "splice the main brace"—issue a double ration of rum to all hands in celebration—be flown from the Admiral's yardarm; and "open gangway"—meaning that sailors were free to come and go as they pleased—had been in effect for more than an hour already, as per the Admiral's original V-Day orders. More than 9,500 sailors were eligible to go ashore.

Even if there'd been time to stop them, Murray had no intention of cancelling his sailors' leaves. After all, the Mayor's official VE-Day Proclamation had invited "all citizens" to participate in the civic celebrations. Were his sailors not citizens? Furthermore, unlike their civilian counterparts, who'd spent the war safe and warm on land, Murray's men had risked their lives—and many had given their lives—to defeat the enemy. So they'd earned the right to savour their victory, and no small-town police chief was going to convince Murray otherwise. Besides, he was convinced that only a few of his sailors had actually taken part in last night's troubles, probably egged on by the local bootleggers and ne'er-do-wells, and they would now be sleeping it off in their barracks. There would be no recurrence of whatever it was the newspapers claimed had happened the night before; he was certain of that.

Ironically, so were the heads of the civilian and military police forces who gathered informally that morning in an open office at the liquor commission headquarters to decide how to protect the liquor stores from further attack. They were so convinced there would be no problems during the day that they decided not to post any special guards at the liquor stores until 8 p.m. That might have been in part because they all assumed there would be few naval personnel on the loose during the daytime. After all, hadn't Admiral Murray made it clear his men had "many duties to perform, V-Day or no V-Day"? During their meetings back in April, some recalled, he'd even suggested "the navy intended to march their service personnel to a brief drumhead service and then march them back to duty."

So much for plans.

Now that the first edition of the *Mail* was on the streets, Eric Dennis could venture outside to see what was happening. As soon as he stepped out the door onto Sackville Street, he was overwhelmed by crowds, mostly civilians, streaming past him up from Barrington Street, their arms full of whatever they could carry from the abandoned downtown shops.

Across the street, a woman walked into Maritime Furriers, ripped a fur coat off a rack, tried it on and walked back out. "I always wanted one of these," she announced to no one in particular. "Now I got one."

Eric headed down to Sackville and Barrington, where Gordon Vincent, the pastor of the West End Baptist Church, had taken over the corner as his pulpit and was cajoling bemused passersby into praying with him for the souls of the sinners. There were certainly plenty of those.

The harbour side of Barrington Street was a particular shambles. The floor of Wallace Brothers', where the drunken sailor had been handing out shoes to passersby in the middle of the night, was now knee-deep in empty boxes. A mannequin that had been dragged from nearby D'Allards Dress Shop sprawled incongruously among the debris. D'Allards itself was denuded, only a half-dozen bedraggled dresses left hanging.

People's Credit Jewellers was in even worse shape. The store, whose few remaining display cases were completely empty, appeared to have been singled out by the vandals. The story Eric heard was that sailors had targeted it for special attention because it was infamous for selling rings on credit to sailors, getting them to make a healthy down payment and then waiting until they were safely out at sea to demand their payment in full. When the payment wasn't forthcoming, they'd send someone to repossess the ring, sometimes literally off the sailor's sweetheart's finger, and then sell it again to another unsuspecting rating. That, at least, was the story.

Last night, it was more than enough.

IT WAS THE SAME—only different. Dangerously different. Shortly after one o'clock, Reg Wood was once again sitting in his Shore Patrol office in J Block at Stadacona when he saw a crowd of ratings attacking a tramcar on Barrington Street. Incredibly, despite what had happened the night before, the city's tramcars were operating again. In fact, it was just like the night before, except that there were now about two thousand sailors instead of only a few hundred, and they weren't in a celebratory mood. The wet canteen had run out of beer and closed, forcing the men into the street, where they initially vented their anger on the canteen itself, hurling bottles and rocks through its windows. Then someone saw tramcar 151 slowly approaching from the north along Barrington. As one they rushed the car, surrounded it and forced the driver and his ten passengers off. A small group of Shore Patrol officers rushed out from the base and attempted to intervene, but they were beaten back by the mob.

When Lieutenant Commander Wood got to the scene, the

hijacked tram was heading south on Barrington Street filled with close to 150 sailors, inside or perched on the roof, and escorted by a running, jostling, belligerent crowd, some now brandishing wooden sticks they'd found somewhere. It was past time, Wood realized, to begin using force to quell the violence. But his initial orders—to avoid arresting the sailors—still held, so the rioters were able to run amok into the downtown, unmolested.

By the time they abandoned the tram a few blocks short of City Hall, their numbers had been augmented by Wrens as well as dozens of women and children, some of whom were returning from downtown with loot from the trashed shops, and most of whom now seemed intent on scooping up whatever additional booty the sailors might leave in their wake. As the mob surged towards the downtown, one small group broke off and smashed its way into Edward Cornelius's grocery store at the corner of Gerrish and Barrington, stealing his supplies of cigarettes and turning his cartons of fruits and vegetables into missiles to smash out windows in houses along their route.

As the mob fanned through the downtown, Shore Patrol and army provost officers massed on Salter Street and began shepherding the mob west, in the direction of the Garrison Grounds at Citadel Hill, where bands and other entertainers were tuning up for the official outdoor thanksgiving service and celebration, scheduled to begin in less than an hour. At first the diversion seemed to be working. The crowd, wrote one reporter the next day, shifted direction and began "shouting its way toward the high ground and away from the commercial area when three civilians staggered into the van of the procession."

"This way to the brewery, boys," one shouted. "This way to the brewery. Let's go and take it." And the mob, as if they'd just been ordered into battle by Churchill himself, suddenly "swung in their tracks and massed into Water Street," defying the military policemen and laying siege to the iron fence that separated them from thousands of gallons of beer held hostage inside Keith's Brewery.

BYRON HIMMELMAN HADN'T PLANNED to venture downtown, but Loretta, his cousin who ran a beauty salon on the second floor of a building at the corner of Sackville and Barrington, was worried what the rioters might have done to her salon, so Byron reluctantly agreed to accompany her there. Besides, it might take his mind off his leg. The treatments weren't going well. The first ointment hadn't worked. Neither had the second. Dr. Koch was now trying a third. Byron had another appointment with him later today.

He and Loretta drove as far as Argyle Street, a block above the rioting, parked, and then slipped down Sackville and into the building's side entrance.

The salon, as Loretta had feared, was in a shocking state. The chairs and hair dryers had been tossed in a pile in the middle of the floor. All the various hairdressing solutions had been emptied over them and the bottles tossed into the mess, as if whoever did this was planning to start a fire but then got distracted by some more interesting vandalism. There was little to be done.

Loretta cried and cried. Byron stood by the window and watched, transfixed, as the riot continued to play out in front of him along Barrington Street. To the south he could see a horde of sailors descending on Bond's Clothing, one of the few shops with its windows intact. They smashed the plate glass windows and stormed inside. There was already so much glass in the street, it reached the curb. Within a few seconds, suits and hats and topcoats were flying out of the shop and onto the street. Others—most of them civilians—stood at the ready to scoop up the booty and make off with it. God knows where they were heading. A minute or so later the crowd spilled back out of Bond's and moved on. Nick Aliotis's tobacco shop was next.

Byron saw another crowd across the street, busily emptying the racks in Zeller's, the big department store at the corner of Barrington and Sackville. Suddenly someone twigged to the fact that there was a liquor store just below Zeller's on Sackville, and the crowd surged as one in its direction. No matter that it had been attacked the night before; there might still be some liquor inside.

This was their chance. Byron quickly turned to the tearful Loretta. "Let's get out of here," he said, "while we still can."

HAVING FINISHED HIS MEETING with the other police force heads, and confident there'd be no problems at least until after dark, Judson Conrod had gone home for a quiet lunch with his wife at their house in the city's west end. He was just sitting down to eat when he got a call from one of his officers. Sailors were swarming police headquarters and looked ready to storm it. Conrod called the Mayor at home, asked him to contact Admiral Murray for reinforcements, and then got in his car and headed back downtown. Would this never end?

Mayor Butler reached Murray at 1:45. "You've got to do something, nip this thing in the bud now," he demanded, after telling Murray what Conrod had told him.

"What would you suggest?" Murray's calmness, almost condescension, irritated Butler, but he tried to control his anger. He reiterated what everyone else seemed to accept as a given, that it was Murray's naval ratings who were the chief culprits, and suggested as delicately as he could that the Admiral should go to the scene and show himself, that the sailors might heed his command.

But what if they didn't? Murray asked himself. It was critical that he continue to be—and be seen to be—in control of his men. If he took to the streets to make a personal appeal to his sailors and, because they were drunk or excited or under the sway of the civilians, they refused to obey his orders or, worse, jostled him or pushed over his car, his whole command would be called into question. "All the Canadian navy under my command who were still fighting the Germans," he would say later, "would have been left without a leader. I would have been the commander who was unable to control his troops." He couldn't allow that to happen.

"I don't think I can do that," he told the Mayor.

Butler was about to press his point when Warrant Officer Barbour, the Shore Patrol's liaison officer to city hall, arrived to report that the mob, led by naval ratings, had the police hemmed in at City Hall, and that there was again rioting and disorder on Barrington Street. Butler tried to relay that to Murray, but the Admiral asked to speak with Barbour himself. Butler couldn't hear what Murray was saying, only Barbour's occasional interjection. "No sir," he kept saying, "it is the navy."

After he hung up, Murray called Captain Balfour, the officer in charge at Stadacona, and ordered him to put sixty-seven more sailors, then in training to be Shore Patrol officers, at Lieutenant Commander Wood's disposal. Then he left for the Garrison Grounds and the official celebrations.

COLONEL SID OLAND was having lunch at the castle on Young Avenue when Whitman, the caretaker down at the brewery on Water Street, called him in a panic. "You'd better get down here, sir," he said. "There's a huge mob and they're going to break in."

They were indeed. The throng, numbering close to four thousand and led by the three civilians, had reached the Salter Street entrance to Keith's Brewery just behind the retreating police and provost forces. The soldiers managed to push the vanguard back and shut the gate against them. At first it seemed as if the forces of law and order would triumph for a change. The prison-like stone brewery complex was surrounded by a five-foot-high stone wall topped by a picket fence and barbed wire, which should have been more than enough to keep the multitudes at bay. One of the guards even manoeuvred a beer truck against the gates to shore them up. But it was impossible to patrol everywhere and, one by one, about two dozen rioters managed to breach the defences and storm the loading platform door, which they smashed in. Encouraged, hundreds more pressed against the gate, and the heavy truck, even in gear with its brakes on, couldn't withstand the crush. They swarmed in and around the helpless provost corps and police officers, and into the brewery. Others had already broken through other entrances to the grounds. Hundreds swarmed into a section of the brewery where the beer was still hot from pasteurization. Not finding this to their taste, they threw it into the street.

By this time Colonel Oland had arrived in his car and hurried to the warehouse, where dozens of sailors were pushing against a heavy door.

"Wait a minute, boys," he ordered. "I'll unlock her for you." Recognizing that the intruders were going to empty his stocks regardless of what he did or said, Oland had resolved to make it as easy as possible for them in hopes that his brewery would be spared. He led them to a shipping room, opened a door onto Water Street, where thousands were milling about, and began handing out cases of beer. "This is to thank you for your service to your country. Now just form a line and pass them along to the fellas outside," he instructed. Remarkably, the sailors did as they were told. Perhaps not so surprising was the fact that the mob left the brewery complex, including its windows, intact.

Within minutes, 118,566 quart bottles of beer had disappeared into the streets and the crowds began to move off. Some, men and women both, staggered south to Cornwallis Park, across from the Nova Scotian Hotel, where they sat on cases of beer and liquor, "drinking, singing [and] intermingling ale with fighting and sex," as Halifax *Mail* reporter Frank Doyle put it. "The scenes of debauchery were rivaled only by those on Citadel Hill and Grafton Park." Others took up residence in spare trams stored on a track above Water Street, where men drank, tossed their half-empties through the windows and opened more from their endless cache. Most, however, headed north, back towards town. A seaman tossed a bottle through a window in the big office building next to the Hollis Street liquor store. As if on cue, bottles rained down on the building's windows. Within seconds, fifty more panes of glass had been smashed.

Back at the brewery, Sidney Oland took a last look around at his now empty warehouse, thanked his lucky stars it hadn't been worse and rushed to his car. There was a ceremony going on up at the Garrison Grounds and he needed to get there. He had to tell the Mayor and the Admiral what was happening downtown. They must do something—and soon.

BILLY MONT WAS RIDING his bicycle north along Granville Street, zigzagging up to the Garrison Grounds to watch the promised military marching bands, when he saw what looked like a human wall pushing south. Billy had heard about the troubles the night before, but he'd been too busy unloading baggage at the train station to join in the excitement. He hadn't expected it would still be going on this afternoon.

He hid his bicycle in an alley and fell in behind a group of a thousand or more sailors, who turned down Sackville and headed towards Hollis, smashing any intact windows they encountered as they passed. At the northeast corner of Hollis and Sackville, Billy followed some ratings into what had been Fader's Drug Store, where he helped himself to a bottle of Iron Brew, the Scottish soft drink that "provides a great taste and is truly as hard as nails" (known as Irn-Bru after the war).

Two doors south he saw men, women and children, piles of clothing slung over their shoulders, pouring out of H. Star and Sons, Naval and Civilian Outfitters. Billy decided there might be a market in the south end for some of those items. By the time he'd filled his arms with suits, however, most of the rest of the crowd had already moved on, and Billy found himself face to face with two uniformed policemen.

"What do you think you're doing?" one demanded.

Billy could have asked the cop what he was doing picking on a fifteen-year-old kid instead of going after some of the tough, drunken sailors at the head of the mob down the street—but he thought better of it. As it was, the cops just took his name, confiscated the suits and sent him on his way.

Disappointed at his failure to collect any merchandise he could peddle, Billy ran to catch up with the mob, which had now gathered outside the Hollis Street liquor store and its adjacent mailorder department in numbers so thick, a reporter would note later, "a drunk would not have had room to fall down if he wanted to." After last night's looting, officials had boarded over the broken windows with sheets of plywood, but they were no match for the determined hordes, who ripped them off and pressed into the retail store to finish what their fellow rioters had begun the night before. The dozen or so Shore Patrol officers who'd been dispatched to the scene as soon as the crowds began massing could only stand by, helpless against the onslaught.

As the crowds surged through the liquor store, looting and smashing and looting some more, Billy found himself next door, outside the entrance to the mail-order department. A burly sailor said, "Here, kid, I'll boost you over," and Billy glanced up at the transom above the entrance door. He would fit. He looked again at the sailor, who had now cupped his hands together to make a foothold so Billy could reach the transom. "Get me some rum," he demanded as Billy put his right foot in the hand-stirrup, grabbed on to the man's hunched shoulders and heaved himself skyward.

Once inside, Billy discovered that looters had already found other ways into the mail-order section, and had formed human chains to pass cases of liquor to their waiting comrades outside. He joined one.

Less than an hour later there wasn't a bottle left on the shelves, though there were plenty of broken ones littering the soaking floor. Billy was sweating and his arms were sore. Worse, he realized he had nothing to show for all his labour. He'd been so busy passing the booze along, he hadn't managed to keep any for himself. It didn't matter much, though: he didn't drink.

BYRON HIMMELMAN'S BROTHER called him just before his afternoon doctor's appointment to tell him sailors were going crazy downtown. They'd broken into the brewery and cleaned it out, he said. Though Byron had already seen the devastation first-hand earlier today, he, like plenty of other Haligonians, was drawn to the scene like a moth to a flame. For many of those not directly involved, the riots had become a kind of spectator sport. Byron decided to drive to the area and see the latest developments for himself.

As he drove past the Nova Scotian Hotel, he glanced to his left at Cornwallis Square. It appeared to be filled with dozens of couples sprawled out on the grass in various stages of undress and sexual activity. Continuing north on Hollis Street, Byron spied pockets of drunken sailors stumbling down the sidewalks and, off in the distance in the middle of downtown, a sea of bodies. He turned left on Bishop Street, beside the Lieutenant-Governor's mansion, and looked for a place to park. No point in driving too close to the action, he thought.

He'd barely pulled to a stop when a half-dozen sailors materialized from an alley and swarmed his car. They were clearly drunk and much the worse for wear. Most were cut and bruised, and their uniforms were dirty, as if they'd been in a few fights already today. They appeared to be hoping for another. One of the sailors poured what was left of a quart of beer over the hood of Byron's Oldsmobile and stared menacingly at him. Another took a leak on his fender. "Goddamned zombie," one shouted at Byron, employing the epithet used to describe army conscripts assigned to home defence. Byron wished he were wearing the merchant navy officer's uniform the *Trontolite*'s captain had made him buy. "Goddamn fucking zombie," someone else chimed in.

Byron looked again at their uniforms. "I just want to thank you guys for all the times you saved my skin in convoys." The words just spilled out of him, quick, desperate, deceitful. The truth, of course, was that the closest he'd come to combat was changing a light bulb on a ship's mast outside Boston harbour; his war wound was the result of banging his shin on a ship's ladder. But the sailors were too far gone to quibble or ask for details. He was now their long-lost brother for whom they would do anything.

All Byron wanted to do was get out of there, and fast. While one of the sailors stood in the middle of Barrington Street halting traffic, Byron drove to the corner, smiled and waved goodbye to his new best friends, and made a right turn towards downtown. It wasn't the direction he should have turned—he was heading into the heart of the riot—so he took the first left up along Spring Garden Road past the cemetery, where sailors had set up shop by the headstones and were selling beer by the case.

When he finally arrived back at his parents' house on Inglis Street, his brother, Forde, a driver for a local news dealer, and a buddy were in the kitchen. They were vigorously shaking bottles of champagne.

"What're you doing?" Byron demanded.

"Seeing how high we can make the corks go," his brother replied, as if there could be no other answer.

"Where'd you get the champagne?"

"Liquor store on Agricola."

ALLAN BUTLER TURNED to Murray, his face flushed, his tone urgent. "If you aren't going to do anything, then I will," the Mayor hissed, trying not to attract the attention of the milling crowds beyond their tight little circle. It was the second time in less than an hour the two men had exchanged something other than pleasantries in a public place.

At 2:25, just before the beginning of the Garrison Grounds ceremony, the Mayor, the Admiral and the heads of the army and air force had conferred briefly as close to twenty thousand Haligonians gathered on the hillside behind them. Six years before, many in this crowd had assembled here to catch a glimpse of the King and Queen during their triumphant royal tour. Since then, Halifax had become a very different, far less innocent city.

Given what he knew of what was happening downtown today—which wasn't even close to the complete story—Mayor Butler told the others he wasn't sure they should go ahead with the afternoon's ceremony. While Murray was able to persuade him that unleashing thousands of disappointed civilians on the downtown area wasn't likely to solve their problems, the Mayor couldn't help but notice that Murray didn't have much else to offer.

The Admiral explained he'd ordered his sixty-seven Shore Patrol trainees be made available for policing duties. In addition, he had come up with a plan to march his four-hundred-member official contingent, at the conclusion of the ceremony, from the Garrison Grounds through the downtown with the band playing, in hopes of creating a diversion and stopping any more window breaking or other property damage, "and [to] give people an opportunity to come back to their senses." Butler thought it was too little too late, but he held his tongue during the service.

Then, as it ended and the band, under Murray's orders, began to march off towards downtown, Colonel Oland arrived with his own update on the worsening situation downtown. Butler had heard enough.

"If you can't do something to stop this," he blustered at Murray, "then I'm going to declare martial law and ask for the military to send in troops to restore order." He paused, unsure of himself. "And if I don't have the power to declare martial law, I'll read the Riot Act. I know I can do that."

Murray listened, but he didn't respond. He was confident his plan to march his sailors through the riot would have the desired effect. Just to be certain, though, he amended the order: after the 375 sailors marched through downtown, they were to halt on the northern outskirts of downtown, where they were to be turned over to the Shore Patrol to help round up any remaining rioters. That taken care of, Murray excused himself, got in his car and told the driver to take him home.

To say the parade didn't produce Murray's desired result would be an understatement. His orders were never carried out. First of all, no one told the officer leading the parade that it was to stop just past downtown and wait for the Shore Patrol to take command. But that didn't matter much, since no one had told Lieutenant Commander Wood that the men were being placed at the Shore Patrol's disposal. Whether Murray had failed to relay his orders down the line or whether his underlings failed to follow orders, the parade fiasco was one more sign the situation had now spiralled totally out of control.

By the time the 375-member contingent led by a navy band made it back to Stadacona, it was only 260 strong. Some, seeing the pandemonium in progress on the streets, had decided to join in. Others were dragged out of the line by their fellow sailors. The end result: another hundred or so recruits for the rioters, who were by then in no need of reinforcements.

To complicate matters even further, Chief Conrod, who was in charge of overall policing, appeared to have lost control of the situation entirely. He forgot to order his own officers to remain on duty after their shifts ended. At four o'clock a full platoon—close to forty policemen—went home.

"WHY NOT RECALL ALL the servicemen to their barracks immediately?" the Mayor proposed.

"What about the civilians?" the Admiral countered.

They had already reached what had become an all too familiar impasse, and the meeting was barely ten minutes old.

The Mayor had asked for this meeting, just an hour after they'd parted company at the Garrison Grounds. It took place in the army commander's office in case they decided to call in troops to quell the disturbances, but Murray, as the senior military officer in the city, still presided. Besides Butler and Murray, those present included the heads of the other forces along with their military police chiefs, the head of the RCMP in Halifax, Chief Conrod, the city solicitor and the provincial Attorney General.

Butler already knew from an on-the-fly conversation he'd had a few minutes earlier with the city solicitor that he didn't have the power to impose martial law himself but that the Attorney General did. J.H. MacQuarrie, the Attorney General, wasn't keen. He feared that bringing in the army could lead to bloodshed, even some civilian deaths. Others, including Brigadier White, the senior army officer in the city, concurred. The army's Halifax-based soldiers were so few in number, so inexperienced and so ill equipped, he told the gathering, they could not be relied upon to put down the disorders. "It would be disastrous to ever get them to start."

In the end they all agreed with Brigadier White's suggestion that the Mayor officially declare VE-Day over at 6 p.m. and impose a curfew effective at 8 p.m. Just in case that failed to have the desired result, the Attorney General would request that a "well-trained regiment" of army troops from the base at Debert, sixty miles outside the city, be dispatched to Halifax to enforce the curfew. Finally, it was agreed that Murray and Butler would drive through downtown streets declaring the celebrations over and ordering everyone off the streets. That decision, Murray would say later, made everyone but the Mayor and himself "very happy." The Mayor, Murray couldn't resist sniping, didn't "wish to be pushed in the gutter by rioting people."

Neither, of course, did Murray. He telephoned Captain Balfour, the officer in charge at Stadacona, and instructed him to send all those who'd returned to barracks from the Garrison Grounds to join the Shore Patrol in sweeping rioting sailors from the streets.

Shortly before 7 p.m., the Mayor and Admiral, in a closed air force sound truck accompanied by nine truckloads of now-armed Shore Patrol officers (Lieutenant Commander Wood had procured 150 heavy axe handles from stores and distributed them to his men) set out for the downtown's glass- and debris-littered streets, Murray in the front seat beside the driver, Butler in back.

"This is Admiral Murray speaking in person," the disembodied voice declared over the truck loudspeaker. "Go to your billets, your ships, your quarters and your homes . . . this applies to both civilians and services personnel."

He handed the microphone to Butler. "Go to your homes. Don't stand about on the sidewalks."

Perhaps it was the voices of authority, or perhaps the mob was merely spent. Whatever the reason, the downtown streets began to empty. "Immediately," a *Mail* reporter would note, "a sobering effect was noticeable. The crowds, which had been menacing in [their] attitudes and moving only slowly as they battered at remnants of windows and strewed the balance of ruined stock on the streets, began to slip away, some up the side streets, others along the principal thoroughfares . . . Within a matter of minutes, jammed streets became merely crowded streets."

It wasn't as easy—or as quick—as the reporter made it sound. Even as Murray and Butler were delivering their message through the downtown, someone set fire to Fader's Drugs, where Billy Mont had made off with a bottle of Iron Brew a few hours earlier. Shortly thereafter, a fire began in the looted People's Credit Jewellers, causing $50,000 damage.

While those sailors too drunk or still too belligerent to heed the admonitions of the Admiral found themselves grabbed by the Shore Patrol and tossed bodily into trucks for the journey back to their barracks, many were not quite ready to go gentle into that good night. At HMCS *Peregrine*, a naval manning depot in the city's west end, drunken sailors smashed windows and toilets in their barracks with axes and clubs before massing on the parade square for an attack on the officers' wardroom. It was only thwarted, some say, when Admiral Murray himself showed up around 9 p.m., walked into the middle of the mob and announced he would "do the best I can for you. Just give me a little time." Whether cowed by the presence of an admiral or mollified by the way he spoke to them— "a man talking to men rather than an officer barking at seamen," as one young sailor later put it—the anger went out of the men and they dispersed. One can only speculate what might have happened had Murray made such a personal pitch to the rioters much earlier, as the Mayor had urged him to do.

By now, however, it was over. All except for the massive job of mopping up. And, of course, the blame-laying.

HE KNEW HE COULDN'T run it—his uncle would never allow it, and readers would be outraged—but what a picture it was. And didn't it say more about the bacchanalian insanity of the last thirty-six hours than all the words they could write, or the dozens of other pictures they could—and would—publish tomorrow? Or perhaps he was just trying to justify the unjustifiable.

Eric Dennis wasn't the only one who felt this way. Most of the editors, reporters and photographers still in the newsroom tonight had gathered around his desk to hold a mock debate over the question—and, of course, to look at the picture. About half were in favour of running it, though most of them, like Eric, knew it wouldn't happen.

"We've got pictures of everything but," argued one.

"Everything but a butt," joked another.

The photo, taken down at Keith's Brewery earlier in the day, showed the back of a Wren being boosted up over the stone wall by a helpful sailor. Her uniform skirt had ridden up to her waist. She wasn't, as the photo clearly showed, wearing any underwear.

Eric listened to their ribald jokes a while longer before finally announcing the inevitable. It would not run, he told them, urging them all back to their desks. They had a paper to put out. And Eric had a story to finish and get to the telegraph office in time to make tomorrow's first edition of the Toronto *Star*.

IT WAS INCREDIBLE, as if all his toy soldiers had suddenly come to life. Quinpool Road was chockablock this morning with army trucks full of army men in full battledress. Harold Masterman wanted to get closer—they were, after all, lined up all along the street in front of his house—but his foster mother wouldn't allow it. So he had to watch from the front window as the soldiers sat in the backs of their trucks awaiting word on whether they'd be needed to keep order.

Harold knew all about the riots. Who didn't? The radio and newspapers were full of stories about what had happened. But Mr. and Mrs. O'Byrne wouldn't let him go downtown with some of the other neighbourhood boys to see for himself. They hadn't let him go to the Garrison Grounds yesterday afternoon, either, even though other kids had told him there would be military bands playing and Uncle Mel entertaining.

So the war was over. What would that mean for him? "You'll be going home soon," Mrs. O'Byrne had said when she heard the news of the German surrender. She looked sad.

Harold didn't feel sad. It would be another adventure. But he had trouble remembering the place he came from, and his parents. He'd been in Canada for half his life.

JUSTICE WAS DISPENSED SWIFTLY, and with good reason: there was no room in the police lock-up to house the miscreants. So many rioters and looters had been tossed into the single cellblock that police couldn't even maintain an accurate count of prisoners. The dispatcher's office had tripled its usual staff in an effort to compile a list of names and addresses of those who'd been arrested, but they couldn't keep up. The detectives' office, which had become the receiving centre for stolen goods, was so full of evidence—shoes, dresses, hosiery, hats, household furnishings, even three battered mannequins—it looked like a department store display. Except, that is, for the cases of liquor piled ceiling high in one corner of the room.

Dozens of conscience-stricken or frightened Haligonians had begun inundating police with VE-Day loot. It arrived by mail, by special messenger, was left—in the colourful turn of phrase of one reporter—"like abandoned babies" on the steps of City Hall and the police station. When police officers weren't examining the voluntarily returned merchandise, they were busy discovering stolen goods in what one referred to as "the strangest places"— above electrical fixtures in offices, in school basements, in the CN baggage and express shed. In the latter place they found huge quantities of jewellery, liquor and other goods, all neatly wrapped in individual packages and addressed to people in cities and towns all over the country. All of it had now ended up at the police station. Much was still unaccounted for, of course, including two fur coats Jean Murray had stored at Maritime Furriers.

One of the other offices at the police station had been turned into a makeshift medical centre to treat the injured, mostly for cuts and bruises. The more seriously injured—twenty-nine in all—were in hospital. Three men were officially confirmed dead. Vern Tucker, a young stoker from Vancouver, had been picked up Monday night after he collapsed on a downtown street. The medical report listed "no obvious cause" for his death, but he, like Ernest Fitzgerald, probably died from drinking too much alcohol. Fitzgerald, a civilian who worked as a helper at an Argyle Street furniture store and was known to have a drinking problem, was found dead aboard a ship Monday night.

By far the most intriguing case involved navy Lieutenant Commander John George Smith, whose body was found near the boiler house on the Dalhousie College campus the morning after the riots. Smith, who'd been at Admiralty House until around eleven o'clock the night before, was considered "a well-liked and popular officer." His skull had been fractured, there were abrasions on his body and he had suffered a severe leg wound. Some suggested he'd been the victim of a hit-and-run driver who'd deposited his body on the campus. Others argued that his killer had used the riots as a cover for a revenge murder, though no one was prepared to speculate on what the revenge might be for. He had survived the war only to die during the celebration of the peace. In any event, no one would ever be charged with the crime.

Because the room in the police station usually used for police court had been turned into a mess hall for city and military police, many of whom had been on the job since Monday night, court had to be moved to the nearby Armouries, where three magistrates were processing cases. There had been 152 arrests for simple drunkenness, while another 211 faced more serious charges ranging from robbery and theft to possession of stolen property. The judges were in no mood to be lenient. Over in Dartmouth, magistrate E.D. Murray thundered from the bench, "I wish to say publicly that I consider you to be the lowest scum of the earth," before sentencing the first two men to face him, a sailor and a civilian, to two years each in Dorchester Penitentiary. Magistrate R.E. Inglis upped the ante by sentencing a petty officer from Saskatchewan to five years in prison. Then, noting where the man came from, he added, in an aside that would soon unleash a firestorm of prairie anger at Halifax: "During the past five years, there have been hundreds like you before this court, yes, hundreds who were so far away from the sea that they, like you, know nothing of naval tradition."

Despite condemnation of the navy by the Mayor, business leaders and newspaper editorialists, only a small percentage of those charged—34 of the 211—turned out to be sailors. That was probably deceiving, however. There was so little room in the city police lockup during the riots that service patrols had been running a shuttle, picking up sailors from the jail and returning them to their barracks, where most were freed without charge.

ALL CIVILIANS, at least in Halifax, agreed the navy was at fault. "While members of the three services took part in these mob scenes, this wholesale destruction and looting," the *Mail* declared in a front-page editorial, "the members of one service—the navy—were most prominent. Men in naval uniform were the ringleaders and represented the main body of the smashers and looters."

Mayor Butler, who fired off a telegram to deputy prime minister J.L. Ilsley demanding compensation for his city, went on the radio to decry the navy. "I speak to the solemn protests of the citizens against the Canadian navy. It will be a long time before the people of Halifax forget this great crime."

A few hours later a reporter from the *Mail* managed to track down Admiral George Jones, the Chief of Naval Staff, who was at the Eastern Passage airport in Dartmouth waiting to board a Trans Canada Airlines flight back to Ottawa. By chance, Jones had arrived in Halifax smack in the middle of the worst of the riots to be with his father, who was gravely ill.

The riots, Jones allowed, were "most disgraceful." While he hadn't had time to investigate the events himself, he said, he would be in his office in Ottawa by two o'clock that afternoon devoting his "fullest personal attention" to the situation. "So far as I'm concerned," he added with a flourish, "the fullest and most sweeping investigation of any part the Royal Canadian Navy played in yesterday's riots will be made." Perhaps it wasn't surprising that Jones didn't call Murray to ask for his views on what had taken place.

> **SHELBURNE, May 14**—A 750-ton grey-black German U-boat, the No. 889 which had prowled the Newfoundland Banks in a futile search for Allied shipping, according to the story told by its 26-year-old captain, and then intended to take up a sniping position off the entrance to New York Harbour, knifed into Shelburne Harbour Sunday afternoon and formally gave up to the Royal Canadian Navy.

Eric Dennis had been writing for more than an hour now, almost without pausing for breath. He ripped one page out of his typewriter, inserted another and began typing furiously again almost before the copy paper had rolled into place. How many pages had he written? He couldn't remember. Plenty, and there was still more to tell. This was the last great end-of-war human drama: the final surrender of the enemy. "Under an overcast threatening sky . . ."

On Thursday, two days after the riots, one of his air force contacts had invited him to join them. "We're going out to pick up some German U-boats tomorrow." After the surrender Führer Dönitz had issued orders to all his submarine commanders to surface and signal their positions so they could give themselves up to the Allies. On Friday, Eric had spent thirteen hours in the cramped, noisy tail section of an RCAF Liberator ten thousand feet over the North Atlantic south of Newfoundland, looking for their whale-like prey. When the crew finally spotted it, the plane swooped down cautiously to make sure the sub was flying the black flag of surrender. Given the fog and poor visibility, it had taken two low, ear-popping passes to confirm that the vessel was really ready to capitulate. After that, the Liberator had little to do except circle overhead, waiting for naval frigates to arrive on the scene and take the sub in tow.

Today, Saturday, Eric had been back on land, but just long enough to get to Shelburne and board the small Fairmile motor launch that served as a press boat to take reporters to a spot about seven miles off Shelburne harbour, where the first Nazi submarine was about to surrender to Canadian forces. The U889, which had left Norway April 5, had been 240 miles south of Newfoundland when word of the German surrender arrived from Berlin.

While the frigates *Buckingham* and *Inch Arran* stood guard near-by, Chief of Staff Captain George Miles, standing in for his boss, Admiral Murray, led a twelve-man boarding party onto the sub shortly after three o'clock to formally accept it from its commander, Korvetten Captain Frierich Breuecker. A Royal Navy submarine crew then took over, raising the White Ensign on the U889's flagstaff, and bringing the vessel and its fifty-three-man crew into the dock at Shelburne harbour.

Eric, who had been allowed to board the vessel with the military police officers, couldn't get over how young the crew was. Breuecker, a slight, handsome, brown-haired man, was only twenty-six, and not only a captain but the owner of an Iron Cross Second Class for sinking a gunboat in the English Channel. He wore the decoration on his chest for his interviews with Canadian reporters. Though they were supposedly nineteen to thirty-three years of age, most of the crew appeared to be fifteen or sixteen years old, and scared to death.

"Are you going to kill us?" one of them nervously asked a Canadian sailor.

"No," the sailor answered.

"We were told if we were caught, we'd be killed."

"No," the sailor said again. Still, the young German flinched noticeably when the sailor reached into his pocket; he seemed convinced the sailor was reaching for a gun. He wasn't. He pulled out a chocolate bar and offered it to the young man.

The captain, perhaps self-servingly, claimed his sub had never sunk a ship while he was in command of U889. Though he claimed to be a "proud Nazi," he also told reporters through an interpreter that "I would like to stay in Canada or the United States after the war. Germany as a political interest is dead."

When one of the reporters asked him if he was happy the war was over, he grinned. "That is quite a question," he said, then added he was glad he'd been captured by the Western Allies rather than the Russians. "We expect better treatment from you."

"We'll look after you OK," one of his naval guards replied ambiguously.

"How do you like the Canadians?" another reporter wanted to know.

"I think I can stand it very much," Breuecker said to laughter.

When Andy Merkel, the Canadian Press bureau chief, asked him if he could live in America and accept democracy, he shrugged. "There is not such a big difference between your government and ours," he said.

It was a fascinating insight into the thinking of people who, until a week ago, had been the implacable enemy of all things American and Canadian. Now, back at his desk in the Halifax newsroom, Eric wanted to squeeze every detail out of his notebook and onto the page for Monday's story.

But first he could use a coffee. He got up to walk across the room to the coffee pot when—God, he felt faint. Jesus, he was falling. He couldn't help himself. He was on the floor, on his back.

He looked up at the gathering crowd of reporters and editors. He could see concern on their faces. He knew they were talking, but he couldn't make out what they were saying. There was an awful ringing in his ears that drowned out all other sounds. He felt like he was going to be sick to his stomach. Suddenly the story didn't seem so important after all. Nothing did.

THE GATHERING AT THE Lord Nelson Hotel on May 12, 1945, was supposed to be a federal Progressive Conservative nominating convention, but virtually everyone among the four hundred delegates, including Harry MacKeen, the party's Protestant candidate in the dual Protestant-Catholic constituency of Halifax, could talk of little else besides the week's riots.

Mackenzie King had called a federal election for June 11 in hopes of capitalizing on the country's post-war euphoria to win yet another term in office for his Liberals. There was, of course, no post-war euphoria yet in Halifax, where citizens were now feeling as besieged by sneering Upper Canadians, snooty editorialists and know-nothing Western farmers as they had been by the rioters themselves.

The Vancouver *News Herald* pontificated that "no thoughtful person" could have been surprised by the riots given "the intense resentment by service personnel of the treatment they have received in Halifax," where they were "mercilessly exploited . . . Service personnel have also been deeply angered at the high prices and insolent reception they have met with in stores, hotels and other commercial establishments . . . More, bigots and fanatics in Nova Scotia have waged an active and irritating campaign throughout the war to curb what they have been eager and anxious to proclaim as 'excesses' . . . It was even seriously attempted at one time to prevent the sale of beer in service canteens." Such discriminatory treatment continued even after the riots, according to many, when Western Canadians in particular appeared to have been singled out by Halifax judges for the harshest punishments. Criticizing the prison sentences given to sailors from his province, the Attorney General of Saskatchewan lamented: "You know how unhappy these boys have been in Halifax . . . men have said what a terrible place it is to live in." Even the Edmonton Navy Mothers' Club got in on the act: "Much as we deplore and regret such riot incidents," they said in a formal statement, "the responsibility should be placed on the citizens of Halifax themselves, who have for the past five years been merciless in their dealings with servicemen—especially the Navy— who have been unfortunate enough to be stationed there."

Marjory Whitelaw couldn't help feeling some satisfaction as she read the reports from Halifax in her Montreal newspaper. The city had got what was coming to it, she knew that. Not that she disliked the place or wished most of the people there ill. In truth, the four years she'd spent in Halifax had been the most exciting of her life. That had become even more apparent now that she was back in Montreal, where jobs were scarce and men even scarcer. The war, she'd come to realize, had transformed the vibrant, cosmopolitan Montreal of her memory into a depressing city of women, old men and young boys while breathing adventure, danger, intrigue and excitement into everyday life in supposedly humdrum old Halifax. She'd felt alive there in ways she still found difficult to understand, let alone explain. Yet she could also understand the impulse among many to tear the city apart. It had been an incredibly frustrating place to live during the war.

Perhaps in retaliation for all the opprobrium being heaped on the city, the local press had taken to identifying those charged or convicted for VE-Day offences by their place of origin. The point was to emphasize that local citizens, service or otherwise, were not at fault. Thus, "Four navy men and a civilian drew a total of 14 years in Dorchester Penitentiary," the *Mail* reported, adding pointedly: "Three were from the Canadian West and the fourth from Montreal. The civilian gave no stated address."

Tensions between sailor and civilian remained high. Many of the local women who had been escorts or volunteer servers in the hostels and service canteens quit or refused to serve sailors at all. There were reports—officially denied—that some tramcar drivers were refusing to transport naval personnel.

Not everyone in Halifax bought this popular troublemaking-sailor-from-away argument. Harry MacKeen, one of the city's most prominent lawyers, hadn't changed his opinion since the temperance ladies and church wardens at Fort Massey conspired to shut down the Ajax Club three years earlier. "In this province, there will be the same amount of drinking, whether we have prohibition, government control or catch-as-catch-can," he declared in his speech accepting his party's nomination as its federal candidate. "But for the insane liquor laws of this province, the more insane administration, the tragedy of Tuesday may not have occurred. One of the underlying causes of that awful scene was the way the government had administered the law."

As the city slowly returned to what passed for normal, Mayor Butler eased off on the nighttime curfew; from the original 8 p.m. he increased it to 10 p.m. Friday night and 12:30 a.m. Saturday night. After being confined to barracks since Wednesday, naval personnel "with clean records" also got their first leave passes. And finally they would have someplace to go: some theatres and dance halls, including the Knights of Columbus Hostel on Hollis, were reopening for business.

While Butler, belatedly recognizing the reality that Halifax was now and would continue to be a navy town, was calling for "tolerance," the navy was doing its best to put a fresh face on its battered administration. Admiral Jones had returned to Halifax this morning to take over command of all naval personnel in the city. For public consumption the new navy minister, Doug Abbott, insisted that he had placed Admiral Murray on leave so he could devote his full attention to preparing the navy's (and his own) case for any tribunals that might be established. That was technically true. J.L. Ilsley, Nova Scotia's representative in the federal cabinet, had already announced that an Ontario judge of the Supreme Court of

Canada, Roy Kellock, had been appointed to investigate the riots and the allegations that "members of the Armed Forces of Canada were in part responsible for the disorders," and the navy was planning to convene its own board of inquiry into the disorders. Nevertheless, many chose to put a more sinister interpretation on Abbott's announcement. Like Murray's wife, Jean, they believed Murray was being set up to take the fall for what had happened—for what had, in fact, been Halifax's fault.

IT MIGHT HAVE BEEN due to euphoria at the war finally being over, or perhaps young Dennis was so embarrassed by his own "latest and wildest" copy that he didn't want the censor to see it. Whatever the reason, Jeff Jefferson hadn't read the story on the riots that Eric filed to the Toronto *Star* until it was reproduced in all its fulsome glory in both the *Chronicle* and the afternoon *Star*. RIOTS LEAVE HALIFAX $1,000,000 HANGOVER trumpeted the Toronto *Star*'s front-page headline over the story, which carried a "By Eric Dennis: Special to the *Star*" byline and began with Eric having just "walked, crawled and climbed through the ruins . . ."

"What Price Sensationalism?" the *Chronicle* demanded in an editorial. "For gross exaggeration and outrageous inaccuracy [Dennis's story] could scarcely have been surpassed by the most sensational Hearst journalism of the twenties." The story gave *Chronicle* editors a glorious opportunity both to rail against the hated Upper Canada and to tweak the nose of its larger rival in the inviting person of the publisher's nephew. It was certainly not about to pass up such a chance. "To remonstrate with the Toronto press for indulging in sensationalism in which its readers obviously delight to wallow is futile," the paper harrumphed. "That there are members of the Fourth Estate in Halifax who are prepared to do a tailor-made job in writing drivel of this sort for the sake of a dollar, who are willing to sell the reputation of the community that provides them with a livelihood for the proverbial mess of pottage is beyond comprehension . . . Yet such is the case."

As an old newspaperman himself, Jefferson could imagine the delight they'd taken in writing that editorial up at the *Chronicle*. He tried to get a rise out of Bob Rankin with it when they talked on the phone, but the *Herald*'s managing editor wouldn't bite.

"How's young Dennis taking it all?" Jefferson asked, trying to get their conversation back on the rails.

"He's sick," Rankin replied elliptically.

In fact, Eric hadn't even seen the *Chronicle* story. After his collapse in the newsroom four nights earlier, he'd woken up Sunday morning barely able to walk a straight line. His doctor couldn't figure out what was wrong with him but told him he needed to take a break, to get away from work and all that had been happening in Halifax. So, with his uncle's blessing, Eric had gone to stay at a friend's house at Port Williams in the Annapolis Valley.

He didn't see the *Chronicle* story—or the rebuttal that appeared two days later in the *Citizen*, the feisty labour weekly that usually didn't have much good to say about any of the city's dailies. The *Chronicle*'s attack on "junior reporter Eric Dennis," it argued, "takes the biscuit . . . for sheer cant, humbug and hypocrisy." Noting that the affronted newspaper had itself compared Halifax after the riots to a city "over which the Luftwaffe had passed," the *Citizen* said the newspaper "owes an apology to the young Halifax reporter."

None was forthcoming.

FOR SOMEONE WHOSE CAREER had been his life and who now faced the very real possibility of a sudden and publicly humiliating end to that distinguished and successful career, Leonard Warren Murray seemed remarkably serene as he awaited the opening of Mr. Justice Kellock's Royal Commission and the beginning of a simultaneous naval board of inquiry into how he'd conducted his command.

Murray even found the time to help a sailor and a Wren get married. They'd arranged for a Halifax church wedding and had invited their relatives from other parts of the country to travel to Halifax for the occasion, but when Murray cancelled all leaves following the riots, they weren't able to get off the base to attend their own nuptials. When he heard what had happened, just before the ceremony was scheduled to take place, Murray not only granted them special dispensation so they could go ahead with the ceremony as planned, but he also arranged for them each to get four days' additional leave so they could enjoy a honeymoon.

In public he continued to exude a stunning if badly misplaced confidence. On the day after the riots Murray issued a statement not only arguing that maintaining law and order was a civil responsibility but also virtually exonerating the navy from blame for the riots themselves. While conceding that "a handful of undisciplined men in naval uniform—I shan't do them the honour of calling them naval ratings—probably not more than 200 in number—by allowing themselves to become the tools of bootleggers and other criminal elements in Halifax have brought disgrace upon a service of 95,000 men," he said he was satisfied that "in almost all cases, civilians led the assault and encouraged service personnel to take part." Civilians, he insisted, were also responsible for a "major portion" of the looting.

The evening of the day Kellock's inquiry opened, Murray and his wife attended the fifth anniversary dinner of the Navy Wives' Club at the Halifax YWCA. Describing the riots as "the matter of last week which is uppermost in all our minds," Murray predicted that when the inquiry concluded, "it will not be the thing for any newspaper or person to mention lightly the Royal Canadian Navy again . . . The navy will stand higher than before."

In private he was hurt and angry. "I alone, of all people in Halifax on those two days, have been put in the 'dog house' and relieved of my command," he complained in a letter to Admiral Jones. "I can only surmise it is due to pressure from newspapers or from individuals interested in keeping the senior officer in this city under local control." He urged Jones to give him back his job immediately, "to reinstate the whole body of the RCN in its own self-esteem, and make people aware there is justice to be had within its ranks . . . I should advise you to consider this advice carefully and come to a quick decision," he added. "You know I want to finish this war up cleanly at sea, and I am not gunning for your job, now or later, but I shall begin to doubt your ability to fill that job if you are not able to make a decision within the next 48 hours . . . I await your command."

The command never came. However, Murray seemed convinced that he—and justice—would ultimately prevail.

In part, Murray's self-assurance stemmed from his unshakeable belief that the navy had a "cast-iron" case, and that Kellock would see through the web of lies the city and its merchants were spinning. The Mayor, he wrote to a friend, was "trying to clear his own yardarm," and the merchants were just blaming the navy so Ottawa would compensate them for their losses. "If it was ever admitted that the local populace did not only an equal amount of damage but the larger part of the looting, there would be no case upon which to base a claim against the federal government for compensation." As for his own culpability for what had happened, Murray was unrepentant. It was the city's job to maintain law and order, he argued, and besides, he had "many other responsibilities that day besides the responsibility to the City of Halifax, and I could not give up my responsibility for the Battle of the Atlantic at that time."

Murray's confidence was also a symptom of his increasing isolation. He rarely spoke to anyone outside his tight little circle of navy supporters—and his wife, of course. Jean's bitterness had become boundless, her view of Halifax even more scathing. When Helen Pullen, the wife of one of Murray's captains, called to commiserate with Jean about her husband's problems, she went on a tirade, complaining how "awful" the citizens of Halifax had been to her husband. She was just as angry at the navy's top commanders, who, she believed, were planning to sacrifice her husband to placate the locals. She had made her husband go to see Jones after his arrival in Halifax to urge him privately not to sell the navy—or Murray—down the river.

Jean's efforts and her husband's self-confidence notwithstanding, by the time Mr. Justice Kellock, in his dark pinstriped suit with the white handkerchief in the breast pocket, formally gavelled the inquiry into session before a packed spectator gallery in the ornate legislative chambers, it seemed as if the die had already been cast.

NOT EVERYONE BLAMED MURRAY or his sailors for the riots. On May 26, 1945, Toronto-based *Saturday Night* magazine published a full-page article under the byline of a Lucy Van Gogh, who was probably the magazine's editor, B.K. Sandwell. While arguing that what had happened in Halifax was a "disorderly celebration" rather than a riot, because everyone was in a "good temper," the article nonetheless managed to eviscerate the city and its citizens for their treatment of military men.

"The servicemen . . . had no great affection for Halifax," it explained, adding: "There was no reason why they should have. In peace it was very much a small port town run by the Big Merchant class, who are very rich, and very much not run by the Proletariat, who are very poor . . . [Halifax] gets along nicely in peacetime under these conditions, but when war comes along and it is suddenly converted into one of the great ports of the world it does not adjust itself to that change with that elasticity and promptitude which would be desirable. In fact, it continues to be a small port town with a way of life and a set of bylaws very much unlike those of other great maritime municipalities." Not that it mattered much, the magazine added, since the city would soon be "back doing the ordinary business of Halifax." To salt the wound, the author added, seemingly gratuitously, that "the illegitimacy rate of Nova Scotia is precisely 60 per cent above the average for the rest of Canada, pre-war."

Predictably, the article provoked howls of outrage from Haligonians. The Reverend W.C. Clarkson of St. Mark's Anglican Church, the original home of the North End Services Canteen, delivered a sermon in which he lamented that "it's all right for the people of Toronto and other cities to talk viciously about Halifax, but if they had the influx of servicemen to tend with, then they would realize what we have come through. If the boys overseas had to depend on Toronto like they have depended on Halifax," he added, "Mr. Goebbels would have been in Casa Loma today." One newspaper editorial dismissed *Saturday Night* for claiming to be *the* Canadian magazine while devoting "much of its space and energies to running the gamut from symphonic snobbery through the parlor-pinkism to world umpiring. So long as it confines itself to its favourite pastimes there will be few to complain, but when it sticks its nose into realistic situations about which it knows nothing the complaints will be loud and insistent . . . People who know the facts," the paper added, "will describe this article as cheap, insulting, patronizing, facetious, a farrago of nonsense and bad taste—and utterly and ignorantly untrue."

The *Saturday Night* article even became a subject for discussion at the Royal Commission, which asked the editor for evidence on which the magazine had based it conclusions. When Sandwell could produce only a single letter from a reader criticizing Halifax, Kellock dismissed the entire article as having "no value at all."

Certainly, there were plenty of people willing to criticize—and defend—Halifax in letters to the editor. "A Visitor" to Halifax wrote: "Through five and a half years of war, most of you, the landlords and merchants, have been profiteering on service personnel and their families. We've paid through the noses for everything we've needed and wanted. I personally think the downtown merchants got exactly what they deserved and it's too bad that others who deserved it were missed." There were swift responses from "True Haligonians," who compared the so-called Visitor to "a relative who comes for a weekend, eats all our food [and] makes use of all our conveniences while we take a back seat."

William Rand of Canning, Nova Scotia, topped most of the vitriol with a commentary in the Halifax *Chronicle* that was later reprinted in the Toronto *Star*. He described the city's critics as "a type of Ontario weasel, mingling with an occasional prairie gopher, [which] darts down to the sight and smell of salt water, which frightens them, and scuttle[s] back to the safety of their holes in Canada to give the press their inspiration." Attacking everything from the "moral delinquency" of Toronto's publishing industry to the "lying, fraud and fakerism" of its mining companies, Rand concluded: "It is quite time that the thick-walled mentality of Ontario should be told where it fits, and that its congenital hypocrisy and bombast should receive from the Maritimes that which it had been asking for."

JUNE 11, 1945, the day Leonard Murray began his testimony at the Kellock Inquiry, also happened to be the day Canadians cast their ballots in the first post-war general election. There were more than a few among Murray's inner circle who would later claim that the confluence of the inquiry and the election was not mere happenstance. They hinted darkly that Prime Minister Mackenzie King, knowing he was in danger of losing the crushing majority he'd won in 1940 (178 out of 245 House of Commons seats) and that every vote might be crucial to his re-election bid, appointed the inquiry largely to shunt the riots off the national political train and onto a siding for the duration of the election. As well, they said, King was seeking to placate Halifax's still-seething business community and vengeful voters, and, perhaps most ominously in their view, to fit the Admiral himself for his new uniform of sackcloth and ashes.

The suspicions were unfounded. Though no great friend to the navy, King had been in San Francisco attending the first meeting of the United Nations during the riots, and there's no evidence he played any direct role in the decision to appoint an inquiry. More importantly, as Doug Abbott, the naval minister, would later argue, the riots were clearly so significant and traumatic an event that the public would never have accepted an internal forces inquiry alone. Appointing a Royal Commission, Abbott said, "simply had to be done. No government could have ignored what happened." And Murray himself could hardly expect to emerge unscathed.

At first Murray had been optimistic about the inquiry. "I have no reason to expect [justice] will not be done," he wrote to a friend shortly after Kellock's appointment was announced, "because the commission is imported from outside Nova Scotia." But that was before he knew much about the man the government had chosen to preside over an inquiry into what some would call "the biggest drunk in Canadian history."

Roy Kellock, a gaunt man with a pinched face and owlish spectacles, who'd been appointed to the country's highest court only the year before, was a puritanical teetotaller who was said to be "paranoid" to be in a room where alcohol was consumed. Worse from Murray's perspective, Kellock had spent World War I in law school, so he brought no military experience of his own to the task of trying to understand what had happened in Halifax. How could the navy—and more particularly, Murray—expect to get justice from a man like that?

He couldn't, Mary Bidwell concluded. The wife of navy Captain Roger Bidwell, one of Murray's staunchest supporters, she sat through every hour of every day of the Kellock Inquiry. It didn't take her long to decide that this was not a dispassionate inquiry into the real cause of the riots, but "a trial: of the navy, of Len Murray." She couldn't understand why the defence department lawyers who were supposed to be representing Murray's interests—armed forces Judge Advocate General Brigadier A.J. Order and Montreal lawyer Hugh O'Donnell, who'd been appointed to represent the department and, by extension, Murray—weren't more aggressively questioning key witnesses hostile to the Admiral, like Mayor Butler, Police Chief Conrod and *Herald* managing editor Rankin. When she asked Murray about that, he confided that his defence department lawyers had told him they planned to mount a case of their own and that the truth would come out then. Unfortunately for Murray, he believed them.

Murray didn't help his own case, either. He spent fifteen awkward, combative, painful, often intense and occasionally dramatic hours in the witness chair over three days. After each day's proceedings he would meet with a private lawyer he'd hired to advise him, and with the captains of the three Halifax shore establishments, to talk about what had happened that day and, as Captain Owen Robertson, the head of HMCS Dockyard, put it, "lay out the campaign for the next day." The problem, Robertson quickly discovered, was that after they left, Murray would talk to his wife, who would "get to [him] and next day he would say things his lawyer advised against. Almost seemed he had a death wish."

By one count the Admiral faced 2,243 questions, many sharply worded ones from Kellock himself, who sometimes sounded more like a prosecutor than a judge. It was Kellock, for example, who pressed Murray on his public statement that no more than two hundred naval personnel had taken part in the disturbances. How had he arrived at such a small number of naval rioters? Kellock demanded.

"I don't think more than two hundred were engaged in actual disorders," Murray reiterated.

Kellock seized on that statement, leafing through the copious notes he'd taken during earlier testimony to find the nugget of information he was seeking. "Nine thousand five hundred and eight [sailors] went on leave," he read, and then, looking up, asked incredulously, "and you have a belief that a smaller number went downtown, and only a small number of ratings took part in the disturbances? Upon what do you base that belief?"

"I had no exact information," Murray was forced to concede. "I'm trying to recall—Would it help you any if I were to say that it was a comparatively small number?"

It would not. "I remind you," Kellock said sharply, "that you said 'two hundred.'"

At another point the judge became so frustrated by what he considered Murray's rambling, evasive answers that he ordered him to answer "yes" or "no," and even admonished him to stop "sparring around. It is a waste of time." He was *not* sparring around, Murray wanted to answer, he was simply trying to prevent Kellock and the lawyers from twisting his words to cast the navy in an unfavourable light.

Kellock wasn't the only one to challenge Murray's recollections or his interpretation of events. C.E. Smith, the lawyer representing the City of Halifax, was especially antagonistic in his cross-examination. He got Murray to admit that when he was planning security for VE-Day celebrations, his prime concern was to prevent damage to military establishments. Murray testified he hadn't considered the possibility that there might be damage to civilian property as well. "You were going to protect government property by turning the men loose in the city of Halifax," Smith needled him, "[because] neither you nor your officers had any faith that you could control your men on VE-Day."

"You are wrong," Murray responded angrily.

"I am not wrong," Smith shot back.

This was not the way Murray had intended, or expected, his testimony to unfold. He had wanted to tell the inquiry how, from the beginning of the war, the local authorities had utterly failed to rein in the gouging landlords and the profiteering merchants, or to control the bootleggers, the blind pigs and the houses of ill fame. However, the defence department lawyers had advised against raising these issues. There was no need to "stir up such matters in public," they told him, adding that they would be dealing with them in their final arguments. They didn't.

Instead, Murray's coached testimony ended up conspiring against his own interests. When Kellock asked him at one point if he could explain why there had been little or no trouble in navy establishments in other parts of the province, or anywhere else in the country for that matter, "and all this trouble in Halifax," Murray had bitten his tongue. "No, not that I can think of, my lord," he had replied.

The whole thing, Murray realized afterwards, had been a "frame-up." He had been had—by the lawyers, by Jones, by Mackenzie King.

King won the election, though with fifty-three fewer seats and only a bare majority this time. Harry MacKeen, the Tory candidate who'd blamed the province's "insane" liquor laws for the riots, lost his bid for a Halifax seat.

DOROTHY HENDSBEE'S WEDDING no more resembled a romantic Hollywood movie than her engagement had. Reg simply told her he had some leave coming up and maybe they should get married while they could. The weekend before the wedding, she and Reg drove up to Berwick in the Annapolis Valley to break the news to his parents.

"What day you planning to have it?" Reg's mother asked matter-of-factly.

"I'd been thinking July first," Dorothy replied.

"Don't make it the first of July," Reg's mother warned. "There's a festival in Harbourville on July first. It's a big day around here and nobody'd come."

So, on July 4, 1945, Dorothy and Reg were married in a small, simple ceremony in Reg's hometown. The wedding was . . . OK, Dorothy thought, but it wasn't like the movies at all. She wondered what might have happened if she'd taken that American soldier up on his offer to fly down to Texas to meet him. It was a crazy thought. Still, it was something to dream about. She still had the photograph he'd sent her. He was a handsome young man. But that was over now.

Also over was the dream she'd once harboured—the one she'd told that newspaper reporter about two years earlier—to make welding "my life profession . . . This is too good to give up for a kitchen," she'd told him then. But now she had. She had no choice, of course. Like most of the thousands of women who'd become skilled tradespeople in order to do their bit for the war effort and make a better life for themselves, Dorothy was now supposed to forget that any of it had ever happened. She was married—for better and for worse.

AT FIRST JEFF JEFFERSON thought it must be some sort of belated VE-Day fireworks display. He'd been doing some paperwork in his office in the federal building tower when, on a whim, he decided to see what was visible through his binoculars. He hadn't picked them up in months, not since the last convoys had passed out of the harbour. Now he panned slowly from the seaward side of the harbour along the south end of the city to the eastern slopes of Citadel Hill, which were dotted with "fugitives from what passes in these parts for a heat wave." It was July 18, 1945, the first "fairly warm" day of the summer, and he could see that the locals were taking full advantage. Then, to the north, Jefferson heard what sounded like rapid-fire gunshots. He swept the binoculars towards the Basin and adjusted the glasses in time to see "fireworks begin to shoot up into the air from just inside the Basin on the Dartmouth side," about three miles as the crow flies from where he was standing. It was a beautiful sight, like a "sheaf of wheat." Could it really be fireworks? He telephoned Lennie back at the hotel. "Go to the window and look up towards the Basin," he told her. When he put the binoculars back to his eyes, that "sheaf of wheat mushroomed into a ball of reddish flame and a huge ball of black smoke soared into the air above it."

These weren't fireworks. The explosions were coming from the Canadian Ammunition Depot, a compound of storage buildings and bunkers on the northeast shore of Bedford Basin. Ships had been tying up at its jetties to offload their stores of ammunition, depth charges and TNT almost continuously since war's end. The St. John's magazine had already been closed and its entire stock of ammunition and explosives transferred to Halifax. There was so much firepower, in fact, the navy had run out of space in its buildings to store it all, so it was piled high on the wharves and even on barges floating beside them: eighty depth charges, four hundred hedgehog anti-submarine bombs, cordite charges, small arms ammunition, anti-aircraft shells . . . Apparently, the ammunition on one of the barges had exploded, touching off fires on the wharves.

If the munitions there exploded, it could set off a chain reaction that might reach all the way into the buildings and bunkers where the bulk of the huge cache of unused explosives and munitions—fifty thousand depth charges for starters—were stored. And if that happened, it would make the Halifax Explosion seem like, well, fireworks by comparison.

Jefferson remembered having been told that "on occasions of this kind" the smartest thing to do is to open the windows to prevent them from being blown in by the force of the blasts. He'd just slipped one window up when he heard the sharp crack of a report and felt "the hot wind of the concussion" on his face.

Within minutes CHNS called. "Can we carry anything on the explosion?" the station's newsman asked.

Realizing that the sound of the blast had probably brought the whole city up short and that, given its history, this could easily provoke a panic among its citizens, Jefferson decided the smartest course would be to let people know immediately what was going on and where; it didn't make sense to wait for official confirmation. "Go ahead," he said, adding almost unintentionally, "shoot the works."

"But what are the works?" the reporter asked. "We don't know much yet."

Jefferson looked out his window again. "From what I can see, it's definitely in the Burnside area, but it could be coming from the magazine or the jetty area. You should call the military to find out more first."

The reporter didn't. Within seconds he was on the air with the first bulletin. The station was in the middle of broadcasting a ball game from the Wanderers Grounds near the Halifax Common. The game, and the broadcast, continued even after the explosions began, but the play-by-play announcer, Ace Foley, interrupted his game coverage from time to time to announce that this or that officer was to report to the dockyard or some other base immediately.

Jefferson listened with one ear while fielding phone calls with the other. Bert Robinson from the *Chronicle* called to tell him that the authorities had decided to evacuate Halifax's north end and the whole of Dartmouth. Jefferson wasn't surprised; he'd already noticed Citadel Hill becoming "black" with fleeing residents.

Thank God Butler was out of town, Jefferson thought. When someone asked Deputy Mayor "Gee" Ahern, a much more can-do politician, whether the city should supply coffee and sandwiches for people who'd fled to the Commons, Citadel Hill and other parks, Ahern didn't even pause to consider the whys and wherefores. "Go ahead and dish them out," he ordered. "We can let the council and the government worry about who's going to pay for them."

The military response was also much better than it had been on VE-Day, in Jefferson's opinion. Within an hour of the first blast, trucks loaded with armed soldiers fanned out to patrol the streets and prevent looting. Ships that had been at anchor in Bedford Basin hurriedly got up steam and retreated down the harbour to anchorages out of range of a possible massive explosion.

There hadn't been one of those yet, but the night sky continued to light up with the "machine-gun-like popping of smaller shells." As well, every once in a while there would be a much larger explosion. At around ten o'clock one bang even shook the thirty-foot-square office tower where Jefferson was. He could feel the whole structure "actually rock back and forth several times on its foundations. I wouldn't have believed it," he wrote later, "if I hadn't seen and felt it." He wondered if it could "stand the gaff if the fire got into the main magazine."

At around midnight the fire seemed to be dying down, so Jefferson left the office and walked south to the hotel, along sidewalks that were once again littered with broken glass.

Soon after he got to his room, another blast cut off the electricity to the hotel. He and Lennie took chairs into the bathroom, the only room without windows, "and made ourselves extremely uncomfortable waiting for the final sockdolager."

By sunrise it seemed the worst was over. While fires still burned, they were not triggering explosions, and it seemed likely the main munitions dumps were no longer in danger. Walking back to work through the downtown, Jefferson could see that the damage, while not as bad as the Halifax Explosion, was certainly worse than what had happened on VE-Day, because the force of the blasts had literally moved buildings off their foundations. Most of the city's downtown office buildings were closed for the day so officials could determine if they were safe for people to work in. He and a few navy signalmen, in fact, were the only souls at work in the federal building that day.

With no pressing censorship business to occupy him—he'd already made it clear to the reporters who called last night that he didn't consider the incident at the munitions dump to be a matter for the censor—Jefferson decided to sit down and write a feature story about what he'd seen. After all, it might be good to get back into practice for when this job ended, as it soon must. Besides, his colleagues in Ottawa would appreciate the yarn. He put a fresh sheet of paper into the typewriter.

"Well, it finally happened," he began.

New paragraph. "On a slightly reduced scale, anyway.

"For the past 26 years, and more particularly in war time, whenever a couple of bum boats chanced to bump in the harbour the local gazettes would invariably shriek SECOND HALIFAX EXPLOSION NARROWLY AVERTED BY A HAIR or words to that general tenor and effect.

"But tonight lightning proved that it can strike twice in the same place."

ERIC DENNIS DIDN'T HEAR about the biggest story since the war until it was all over. He was still in the Annapolis Valley recovering from the mysterious ailment that had felled him more than two months earlier. His doctors hadn't yet figured out what had caused him to collapse in the newsroom that night. While he still had occasional dizzy spells, they were occurring less frequently these days, for which he was grateful.

He was grateful now too that he'd been turned down for service overseas. He'd had some time to think about it all. He knew too many men who'd gone over and hadn't come back. Like the fellow in the composing room who used to get on the phone every night after work to try to woo the operator over at the Victoria General Hospital. He'd been one of the first to die when the Canadians went into Sicily. And then there was the reporter on the night shift who'd got married shortly after he was accepted into the armed forces. Eric and all the other reporters had gone to his wedding. A few months later he went overseas. He died crossing the English Channel on D-Day.

If he'd got his wish, where would he be now? Eric wondered. He might not have a wife and two healthy children. He might not even be alive.

The sound of two cars pulling into the driveway brought him out of his reverie. Eric Balcom, the man in whose house he was staying, hopped out of the lead car. His face was flushed.

"Did you hear what happened in Halifax?" he demanded. "There's been another explosion. At the ammunition magazine in Bedford. Don't worry, Maxine and the kids are OK. But I've arranged a car and driver for you so you can go back to Halifax and see them."

On the drive back Eric wished he'd been in Halifax for the explosions. It would have been such a great story.

MRS. O'BYRNE WAS CRYING, just like his mother had done five years before on the other side of the Atlantic. *His mother*. Harold tried to remember what she looked like. He'd had enough trouble recognizing his sisters, Marion and Elizabeth, when they arrived at the dock this morning wearing their new matching skirts and argyle sweaters. Marion was now thirteen, Elizabeth fifteen. When they first arrived at this very dock in the summer of 1940, Elizabeth had been ten, Harold's age now. It seemed a lifetime ago. Harold had seen his sisters only three times in the last five years. Even though he'd seen his brother more often, Jack looked different today too. Perhaps the fact that he was so nattily dressed in a sports jacket, tie and fedora just made him seem older than his seventeen years.

They were going home. There were 101 of them altogether, guest children like Harold and his siblings, all being repatriated to their families back in England. In place of the small single suitcase he'd arrived with, Harold would be returning with a huge trunk full of possessions. Mr. O'Byrne had packed Junior's train set and his collection of toy soldiers, as well as all the soldiers he and Mrs. O'Byrne had bought especially for him. And of course his prized Maple Leafs sweater was in the trunk too. He couldn't wait to show it to his parents and the kids on his street. If only he could remember some of their names . . .

He really wished Mrs. O'Byrne would stop crying. Usually she only cried when she was thinking about Junior.

GIVEN THE TENOR of the hearings, the final *Report on the Halifax Disorders* by Hon. Mr. Justice R.L. Kellock, Royal Commissioner, came as no surprise to anyone, including Leonard Murray.

On June 21, two days after Kellock wrapped up his hearings and returned to Ontario to write his final report, Murray fired off a scathing letter to Jones, venting his indignation at what he believed was the navy's abysmal failure to properly defend itself—and him—before the Royal Commission. Murray's pent-up resentments spilled out in sentence after sentence, paragraph after paragraph, page after page of green ink. When it was later typed—single-spaced on legal paper—Murray's letter would run to eight acid pages of accusation and anger.

> From the trend of events . . . it became increasingly evident that the "inquiry" was developing into a "trial" of the services, on charges made by the Halifax newspapers, and by the citizens of Halifax as expressed by the mayor . . . though these charges were never properly formulated so that a defence could be prepared . . .

The naval organization was thrown wide open, and examined under a microscope with any of its weaknesses brought under the severest criticism. The organization of the city authorities, control of the police force, control of bootleggers and "blind pigs," or lack of it, and control and ownership of houses of ill fame were not, at any time, under review . . .

It is most respectfully submitted that the evidence presented to the commissioner at this inquiry is so incomplete and so biased, that it will not be possible for him to come to a conclusion which will do justice to the city of Halifax or to the 95,000 men of the Royal Canadian Navy . . .

Worse, he wrote, he now suspected the failure might have been more than simple lawyerly incompetence. "I may be doing the Judge Advocate General and Mr. O'Donnell [the defence department's lawyers] an injustice because it is possible they had instructions from higher authority to placate Halifax and not to expose their bad drains," he told Jones. "If such is the case I should be glad to know in order that I may revise my own judgment." Given that the navy had not had the opportunity to present its side of the story, Murray wanted Jones to write Kellock and request the hearings be reopened to hear "further evidence."

The accusatory, vitriolic letter earned Murray a trip to Ottawa and a dressing-down by the minister himself. At the meeting, Murray said later, he was up against "the entire weight of the department," including one of the defence department lawyers from the inquiry, "who warned me that if I ever said any of the things I had written, in public, he would be down on me for libel." A few days later Murray formally withdrew the letter, but by then he'd already decided what he would do once Kellock's report was made public.

He didn't have to wait long. On July 28, 1945, less than three months after Ottawa appointed him to look into the disorders, Mr. Justice Kellock published his final report. After considering the two thousand transcribed pages of testimony from ninety witnesses over eighteen days of hearings, Kellock had come to one simple conclusion: Royal Canadian Navy Rear Admiral Leonard Warren Murray, CB, CBE, Commander-in-Chief, Northwest Atlantic and the only Canadian military man ever to be in charge of an entire theatre of war, was to blame for virtually everything bad that had happened in Halifax on May 7 and 8.

Kellock's statistical cataloguing of the extent of the disturbances was staggering: the theft of 6,987 cases of beer, 1,225 cases of wine and 55,392 bottles of spirits from the liquor commission in Halifax; another 5,256 quarts of beer, 1,692 quarts of wine and 9,816 quarts of liquor from the commission in Dartmouth; and 30,516 quarts of beer from Keith's Brewery; not to forget 2,624 pieces of plate and other glass broken; 207 businesses looted and 564 damaged; and, of course, 363 people arrested, 211 for offences more serious than simple drunkenness.

"The disorders," Kellock wrote in the introduction to his sixty-one-page report, "owe their origin, in my opinion, to failure on the part of the Naval Command in Halifax"—for which, read Admiral Murray—"to plan for their personnel . . . Once started, the development and continuance of the disorders were due to the failure of the Naval Command to put down the initial disorders on each of the two days . . . Subsequently the insufficiency of the police forces, service and civilian, employed, as well as their faulty direction on both days, and the passive conduct of the Naval Command in allowing naval personnel to continue unchecked on the afternoon of May 8 without taking any steps to deal with the situation until a very late hour, when the disorders had begun to play themselves out, explain the length of time during which the disorders continued."

Kellock dismissed Murray's contention that naval personnel had played only a minor role in the disturbances. "Had it not been for the presence on the streets of a large number of naval ratings," he wrote, the riots would not have happened. The fact that those sailors were on the streets, he added, was the result of Murray's failure to make sure there were enough interesting and diverting programs on the bases on VE-Day "to occupy the minds and the time of ratings and keep them from wandering in large parties about the streets." The fact that they felt free to loot and pillage the city could also be traced back to Murray: his approval of "rather strange" instructions to the Shore Patrol not to arrest anyone if they could avoid it made it clear to sailors, Kellock concluded, "that they had very little to fear" from the military police. To compound all his other sins, Murray was also to blame for "failing or refusing to accept the actual facts of the situation" not only on Tuesday afternoon, when the Mayor and others were begging him to take action, but also all the way back to his failure to acknowledge the problems of naval discipline that Rankin had raised in his correspondence with Admiral Jones.

Murray wasn't the only one who failed, or refused, to accept reality. While Kellock claimed the inquiry "endeavoured to ascertain from various witnesses whether there was discontent with Halifax conditions, on the part of service personnel, sufficient to establish the damage done on May 7th was premeditated and in the nature of a quid pro quo," it didn't find any. "If there were in fact any underlying discontent or feeling of resentment on the part of service personnel in Halifax on May 7th or 8th, the evidence failed to establish it, or that it had anything to do with the outbreaks."

The problem may have been that Kellock didn't ask the right people. Although the commission published ads inviting "all persons in a position to testify or to give information" to come forward, not a single rating appeared as a witness. Instead, most of those who testified were either civic leaders, like the Mayor, the police chief and local businessmen, or military officers, like the heads of the armed services and of the military police, most of whom would have had no personal experience of what life was like for the men under them.

Kellock himself certainly didn't. Although he took note of the fact that the local liquor commissions, theatres and restaurants were all shuttered on VE-Day, the teetotalling judge didn't seem to understand the frustrations such privations might cause ordinary sailors who wanted nothing more than to celebrate their great victory, or how such seemingly minor inconveniences, piled on top of five and a half long years of grievance and resentment, could suddenly explode in anger and violence.

The Kellock Report, journalist Doug How would write in a draft of his MA thesis twenty-five years later, was "notable for those things it did say and for the things it did not. It did not lash the sailors for their conduct. It did not lash civilians for their looting. It did not question the government's attitudes which for six years largely let difficulties compound and fester. Apart from comments on police control, it did not criticize the city. It did not dwell on the denial of liquor as an explosive factor . . . [Kellock's] belief was that the onus had been on the instruments of authority, chiefly the naval command, to anticipate and prepare for trouble, and to curb it when it came."

The reality is that there was more than enough blame to share out. Kellock's criticisms of Murray were certainly not unjustified—he was, in part, the author of his own misfortune—but the riots had plenty of other authors. The federal government had failed to recognize the enormous pressures the war had placed on Halifax, and had done little to help the city cope with the massive influx of people and the resulting strains on local services. For its part, the city seemed more interested in the sailors' paycheques than in the sailors themselves; their presence was often barely tolerated. And of course the sailors themselves couldn't—or wouldn't—comprehend that Halifax wasn't Toronto or Montreal or Vancouver, that it simply didn't have the resources to provide them with the services and amenities they wanted.

None of this mattered much to Murray now. He had to decide what to do next. One option was to demand a court martial in hopes it would ultimately vindicate him. Shortly after Kellock's report was released, Murray invited Louis Audette, one of his frigate captains who also happened to be a lawyer, to lunch to discuss the idea. Audette, who was sympathetic to his boss's situation, nevertheless warned him that asking for a court martial would be "the height of human folly." If he won, he told the Admiral, "everyone will think your friends and colleagues rallied to your help through affection and prejudice in order to contradict the report of a completely detached Justice of the Supreme Court of Canada." If he lost, Audette added, "you will be even worse off."

Although Murray accepted his advice, albeit reluctantly, Audette's mild criticism over pre-lunch drinks of the Admiral's performance at the inquiry so irritated Jean that "she broke into a violent speech against me—really couched in terms to which I was unused in a lady's speech," he would later recall. Offended, Audette got up to leave. Murray himself eventually had to intervene to persuade him to stay for lunch.

Even though he explored the idea of asking for a court martial, Murray, in truth, had pretty much decided after his meeting with navy minister Doug Abbott in Ottawa the month before that he would retire when the report came out. The only problem was that he wanted the navy to fire him; if he was fired, he would get 20 percent more in his pension cheque. Ottawa obliged. When he'd initially been relieved of his command after the riots, he was told, "it was further stated to you that no suitable new appointment was available immediately in the RCN for an officer of your seniority but that the matter would be taken under advisement." After the Kellock Report was released, the navy quickly concluded there was "no suitable appointment available . . . The minister has decided to retire you."

For his thirty-four years of distinguished service to King and country, he would receive an annual pension of $5,624.

"Want a swig?" the American sailor asked, holding up a bottle in Byron's direction.

Why not? Byron Himmelman finally had something to celebrate, and it wasn't just the fact of VJ-Day, which was what his hospital roommate was toasting with his smuggled-in bottle of booze.

Unlike the riots of VE-Day, celebrations of the Allies' ultimate victory over the Japanese had been incredibly low-key in Halifax. That was perhaps understandable, given not only the hangover from the city's last victory party but also the fact that the war in Japan had always seemed so far away, and victory in it came as such an anticlimax after what Halifax had gone through to win the Battle of the Atlantic. But there were other reasons as well. The navy, and Halifax, had learned a lesson. This time, sailors were permitted to buy a bottle of rum, even if they'd bought one the day before. The breweries donated free beer to serve in the wet canteens. And the theatres were open.

Byron Himmelman's victory, however, was personal: he had triumphed over amputation. Ten days ago it appeared inevitable he would lose his leg. Dr. Koch had prescribed every ointment imaginable, all without success. The sores refused to heal. Eventually, Koch had admitted defeat and admitted him to hospital for the operation. There, a young intern assigned to his ward examined his chart more carefully. "Have we tried saline compresses?" he asked the surgeon. They hadn't.

Twice a day for the next week, nurses applied saltwater-soaked bandages to his sores. Within days he could see new skin growing over the wound. He would keep his leg after all. He took a swig of the sailor's rum. It burned his throat. It felt good. The war was over—and he could get on with his life.

"DEAR MR. CRUIKSHANKS," Jefferson typed. "It would be too optimistic to expect you to remember my name, after only one meeting, but it may help your recollection . . . if I mention that I am the chief press censor who met you at Halifax pier when you arrived with Mr. Churchill."

Jefferson had been busy these last few days closing down the office he'd occupied for nearly six years: cancelling newspaper subscriptions; cataloguing the thousands of photos he'd taken of convoy ships coming and going in the harbour in front of his office window;

gathering up his boxes and boxes of official files, letters and reports; making notes of some of the nagging questions to which he still wanted answers (he wanted to ask Admiral Jones if there had really been a mutiny on the *Pasteur* back in 1940, and also if it was true, as the British Admiralty had said, that Halifax had been the "busiest" port on this side of the Atlantic until the fall of 1942); itemizing and returning his office equipment, including the four gooseneck lamps, to Public Works; and finishing up some final personal correspondence, like this letter to Churchill's press agent.

He'd already written a similar letter to Admiral Bonham-Carter, reminding him of their discussions following the sinking of the *Jervis Bay* in 1941 and asking him to autograph a photo he was enclosing. "I would have preferred a picture of yourself alone," he wrote, "but it happens that this with Admiral Jones is the only type available to me at present." He'd had the same problem finding a suitable photo of Churchill and had ended up selecting one of the Prime Minister with Admiral Murray, walking along the Halifax seawall.

Ah yes, Admiral Murray, Jefferson thought. It was sad. Two days earlier Jefferson had watched Murray and his wife board a ship bound for England. He'd retired or been fired—no one was saying—and was going into voluntary exile across the pond. His wife's choice, everyone said. She thought the navy and the city had treated her husband "shamefully and shabbily." The only positive note was that several hundred sailors had come down to the dock to give him a final salute, some with tears in their eyes. (Though he was at work in Cornwallis that day, Debby Piers had cried too.)

Jefferson turned his attention back to the letter he was writing. "It happens that I am the only local civilian who was officially present at all the comings and goings of Mr. Churchill to and from Halifax, and I am most anxious to have a special memento of these red-letter occasions in the life of a censor at a port which has not been the most inactive port in the Empire during the late hostilities . . ."

Not the most inactive port. Yes. Jefferson liked the modest, understated sound of that.

POSTSCRIPT

2002

M any of the old landmarks have disappeared or magically meta-
morphosed into something unrecognizable, even unimaginable,
to those who inhabited Halifax during the war years.

The grimy harbour-side docks where Billy Mont scavenged for
scraps and scrap metal have been either dismantled or made over.
What remains of the rabbit warrens of wartime waterfront warehouses are now mostly trendy boutiques selling handicrafts and
high fashion, and connected by ribbons of weatherproofed board-
walks that boast spectacular views of the harbour unobstructed by
the inconvenient sight of ships or stevedores. Few of those who
gaze out at the harbour realize that the ammunition scuttled with
the burning *Trongate* in 1942 still litters the harbour bottom.
Canada's last corvette, the HMCS *Sackville*, is a naval memorial and
tourist attraction. Halifax's famous Pier 21 has become a museum.

Billy's Greenbank shantytown is gone. The Oland castle on
Young Avenue stands empty. Sidney Oland's family brewing com-
pany was swallowed whole by the Labatt's empire in 1971. And
Keith's Brewery, the stone Water Street labyrinth where Sidney
Oland handed out beer to rioting sailors in 1945, has been converted
into an eclectic collection of restaurants, bars and specialty shops.

Norman's, the restaurant of choice for discerning wartime

diners like Jeff Jefferson, now houses a public relations firm. The tower on top of the old downtown federal building, where Jefferson performed his censorship duties, no longer dominates the waterfront skyline. Though the building still houses federal offices, the tower itself is no longer used because Public Works officials consider it unsafe. The Nova Scotian, the Canadian National Railway hotel where Jefferson and his wife lived, and where thousands of sailors and their girls came to dance and fall in love during the war, stood closed and vacant for many years but has recently been refurbished and reopened as part of the Westin hotel chain.

The temperance movement no longer holds sway over the city. In fact, the teetotallers would be appalled to know you can buy booze with your meal in most restaurants and, worse (or better, depending on your perspective), that the city now boasts 135 licensed liquor establishments within sixteen downtown blocks.

The Odell estate that housed Dolly McEuen's Ajax Club in the early years of the war has been torn down and long since replaced by apartments and condos. Fort Massey, the church that was the Ajax Club's nemesis, still stands, although, like many churches these days, its congregation is aged and dying. The Maritime Command Building on South Street, from which Admiral Murray organized the wartime convoys, was demolished in 1998 without a word of preservationist protest. Even the red brick house at 51 Hollis Street where Germaine Pelletier's girls plied their trade is now a parking lot for the union hiring hall next door. But the upper-middle-class west-end house Pelletier listed as her residence is still occupied, probably by a family that has no idea just how infamous their predecessor was.

They wouldn't be alone in their ignorance of the history that surrounds them. Halifax has done remarkably little to memorialize its pivotal and colourful wartime role. Halifax's most fondly remembered fifteen minutes of fame remains the 1917 Halifax Explosion, which, like the city's role in the sinking of the *Titanic* in 1912, offers the comfort of having been man-made but also an act of God.

Perhaps because what was arguably Halifax's finest hour on the world stage ended so ingloriously, Haligonians prefer to gloss over the story. They'd rather talk about the city's present and future.

The Halifax Regional Municipality's population now nudges 350,000, which is nearly three times as many as crammed into the city during the busiest years of the war, but they no longer seem quite so squeezed. Thanks to two cross-harbour bridges built in the post-war era, as well as a spiderweb of modern multi-lane highways snaking in and out of new suburban enclaves, the city has developed a comfortable middle-aged spread. While wartime Halifax repelled many of those forced to endure life here, the city has now become a powerful magnet for newcomers.

Although the sea continues to shape and define the city, the navy is not nearly as important as it was in wartime. Neither is the Shipyards, whose workforce now numbers a few hundred instead of the thousands in Dorothy Hendsbee's day. These days it is the offshore oil and gas discoveries of the seventies that are finally beginning to bear economic fruit. And Halifax has become a prosperous regional centre for education, research, government, business and finance.

If the city has changed in the years since 1945, so too have the people who helped change it during the war years.

Harold Masterman

Back in England, Harold Masterman was teased by the neighbourhood children. Unlike Harold, they hadn't had the chance to hide in Canada while German bombs were falling on their homes. Harold was one of only two kids his age on his old street who was evacuated during the war, and the others clearly resented him for it.

"It didn't take long," Harold says today, "six months maybe, and I was ready to go back home to Canada again."

Understandably. He'd spent his most formative years—from five to eleven—living another life in another country with another family. The O'Byrnes had become his *real* family. When the *Pasteur* docked in Liverpool after the voyage back from Halifax in 1945, Harold recalls, "I ran right past my mother and father. I didn't even know them."

Whatever privations Haligonians endured during the war years, Britons had suffered more, and continued to do so even after the hostilities ended. "Everything was still rationed, or too expensive."

Within six months Harold, who'd barely written home from Canada to his biological parents, had composed a heartfelt letter to the O'Byrnes, asking them to take him back. With the reluctant concurrence of Harold's parents, the O'Byrnes agreed, and in 1947, Harold, now twelve, returned to Halifax. His sisters and brother remained with their parents in England.

Except for a year in Vancouver, he's lived in Halifax ever since. He grew up, married, had two sons and spent most of his working life as an administrator for the Nova Scotia Department of Agriculture. Ironically, he worked two floors below Fred MacKinnon, the deputy minister of welfare who oversaw the child evacuee program. "I got to know him well," Harold says. "He was a very nice man." Masterman retired in 1994.

In 1990 he attended a reunion in Halifax to mark the fiftieth anniversary of the arrival of the guest children in Canada. There, he discovered that many of his fellow evacuees had also chosen to return to Canada to live after the war. Though they were inextricably linked by the circumstances of their childhood, it was the first time he'd met most of them. "That was an eye-opener, I'll tell you. I discovered there'd been a lot of abuse of some of those kids. I never knew anything about it. My brother, my sisters and I were very fortunate.

"You know," he says, "I still have that shoelace and the plastic tab, the ones with the number they gave us to wear around our necks when we left England the first time. Twelve—that was my number. I still take 12 in the 6/49 lottery."

Eric Dennis

In 1947 a specialist in Montreal finally told Eric Dennis why he'd collapsed that night in the newsroom in May 1945. He was suffering from Ménière's disease, a condition of the inner ear whose symptoms include recurrent attacks of deafness, ringing in the ear, dizziness and nausea, probably triggered by stress and the effect of spending the day before the first attack swooping over German U-boats in a noisy, unpressurized RCAF Liberator. The doctor prescribed medication, which cleared up the problem.

Eric spent more than thirty-five years with what became, as a result of a 1949 merger, the Halifax *Chronicle-Herald* and *Mail-Star*. In the fifties and sixties he served as the paper's bureau chief in Ottawa and London, and reported regularly from Washington. He returned to Halifax in the early 1970s to run a new provincial communications and information agency. Maxine died in 1977. Eric remarried in 1982. He and his wife, Margaret, now live in Oakville, Ontario, near their children and grandchildren.

H.B. Jefferson

During the 1950s, Jefferson was editor of Hansard, the proceedings of the Nova Scotia legislature. Between 1957 and 1961 he wrote a freelance series of nearly two hundred articles for the Halifax *Herald* about one of his many passions: Nova Scotia's steam railway system. In semi-retirement he also became a writer of feisty, often controversial letters to the editor. His last letter to the editor dealt with the shooting of four students at Kent State University during a 1970 anti–Vietnam War protest. Getting shot, he wrote, "served them right." He died in 1970 doing what he loved most—editing a new weekly newspaper he helped set up back in his hometown of Moncton, New Brunswick.

Though he and Lennie never had any children, the thirty boxes of writings, photographs and notes he donated to the Public Archives

of Nova Scotia—much of it dating from his days as regional censor—
represent a rich legacy for students of life in Halifax during those years.

Billy Mont

Bill Mont turned his boyhood penchant for scavenging and hus-
tling into a successful career. He attended his first auction shortly
after the war, bought a baby grand piano for $100 and sold it to a
"south-end swell" for $1,000. He didn't look back. Eventually he
bought the auction house, not to mention his original family home
in Greenbank and the Oland castle on Young Avenue, which he
soon sold. These days he's married with a grown family, works out
of an office in the old CN railway station where he once worked—
and scavenged—and is known as "Nova Scotia's flea market king"
because of the huge weekend buy-and-sells he runs.

The war, he says, was "a good time."

Byron Himmelman

In 1993, Byron happened to see a notice that the annual convention
of the Canadian Merchant Navy Veterans' Association would be in
Halifax that year. He went and eventually joined the organization,
which lobbies for improved recognition and compensation for merchant navy veterans. Today he is its Nova Scotia president and
regional director.

He says the leg he injured changing the light bulb on the
Trontolite's mast back in January 1945 still gives him "trouble" from
time to time. Now, at least, he knows what caused it: doctors eventually diagnosed his problem as a varicose ulcer.

Debby and Janet Piers

Debby Piers's memo to Ottawa headquarters complaining about the
navy's lack of modern equipment in the aftermath of his disastrous

1943 convoy helped change the course of the war, but Debby didn't know that for twenty years. Officially, he "never heard a word" about the memo, which he assumed had been filed and forgotten. In truth, academic researchers would later conclude his "Comments on the Operation and Performance of HMC Ships," along with two other similar memos from on-the-water officers, helped trigger an internal investigation that not only led to the strengthening and updating of naval equipment but also eventually resulted in the government's decision to replace Percy Nelles as Chief of Naval Staff.

Neither the disastrous convoy nor his memo ultimately hurt Piers's military career. He became a rear admiral, retiring in 1967. Ten years later the Nova Scotia government tapped him to be its agent general in London for two years. These days he and Janet divide their time between an apartment in Halifax and the Piers family home in Chester.

They celebrated their sixtieth wedding anniversary in 2001.

Marjory Whitelaw

Marjory saw Thane Parker one final time shortly after the war. Having recovered from the sinking of the *Lady Somers*, Thane was back in London as the business manager for the Sadler's Wells ballet company. Marjory happened to be in London for a week, on her way to take up a new job at the International Labour Organization in Geneva, when she saw his name in a newspaper story. She called him up.

"Good God," he said when he realized who was on the phone.

That afternoon he took her to a pub, told her about all the "awful circumstances" he'd encountered since he saw her last, then invited her home to have dinner and meet his wife. Though devastated at the time—"I'd still have gone off and married him the next day if I could have"—Marjory is philosophical today. "I wasn't surprised, I wasn't disappointed," she says. "There were so many girls I knew in those days who'd had these sorts of intense, passionate love affairs with British sailors, and then they'd go back to England and that would be that."

Though she never married, Marjory did not lose her taste for adventure, or for the place and time where her life's adventures began. After a stint as the fiction editor for *Weekend Magazine* in Montreal, Marjory returned to Halifax in the late 1960s, where she became a successful freelance author and broadcaster. In 1975 she produced an hour-long national radio documentary on what life was like for women in Halifax during the war years.

These days she lives in a senior citizens' home in Bridgetown, Nova Scotia.

Leonard Murray

The Murrays' decision to leave Canada was largely Jean's, but Leonard seemed sanguine about it. "Except for leaving the service, it was no great hardship for me," he wrote to a friend. "I had a house in England waiting for me . . . two sons were in the Royal Navy . . . Besides, I was very tired after five-and-a-half years of war and, for the last four of it, running the Operations of the Northwest Atlantic with inadequate staff."

Murray's choice of a new post-war career arose largely from his unhappy experiences at the Kellock Inquiry. After studying law at the Inns of Court Law School in London—where his fellow students elected him class president—he was called to the bar in 1949 and began practising in the Admiralty Division of the High Court in London. Within a few years, however, Jean was diagnosed with cancer and they retired to West Hoathly, Sussex, where Murray became a dominant figure in local politics and society.

In 1963, a year after Jean died, Murray married Nin Sergeievna Shtetinin Seaford Warwick, an ophthalmic surgeon, and they settled in Derbyshire. According to Douglas How's thesis on Murray, the former admiral "led a full life. He never missed a yacht race. He golfed. He worked in elections. He went each year to the annual banquet of veterans of Western Approaches. He enjoyed being near his two sons."

What he didn't do was talk about the past—even with members of his own family. His son Hugh says he didn't come to understand the impact of the riots on his father until after Murray had died and Hugh finally got the chance to read his papers. "I was amazed and deeply touched to discover that it should be as burning a subject to him," he explained. "It must have wounded him beyond all possibility to heal."

There were other wounds too. Though the United States government named Murray a Commander of its Legion of Merit in 1946 for his outstanding work under American commanders in Newfoundland during the Battle of the Atlantic, there would be no more honours for him from Canada. Dalhousie University in Halifax turned down the idea of awarding him an honorary degree; the federal government said no to giving him the Order of Canada. And when Murray lobbied for an ambassadorship, the Department of External Affairs made it clear it had nothing to offer him.

Even in his self-imposed exile, Murray remained very much a Canadian. "One impression I must correct," he noted pointedly in a letter to Eric Dennis turning down a request for an interview. "I am not a 'former' Canadian. I am a Canadian. I retain my Canadian domicile and have kept a small portion of the family property upon which I intend to settle when the time is ripe."

He never got the chance. Leonard Murray died in England on November 25, 1971.

He did, however, come home to Nova Scotia for good. In 1972, at a memorial service attended by more than seven hundred former colleagues and friends, his ashes were laid to rest in a naval vault in the basement of St. Paul's Church in downtown Halifax.

Dorothy Hendsbee

Dorothy Chisholm smiles and suddenly, magically, the years and the age lines and the disappointing life she has lived melt away. For a brief moment she is Dorothy Hendsbee, that "dark-eyed, dimple-cheeked . . . comely maid" in the welder's coveralls in the 1943 newspaper photograph.

It is easy, looking back now, to see those nine brief months between April and December 1943, when Dorothy was one of Canada's first female welders, as the best, most exciting, most satisfying, most successful days of Dorothy Hendsbee's life. It is easy to understand why she is eager to recall that moment in time whenever she is offered the chance.

Reg Lutz didn't turn out to be the man of her dreams. He was an abusive drunk. But she stayed with him—"that's just the way it was then"—through seventeen years and three children. They finally divorced in 1975; he died in a house fire on New Year's Eve in 1979.

Nowadays, Dorothy Hendsbee—who was given her last name by her hated stepfather and then became Dorothy Lutz by virtue of her marriage to the alcoholic Reg—calls herself Dorothy Chisholm. "Chisholm was my real father's name," she explains. She discovered that from old church records. "So I took it from then on as my name."

With no education to fall back on and a skill—welding—that remained "man's work" until she was too old to go back to it, Dorothy eked out a living as a shop clerk and waitress. Until she turned sixty-five in 1991 and qualified for Canada's old-age pension, she admits she was "financially embarrassed" most of the time.

Dorothy's post-1943 life may help to explain why, in 1987, she wrote a letter to the editor of the Halifax *Daily News* seeking other members of the Electric Five for a forty-five-year reunion. After only a few days she got a "yes let's" letter from Bertha MacKeigan, née Roche, the woman with whom she'd lived while she worked at the Shipyards in 1943. Bertha was seventy now, widowed and living just a few blocks from Dorothy's small Halifax apartment. A few weeks after that, a letter arrived from Helen Pilicoski (Rice) in Toronto. She was a widow too, retired now from a job in an insurance company.

Dorothy tried without success to track down the others. "But the three of us decided to get together anyway. We were always so giddy back then, and I wanted to find out if we were still as crazy as we used to be." They were. "A little fatter now," she joked with a newspaper reporter who came to do a story about their reunion. "We've all changed our hair colour a few times, but we haven't really changed."

They posed for photographs holding pictures of their younger selves, laughed at the yellowed newspaper clippings in Dorothy's scrapbook, tried on the welder's goggles Dorothy had kept as a souvenir, and reminisced about what life had been like for them back then.

They all agreed it had been a good life. A very good life.

- SELECTED BIBLIOGRAPHY -

Amey, Gerald. *The Halifax Club: 1862 to 1987*. Halifax: Halifax Club, 1987.

Bard, Mitchell. *The Complete Idiot's Guide to World War II*. New York: Alpha Books, 1999.

Blakeley, Phyllis R. *Glimpses of Halifax*. Belleville, Ontario: Mika Publishing, 1973.

Borrett, William Coates. *More Tales Told Under the Old Town Clock*. Halifax: Imperial Publishing, 1943.

———. *East Coast Port and Other Tales Told Under the Old Town Clock*. Halifax: Imperial Publishing, 1944.

———. *Historic Halifax in Tales Told Under the Old Town Clock*. Toronto: Ryerson Press, 1948.

Bruce, Harry. *Down Home*. Toronto: Key Porter Books, 1988.

———. *An Illustrated History of Nova Scotia*. Halifax: Nimbus, 1997.

———. *Lifeline*. Toronto: Macmillan, 1977.

Calhoun, Sue. *The Lockeport Lockout*. Halifax: Lockeport Lockout, 1983.

Cameron, James M. *Murray: The Martyred Admiral*. Halifax: Lancelot Press, 1980.

Chisholm, Anne, and Michael Davie. *Beaverbrook: A Life*. London: Hutchinson, 1992.

Coade, Jessie. *Messdeck News*. Charlottetown: Ragweed Press, 1985.

Dennis, Eric R. *The Dennis Saga*. Halifax: Chebucto Agencies, 1984.

Draper, Alfred. *Operation Fish*. Don Mills, Ontario: General Publishing, 1979.

Edwards, Devonna. *Wartime Recipes*. Halifax: Nimbus, 2001.

Eggleston, Wilfrid. *While I Still Remember*. Toronto: Ryerson Press, 1968.

Erickson, Paul A. *Halifax's North End*. Hantsport, Nova Scotia: Lancelot Press, 1986.

German, Tony. *The Sea is at Our Gates*. Toronto: McClelland and Stewart, 1990.

Haliburton, G. Brenton. *What's Brewing*. Tantallon, Nova Scotia: Four East Publications, 1994.

Hawkins, John. *The Life and Times of Angus L*. Windsor, Nova Scotia: Lancelot Press, 1969.

How, Douglas. "The Career of Rear Admiral Leonard W. Murray, CB. CBE. RCN, 1896–1971." Master's thesis, Dalhousie University, Halifax, 1972. Public Archives of New Brunswick, Fredericton.

Jaikings, John. "The German U-Boat Attack on Convoy OB217." Memoir of the journey of a British guest child in 1940. Privately printed, April 1999.

Jangaard, Nils. "Norwegians in Nova Scotia: 1941–45." Privately printed memoir of the wartime Norwegian vice-consul in Halifax.

Jefferson, H.B. Papers, 1939–45. Public Archives of Nova Scotia, Halifax.

Jenson, Latham B. *Tin Hats, Oilskins & Seaboots*. Toronto: Robin Brass Studio, 2000.

Kellock, Mr. Justice R.L. *Report on the Halifax Disorders, May 7th–8th 1945*. Ottawa: King's Printer, 1945.

Kjelsrud, Jostein A. *"Somewhere" on the East Coast of Canada*. Head of St. Margaret's Bay: Camp Norway Foundation, 1999.

Lamb, James B. *The Corvette Navy*. Toronto: Stoddart, 2000.

Lawrence, Hal. *A Bloody War*. Scarborough, Ontario: New American Library of Canada, 1979.

Leacock, Stephen, and Leslie Roberts. *Canada's War at Sea*. Vols. 1 and 2. Montreal: Alvah M. Beatty, 1944.

MacKinnon, Fred. "British Guest Children: History and Working Papers." Halifax: privately printed, 1986.

MacLean, Grant. *Walk Historic Halifax*. Halifax: Nimbus, 2001.

MacNeil, Robert. *Wordstruck*. New York: Viking, 1989.

March, William. *Red Line: The Chronicle Herald and Mail Star 1875–1954*. Halifax: Chebucto Agencies, 1986.

Metson, Graham. *An East Coast Port: Halifax at War*. Toronto: McGraw-Hill Ryerson, 1981.

Milner, Marc. *North Atlantic Run*. Toronto: University of Toronto Press, 1985.

Mitic, Trudy Duivenvoorden, and J.P. LeBlanc. *Pier 21: The Gateway that Changed Canada*. Hantsport, Nova Scotia: Lancelot Press, 1988.

Morton, Desmond. *A Military History of Canada*. 4th ed. Toronto: McClelland and Stewart, 1999.

Murray, James Frederick. "The Murray family in Pictou County." Privately printed, 1991.

O'Brien, David. *HX72: First Convoy to Die*. Halifax: Nimbus, 1999.

Parker, Mike. *Running the Gauntlet*. Halifax: Nimbus, 1994.

Piersdorf, Kay. "Anybody Here from the West." *Nova Scotia Historical Review*, vol. 5, no. 1 (1985).

Pugsley, William. *Saints, Devils and Ordinary Seamen*. Toronto: Collins, 1945.

———. *Sailor, Remember*. Toronto: Collins, 1948.

Purcell, Gillis. "Wartime Censorship in Canada." Master's thesis, University of Toronto, 1946.

Raddall, Thomas. *Halifax: Warden of the North*. Toronto: McClelland and Stewart, 1971.

———. *In My Time*. Toronto: McClelland and Stewart, 1976.

Reader's Digest. *The Canadians at War 1939/45*. Vols. 1 and 2. Montreal: Reader's Digest, 1969.

Redman, Stanley. *Open Gangway: An Account of the Halifax Riots, 1945*. Hantsport, Nova Scotia: Lancelot, 1981.

———. *Behind Open Gangway*. Toronto: Lugus, 1999.

Regan, John W. *Sketches and Traditions of the Northwest Arm*. 3rd ed. Halifax: Phillips & Marshall, 1928.

Repka, William and Kathleen. *Dangerous Patriots*. Vancouver: New Star Books, 1982.

Settle, Victor. "Halifax Shipyards, 1917–1978: An Historical Perspective." Master's thesis, Saint Mary's University, Halifax, 1994.

Tucker, Gilbert Norman. *The Naval Service of Canada: Its Official History*. Vols. I and II. Ottawa: King's Printer, 1952.

Wagner, Earle. "A Mariner's Memoirs." Privately printed memoir of a merchant navy veteran.

Watt, Frederick B. *In All Respects Ready*. Toronto: Prentice Hall, 1985.

White, J.F. "The Ajax Affair." Master's thesis, Dalhousie University, Halifax, 1985.

———. "Sleepless and Veiled Am I." *Nova Scotia Historical Review*, vol. 5, no. 1 (1985).

———. "Stadtenim Zweiten Weltkrieg: Halifax, Nova Scotia—A Canadian Staging Area." Paper presented to the International Colloquium on Cities in the Second World War, Stuttgart, West Germany, 1989.

———. "Conscripted City: Halifax and the Second World War." Ph.D. diss., McMaster University, Hamilton, Ontario, 1994.

Wright, H. Millard. *The Other Halifax Explosion*. Halifax: privately printed, 2001.

– ACKNOWLEDGEMENTS –

I'm grateful to John Pearce, the then Editor-in-Chief at Doubleday, for recognizing there was a fascinating, still-to-be-told tale about life in wartime Halifax and for encouraging me to take it on; and to Meg Taylor, Doubleday's Senior Editor, for supporting the project through its inevitable ups and downs.

I was privileged to meet and talk with so many men and women whose memories of those long-gone days are still fresh and vivid, and who generously agreed to share their stories—and their lives—with me. They invariably indulged me without complaint when I returned time and again to ask them to expand on this event, or clarify that relationship, or sort out that chronology, or simply tell me more of their spellbinding stories about what they remembered of that incredible time. You'll find many of their names and stories in this book. But I also importuned plenty of others, some of whom were in Halifax then too, and some of whom later became experts on that time and place. They provided me with the multi-layered background and context I needed to add flesh to the bones of my narrative.

I am indebted to them all: Arne Benson, Gary Burrill, Dorothy Chisholm, Helen Chute, Elizabeth Curry, Eric Dennis, Carolyn Doig, Mike Earle, Ron Grantham, Charlotte Guy, Shirley Haggarty, John Haikings, Byron Himmelman, Doug How, Heather Inglis, Dean Jobb, Carl Kaizer, Lulu Keating, Emily Kimber, Tania Li, Dianne Liddell, David MacKeen, Shelagh MacKenzie, Fred

MacKinnon, Guy MacLean, Judy MacLean, Harold Masterman, Robert Mitchell, Grace Molineux, Bill Mont, Judy Moreira, Bob Mottley, Bruce Oland, Bill Phillips, Desmond Piers, Janet Piers, Walter Piers, Helen Pilicoski, Berit Pittman, the staff of the Public Archives of Nova Scotia, Ed Rubin, Carol Salton, Margo Pullen Sly, Molly Smolenski, Robert Sutherland, Alice Swales, Murray Westgate, Marjory Whitelaw, Budge Wilson, Peter Wooten and Sarah Yablon.

During the writing, many people have generously read drafts of the manuscript and offered helpful critiques and suggestions, including: Phil Gerard, Kevin Kerrane and Leslie Rubinkowski, my mentors at Goucher College in Baltimore; Molly Kalkstein, my fellow student and friend from Goucher; Dan Conlin, the Curator of Marine History at the Maritime Museum of the Atlantic; Marilyn Gurney, Director of the Maritime Command Museum in Halifax; Dr. Jay White, a professor of history at Dalhousie University, who is the acknowledged academic expert on wartime Halifax; Bill Turpin, my friend and former editor at the Halifax *Daily News*; and Marion Kimber, my mother, whose own recollections of life in Halifax during the war saved me from many an embarrassing gaffe.

My editors at Doubleday—Pamela Murray, who helped shape my initial thinking about the structure of the book, and Meg Masters, who helped define and refine it with her careful and thoughtful reading and insightful suggestions—were incredibly helpful. As was copy editor John Sweet, whose eye for detail and meticulousness improved the final manuscript immeasurably. I would also like to thank my agent, Anne McDermid, who was, as always supportive.

Finally, of course, neither this book nor any of the others I've written would have been possible without the continuing support and forbearance of my wife, Jeanie, and our three children: Matthew, Emily and Michael. I cannot thank them enough.

-INDEX-

Index

Index

MacMillan, Mrs. Stirling, 132
MacNeil, Robert, 11
Macneill, Anne (daughter of Janet),
  14–15, 54
Macneill, Edith (Janet's older sister),
  13–15, 43, 80–81, 104
Macneill, Isabel (sister of Janet), 43, 80–81
Macneill, Janet. *See also* Piers, Janet
  avoids tragedy at sea, 13–15
  gets engaged and married, 104–5
  hears from Debby, 25–28
  volunteers locally, 54–56, 80–81
Macneill, Murray, 215
MacQuarrie, J.H., 280
Mahon, Arthur S., 130, 242, 247
Manfield, W.A., 87–90
Maritime Furriers, 267, 284
Marshall, General George, 89
Martin Van Buren (ship), 236
Massey, Vincent, 32
Masterman, Elizabeth (Harold's oldest
  sister), 56, 72, 307
Masterman, Harold, 125
  arrives in Halifax, 66–67
  introduction to, 56–59
  love of hockey by, 135–36
  meets the O'Byrnes, 71–72
  plays soldiers, 205–6
  his post-war life, 319–20
  returns to England, 307–8
  at VE time, 282–83
  visits with brother Jack, 100
Masterman, Jack (Harold's older brother),
  56, 72, 100, 308
Masterman, Marion (Harold's older sister), 56, 72, 307
McEuen, Janet ("Dolly"), 43
takes on Ajax Club, 79–82, 130–35
McEuen, Dr. Stuart (husband of Dolly),
  80
McNab, Archibald P., 41, 44, 68
McNaughton, Major General A.L., 88
Merkel, Andy, 288
Micmac, 185–87
Miles, Captain George, 260, 266, 287
Mills, Hugh, 64
minesweepers, 203

Mitten, Marjorie, 148
Mont, Alice (wife of William), 13
Mont, Billy, 121, 317
  collects scrap, 144–47, 183
  his post-war life, 322
  his schooling, 8–9, 11–13, 83, 103–4
  at VE events, 274–75
Mont, Mary, 12
Mont, William (Billy's grandfather), 13
Mont Blanc (ship), 21, 137
Montgomery, Sir Bernard, 224
Montrolite (ship), 92, 184
Morrisey, Michael, 219
Mountbatten, Lord Louis, 189
Mount Saint Vincent (college), 63
Murray, Alexander (son of Leonard), 38
Murray, Charlie, 149–51
Murray, Magistrate E.D., 285
Murray, Jean (Mrs. Leonard), 243
  disliked by others, 211
  introduction to, 37–38
  leaves Canada with Len, 315, 324
  lost fur coats of, 284
  love of fishing, 173
  mistrust of the Kellock Inquiry,
    292, 300
  post-enquiry bitterness of, 295–96,
    313
Murray, Rear Admiral Leonard W., 1–2,
  18, 120, 219, 315, 318
  anger at Kellock Inquiry proceed-
    ings, 308–13
  anger at his superiors, 114–15
  called to new command, 119
  commands N. Atlantic sea efforts,
    173–75
  escorts Churchill, 189
  inspires Debby Piers, 28
  introduction to, 37–40
  Kellock finds him largely responsi-
    ble for VE riots, 310–12
  the Kellock Royal Commission
    and, 291, 293–301
  learns of VE day riots, 271–74, 265–67
  loses out to Jones, 202
  naval discipline and, 213–15
  not notified during VE riots, 260